Assuming a Body

ASSUMING A BODY

Transgender and Rhetorics of Materiality

Gayle Salamon

COLUMBIA UNIVERSITY PRESS
NEW YORK

Columbia University Press
Publishers Since 1893
New York Chichester, West Sussex
Copyright © 2010 Columbia University Press
All rights reserved

Library of Congress Cataloging-in-Publication Data
Salamon, Gayle.
Assuming a body: transgender and rhetorics of materiality /
Gayle Salamon.
p. cm.
Includes bibliographical references and index.
ISBN 978-0-231-14958-7 (cloth: alk. paper) —
ISBN 978-0-231-14959-4 (pbk.: alk. paper) —
ISBN 978-0-231-52170-3 (e-book)
1. Transgenderism—Psychological aspects.
2. Transgender people—Psychology.
3. Gender identity.   I. Title.

HQ77.9.S25   2010
306.76'8—dc22   2009031454

References to Internet Web sites (URLs) were accurate at the time of writing. Neither the author nor Columbia University Press is responsible for Web sites that may have expired or changed since the book was prepared.

FOR JULIE

who helped me make it out and
who has always taught me about sameness and difference

CONTENTS

ACKNOWLEDGMENTS

First and last thanks go to Judith Butler, whose inspiring work and unfailing support made this book possible.

Thanks to my editors Wendy Lochner and Susan Pensak at Columbia University Press, and to three anonymous reviewers, whose helpful suggestions strengthened this manuscript.

Thanks to Princeton University and my colleagues and friends there including: Eduardo Cadava, Zahid Chaudhary, Anne Cheng, Jim Clark, Isabelle Clark-Decès, Jill Dolan, Jeff Dolven, Diana Fuss, R. Marie Griffith, Daniel Heller-Roazen, Claudia Johnson, Meredith Martin, Deborah Nord, Jeff Nunokawa, Nigel Smith, Val Smith, Alexandra Vazquez, Stacy Wolf, and Michael Wood. Thanks also to the Society of Fellows at Princeton whose support gave me the time to complete much of this work: Leonard Barkan, the indefatigable Mary Harper, Carol Rigolot, Cass Garner, and Lin DeTittia, with particular thanks to fellow fellows Margot Canaday, Jen Rubenstein, Ben Kafka, Graham Jones, Miriam Petty, Mendi Obadike, Bianca Calabresi, and Martin Scherzinger. Thanks also to the Fund for Reunion and Debbie Bazarsky at the LGBT Center at Princeton.

Profound thanks to Alan Schrift and Johanna Meehan, without whose early and continued encouragement I would not have found this path. Thanks to James Kissane and Knut Tarnowski for meeting impatience with kindness and intellectual generosity.

I am deeply glad for the good company of Kaja Silverman, Joan Scott, David Kazanjian, Josie Saldana, Ken Corbett, David Eng, Teemu Ruskola, Zrinka Stahuljak and Laure Murat. Thank you to Gail Weiss, Ewa Ziarek, Angela McRobbie, Penny Deutscher, Ann Murphy, Samir Haddad, Mary Beth Mader, Diane Perpich, Kelly Oliver, Denise Riley, Petra Kuppers, Elizabeth Weed, Anne Fausto-Sterling, and Carol Armstrong. I have benefited from the wisdom of C. L. Cole, Jack Halberstam, Lisa C., Erik Schneider, Dylan Scholinski, and Patrick Letellier in conversations about trans issues.

Thanks go to friends and colleagues during my time at UC Berkeley: Homay King, Catherine Zimmer, Jill Stauffer, Beth Ferguson, Gillian Harkins, Katrin Pahl, James Salazar, Rob Miotke, Emma Bianchi, Felipe Gutterriez, Jane Taylorson, Maxine Fredericksen, and Carl Fredericksen.

Thanks to Judith Butler, Kaja Silverman, Sharon Marcus, and David Hoy for invaluable comments and advice on the project while still in the form of a dissertation. I am grateful for comments on the first chapter from Karl Britto, Michael Lucey, Charis Thompson, Paola Bacchetta, and Leigh Gilmore. Thanks to my students at Berkeley and at Princeton, with particular thanks to Cathy Hannabach.

For true friendship and sustaining kinship, I am grateful to Dustin Ray Jermier, Armon Kasmai, Miss A, Mike Nield, and Lila Thirkield. Thanks to the Lexington Club and to Sunny, Ace, Danny, Libby, Yvette, Kelly, Steph, Bre, and Kiki. I am grateful for the keen eyes of Ace Morgan, Lily Rodriguez, and Allison Wykoff.

For various forms of shelter while writing, thanks to Jane Huber and Gerry Kiwanuka, Patrick Letellier and Keith Hodge, Nello Carlini, Ben Kafka and Julie Coe, and Wendy Brown.

Thanks to Julie Salamon, Cheryl Clark, Richard Salamon, and Marilyn Ayers-Salamon.

Finally: gratitude beyond measure, in every register, to A. B. Huber. You are my magnetic north.

Chapter 1 appeared first as "The Bodily Ego and the Contested Domain of the Material," in *differences: A Journal of Feminist Cultural Studies* 15, no. 3 (2004): 95–122. Chapter 2 appeared first as "The Sexual Schema: Transposition and Transgenderism in the *Phenomenology of Perception*" in Laurie Schrage, ed., *You've Changed: Sex Change and Personal Identity* (Oxford University Press, 2009). Chapter 3 appeared first as "Boys of the Lex: Transgenderism and Rhetorics of Materiality in *GLQ: A Journal of Lesbian and Gay Studies* 12, no. 4 (September 2006): 575–597. Parts of chapter 4 appeared first as "Transfeminism and the Future of Women's Studies," in Joan Scott, ed., *Women's Studies on the Edge* (Duke University Press, 2008), and as "Transmasculinity and Relation: Commentary on Griffin Hansbury's 'Middle Men'" in *Studies in Gender and Sexuality* 6, no. 3 (2005): 265–275.

Assuming a Body

INTRODUCTION

Assuming a Body is a project that works questions of embodiment through phenomenology (primarily the work of Merleau-Ponty), psychoanalysis (the work of Freud and Paul Schilder), and queer theory in order to consider how each of these disciplines conceives of the body. I seek to challenge the notion that the materiality of the body is something to which we have unmediated access, something of which we can have epistemological certainty, and contend that such epistemological uncertainty can have great use, both ethically and politically, in the lives of the non-normatively gendered. Throughout, the book takes up recent theorizations of transgendered and transsexual bodies to suggest both that those theorizations might benefit from phenomenological and psychoanalytic understandings of the body and, perhaps more crucially, that our current ideas of what a body is will be irremediably diminished until trans bodies and subjectivities are considered in a more thorough way. The project thus wants to mark the specificity of trans bodies and subjectivities and also to resist the temptation to define that specificity in resolutely material terms. I am not arguing that the

transgendered body has a material specificity that marks it as different from a normatively gendered body, but rather that the production of normative gender itself relies on a disjunction between the
"felt sense" of the body and the body's corporeal contours and that
this disjunction need not be viewed as a pathological structure.

In this book I examine the relation between the material and
phantasmatic in accounts of bodily being and hope to show that
this need not be a relation of incompossibility, but can be characterized by a productive tension that accounts for ways in which
the materiality of the body is present to consciousness as well as
importantly, the ways it absents itself from consciousness. I read
theories of embodiment offered by Maurice Merleau-Ponty, Sigmund Freud, Paul Schilder, and Judith Butler, questioning how
the relation between the phantasmatic and the material contained
within those theories might contribute to a better understanding of
trans bodies. At the same time, I ask how a consideration of trans
bodies might help us understand how relations between the phantasmatic and the material can be embodied and lived. Each of these
inquiries opens up onto the broader question of what it means to
be embodied. Throughout, I rely on the notion of the phantom or
ambivalent presence to complicate suppositions about the nature of
bodily being, where that phantom is sometimes textual and sometimes material, sometimes designating the ambivalent presence of
a particular region or part of the body and sometimes indicating a
characteristic of embodied subjectivity in general.

Phenomenology, psychoanalysis, and queer and transgender theory each approach the question of what it means to assume a body
by asserting the primacy of a "felt sense" of the body, and the different means by which each discipline does so, when examined in
conjunction, can begin to delimit the contours of this body whose
felt sense is usually unquestioned. Phenomenologists understand
this felt sense as *proprioception*, psychoanalysis thinks of it as the
bodily ego, and it has sometimes emerged in transgender theory as
the grounds for claims about identity and "realness." Each of these
disciplines contends that this meaning, and ultimately the body itself,
hinges on a felt sense. It is my contention that one can acknowledge
the ways in which this felt sense is a product of, and also subject to,

cultural interpretations without disavowing or dismissing the persistent importance of this sense. In conjointly utilizing the conceptual tools offered by these discourses, it is my hope that discussions of transgenderism and transsexuality might not be so problematically reliant on "the real," a phrase that, it seems to me, can never quite shed its normativizing and disciplinary dimensions.

Part 1 addresses the ways in which presence and absence, material substance and immaterial feeling have structured theories of bodily being in psychoanalysis and phenomenology. In a number of works theorizing transgenderism and gender dysphoria, discussions of the nature, origin, and meanings of the body have tended to treat the materiality of the body as self-evident and given, alligning the body with substance and presence, thought in simple and stark opposition to that which is absent, immaterial, or ideal. Such accounts produce a theory of embodiment in which both gender and gender dysphoria are considered to be the products of bodies whose presence is asserted as an indisputable fact and whose materiality is thought to secure both identity and subjectivity. And yet, those immaterial structures which subtend the body's materiality, such as the felt sense that delivers the body to consciousness, cannot be accounted for within a theory that understands the body to be a plenitude of materiality and meaning, a substance without rupture or discontinuity, nor can the problem of correspondence between a subject's felt sense of the body and its corporeal contours be addressed within a strictly materialist framework.

Chapter 1, "The Bodily Ego and the Contested Domain of the Material," looks at psychoanalytic conceptions of the bodily ego. I consider Paul Schilder's account of the development and function of the body schema, Didier Anzieu's formulation of the "skin ego," and Freud's famous assertion that the ego is "first and foremost a bodily ego," along with the recent scholarship that has amassed around Freud's claim. I argue that the body one feels oneself to have is not necessarily the same body that is delimited by its exterior contours, and that this is the case even for any normatively gendered subject. Transpeople have been justifiably wary of psychoanalysis because of the ways it has been used to pathologize gender variance and gender-variant people. Nevertheless, psychoanalysis, perhaps more than any other discourse, has provided the most thorough and detailed examination of the elaborate set of mechanisms by which a subject "knows" her own body, and psychoanalysis can give us a richly productive way of describing that join between the psychic and the material—if its more homophobic and transphobic tendencies can be curbed. Since psychoanalysis deals with the construction of the self, and the way in which that self inhabits a body, it can complicate the assumption that the material body is unproblematically available to us; within psychoanalysis, the body is available to a subject only through a complex set of mental representations, of psychic images, designated alternately as the bodily ego or the body schema. This concept can be of use to genderqueer communities because it shows that the body of which one supposedly has a "felt sense" is not necessarily contiguous with the physical body as it is perceived from the outside, thus complicating the notion of the subject's relationship to the materiality of her own body.

The second chapter, "The Sexual Schema: Transposition and Transgenderism in *Phenomenology of Perception,*" considers phenomenological accounts of the body that employ the concept of a body schema and focus directly on the felt sense of the body. I take up Merleau-Ponty's phenomenological exploration of embodiment and examine his radical proposition that attention to the felt sense of the body need not require the assertion of a body that stands behind, or exists prior to, our perceptions. I turn to his account of bodily being in *Phenomenology of Perception,* in which subjectivity itself is achieved through the construction of a body image. In this phenomenology there is no easy recourse to a materiality that would definitively answer the question of embodiment, because for Merleau-Ponty "body parts are not objects, but potentialities." The body is, instead, "a nexus of living meanings," gaining these meanings through proprioception, the primary but unlocatable "felt sense" that allows a body to be experienced as a coherent whole rather than a collection of disparate parts. The implications of these ideas for thinking transgenderism are quite promising, and several trans writers have described this disarticulation between felt and observed gender in language that is deeply resonant with phenomenological accounts of embodiment. Transgender theorist

Jason Cromwell, for instance, suggests that the sex that one's body manifests, the sex one can *see*, need not be the sex one can *be*, but does not give a thorough account of bodily being that would explain this disjunction in detail; Merleau-Ponty's work provides just such an account. Merleau-Ponty challenges both philosophical accounts of embodiment that rely upon a dualistic conception of body and self and mind/body theorists whose conceptions of the body are predicated on starkly drawn models of inside and outside. Instead, he suggests that our bodies are inextricably intertwined with both our selves and the worlds in which our bodies are situated. I consider his claim that bodies become material only through relations with others and explore the consequences that this might have for theorizing transsubjectivity.

Part 2 engages visual representations of transpeople in photography and the popular media. In chapter 3, "Boys of the Lex: Transgenderism and Social Construction," I examine a growing number of texts that are grouped under the rubric of "transgender studies," first surveying transgender studies' vexed relationship to, and emergence from, discourses of feminist and queer studies. Some feminist theorists have claimed that transsexuality merely reifies gender norms rather than challenging them. Transgender authors, in turn, have charged that feminist theory has been inattentive to the lived experiences of transgendered people. I consider the history of this debate and the ways in which transgender theory has offered new and productive understandings of gendered embodiment. Second, I interrogate some of the problematic claims about bodily materiality that transgender theorists have advanced. Jay Prosser's goal, for example, is to "substantiate transsexual identity, to reveal the materiality of the figure of transition," and to "foreground the bodily matter of gender crossings" that would "reveal the extent to which embodiment forms an essential base to subjectivity." Prosser's account focuses on embodiment as a strategy to combat the invisibility of transsexual and transgendered persons within gay and lesbian discourses. I am sympathetic with these aims, which I take as indicative of a desire to counter a historic absence of recognition with an emphatic and embodied presence and to pinpoint the specificity of a transsexual subjectivity. I worry, however, that the attempt to pinpoint this difference of transsexuality by asserting that the transsexual body is "unimpeachably real" unwittingly falls back in a problematic slippage between the assertion of a felt sense of the body (which is surely necessary) and the consequent claim that what a body is and how it is assumed are self-evident things (which is not).

The fourth chapter, "Transfeminism and the Future of Gender." asks after the relationship between women's studies, feminism, and the study of transgenderism and other non-normative genders. In asking after the place—or lack of place—of transgender studies within the rubric of women's studies, I want to suggest that feminism, particularly but not exclusively in its institutionalized form, has not been able to keep pace with non-normative genders as they are thought, embodied, and lived. Recent contestations around the term *transgender* echo some of the same concerns about referentiality and identity that have surfaced with the circulation of the terms *queer* and *woman* within feminist discourses. I have three aims in this chapter. First, I want to suggest that, if it is to reemerge as a vital discipline, women's studies must become more responsive to emerging genders. Genders beyond the binary of male and female are neither fictive nor futural, but are presently embodied and lived. Women's studies has not yet come to terms with this and is thus unable to assess the present state of gender as it is lived, nor is it able to imagine many of its possible futures. The antagonism that women's studies sometimes displays toward transgenderism is iterated otherwise in the mutually antagonistic relationship between lesbian communities and transmen asserted in the popular press. My second aim is to explore that representation of antagonism and the role that fantasies of violence and figurations of transpeople as predaceous have in shaping that representation. The third aim is to read other ways of figuring the relationship between trans and lesbian communities, and the chapter closes with a reading of photographs of transmen as documented by two lesbian photographers.

Part 3 looks at philosopher Luce Irigaray, who has famously posited sexual difference as the major philosophical issue of our age. Chapter 5, "An Ethics of Transsexual Difference: Luce Irigaray and the Place of Sexual Undecidability," considers feminist reimaginings of sexual difference and corporeal materiality through Irigaray and her reception among feminists trying to challenge and complicate the issue of the materiality of the body and its limits. I address the idea of a sexuate limit which is both implicit and explicit in these feminist challenges to materiality, especially in the work of theorists such as Elizabeth Grosz who question traditional philosophical notions of the body's corporeal limits, and expand the horizons of what "counts" as a body. I argue that this notion of the limit is challenged, but also transferred; questions about the limits of bodily plasticity become displaced into questions about the limits of gender plasticity, where the foreclosure of gender plasticity in the form of transsexuality is intended to secure the body as a site capable of almost limitless physical reconfiguration.

Chapter 6, "Sexual Indifference and the Problem of the Limit," continues to work with Irigaray's notion of sexual difference through a reading of Irigaray's "Place, Interval" and asks whether a nonheteronormative reading of body and relation is possible within the logic of that essay and, if so, what room might be made for sexual relationships that fall outside the scope of the strictly heterosexual or bodily and identificatory configurations that cannot be understood as strictly male or female. I explore Aristotle's conception of place as articulated in *Physics*, focusing on the ontological primacy offered to place and Aristotle's use of relation, containment, and mutual replacement in order to secure a coherent definition of place. Irigaray reads Aristotelian place as figuratively gendered and engages Aristotle both to critique this figuration and to theorize relations across the bridge of sexual difference. The question of sexual difference ends at an impasse in "Place, Interval," and this impasse stems from Irigaray's fundamentally *hylomorphic* understanding of sexual difference: a conviction that male and female, like matter and form, are necessarily ontologically conjoined and that any one sex cannot find expression or existence without the other. The chapter concludes by considering the place of sexual difference itself within Irigaray's schema. I read some of her own equivocations about "the interval" as that which must be preserved in order to ground ethical relations across sexual difference, but also as a gap that needs to be bridged so that the sexes might coexist with one another. The chapter tries to extend this cartography of difference by considering bodies and psyches that do not find easy home in either the category of male or female and suggests a possible paradigm for understanding "sexual difference" not as a boundary, mapped onto the body in strictly determinative ways, but as a marker of difference that can be operative not only across the categories of male and female but within them as well.

The concluding chapter, "Withholding the Letter: Sex as State Property," reads Jan Morris's autobiography *Conundrum* alongside recent legislation regulating gender and transpeople to consider sex as a bureaucratic entity. My argument about trans specificity is at its most emphatic here, and I argue that sex is analogized to property or understood metaphorically as property in much literature, but sex is treated as material property in transpeoples' dealings with medical and state bureaucracies and functions specifically as state property rather than private property for transpeople in a way that it does not for the normatively gendered.

Assuming a Body thus reads from a number of disciplinary traditions in an attempt to show that a critical phenomenological analysis of what a body is and how it comes to be one's own can enrich and broaden the mostly gender normative accounts of bodily materiality offered by psychoanalysis and phenomenology and that phenomenology and psychoanalysis can help us understand transgendered bodies as embodying a specificity that is finally not reducible to the material. I hope then to engage with current dialogues about embodiment happening simultaneously, yet unconnectedly, in (at least) two different fields. Philosophical and theoretical considerations of embodiment have been historically neglectful of sexual difference, and those theories of embodiment that do attend to sexual difference have often considered non-normative genders to be pathological. Canonically philosophical considerations of embodiment have rarely considered the ways in which gender variation can both supplement and challenge traditional notions of corporeality, or what kinds of gendered embodiments are legislated and what kinds are prohibited by philosophical accounts of embodiment. What new forms of embodiment does a transgendered subjectivity enable? Conversely, the newly emerging field of trans studies doesn't yet engage with those philosophies of embodiment that might strengthen some of the political claims it wants to make, and few trans writers have yet availed themselves of the promising tools that phenomenology and psychoanalytic theory offers, their richly descriptive means of detailing the relation between body and feeling, and understanding disjuncture there as a potentially powerful facet of embodied subjectivity rather than a mark of pathology. In *Assuming a Body* I hope to draw on those insights, the unyoking of bodily materiality from bodily feeling, to move the current conversation about transsexuality and transgenderism beyond the decidedly Cartesian frame in which it sometimes finds itself, even as it should be noted that transgender studies as a field is growing so quickly and robustly that it is in many ways already becoming something other than what I describe here. It is my aim to bring psychoanalytic, phenomenological, and transgendered bodies proximate enough so that their similarities might become more visible and their differences might be brought into productive tension with one another.

A note on language and pronouns: if the pronomial preference of an individual is clear, I have honored that prefererence. This has meant sometimes using gender-specific pronouns and sometimes using gender-neutral ones, and I have deliberately tried to retain that inconsistency in pronoun usage throughout the text.

The book discusses both FTM and MTF transpeople, though my general discussions of trans will often take FTM experience as my focus, in a reversal of what has historically been a conflation of trans experience with MTF experience.

I

WHAT IS A BODY?

I

THE BODILY EGO AND THE CONTESTED
DOMAIN OF THE MATERIAL

Every body contains in itself a phantom (perhaps the body itself
is a phantom).

— PAUL SCHILDER,
THE IMAGE AND APPEARANCE OF THE HUMAN BODY

Of what use might psychoanalytic theory be to those of us trying
to bring attention to transgender within contemporary discussions
of embodiment and gender? I would suggest that recent writings
on transgender share a number of concerns and questions with
the domains of psychoanalysis and phenomenology: how does
the body manifest a sex? How can we account, in a nonpathol-
ogizing way, for bodies that manifest sex in ways that exceed or
confound evident binaries? An understanding of transgender that
wants to proceed by challenging a rigidly binaristic understanding of sex might find useful tools in theories that put similar pres-
sure on the binary relation between body and psyche. Transpeople have tended toward suspicion of psychoanalytic accounts of
gender—and justifiably so, since psychoanalysis has historically
been used to relegate them to the realm of pathology and abjection. Indeed, this tradition continues within some psychoanalytic
circles.[1] And yet, psychoanalysis, perhaps more than any other discourse, has provided the most thorough and detailed examination
of the elaborate set of mechanisms by which a subject "knows"

her own body. Since psychoanalysis deals with the psychic construction of the self and the way in which that self inhabits a body, it can complicate the assumption that the material body is unproblematically available to us as a perfectly faithful reflection of the psychic self. Freud can help us describe the psychic conditions under which the body assumes a sex and consequently is useful in discussions of sexed embodiment in which we understand sex to be something other than a binary.

In what follows, I reexamine two Freudian concepts of particular relevance to discussions of transgender. First is Freud's critique of a binary model of sex in his discussion of hermaphroditism, a critique that has received surprisingly little attention. Second, I attempt something of a guided tour of his schematization of the bodily ego and the use to which it has been put by writers grappling with questions of gender, body, and identity. The concept of the bodily ego is of particular use in thinking transgender because it shows that the body of which one has a "felt sense" is not necessarily contiguous with the physical body as it is perceived from the outside. That is, the body one feels oneself to have is not necessarily the same body that is delimited by its exterior contours, and this is the case even for any normatively gendered subject. Taken together, these two models offer a theory of gendered embodiment in which the body is understood to be something more complex and capacious than a unitary formation of matter, singularly given to or claimed by only one sex. To understand embodiment as necessarily routed through a bodily ego is not to contend that body and ego are coterminous or selfsame, but to assert that projections of various kinds are required in the construction of both the ego and the body, that the ego is itself a projection, and that difference, distance, and otherness are at the heart of the ego and the body.

INTERSEXUAL CHARACTERS, BINARISM,
AND FREUD'S TEMPTATION

Freud opens *Three Essays on the Theory of Sexuality* with a string of provocative claims. The most startling among them is offered at the beginning of a discussion of his well-known theory that human beings are innately bisexual. "It is popularly believed," Freud begins, "that a human being is either a man or a woman."[2] Freud goes on to suggest that popular opinion on the subject might be mistaken, and that science "knows of cases in which the sexual characters are obscured, and in which it is impossible to determine the sex." In his discussion of hermaphroditism, conditions that we today would describe as intersexuality, Freud addresses the assumption that human beings are either male or female and suggests that this assumption is at root an error. He marshals the authority of science as evidence, where science possesses knowledge simultaneously secret (science knows about things of which popular opinion is ignorant) and authoritative (what science knows trumps what popular opinion assumes). In the case of sexes and bodies, what science "knows" are instances in which the sex of a body cannot easily be read from its surface and that, consequently, human beings are not always easily divisible into male or female. It is the science of anatomy upon which Freud is most reliant here—and, even more particularly, the anatomy of genital morphology, the reading of the sexual surfaces of the body in order to ascertain (or, in this case, confound) the interior "truth" of the body's sex.

Freud suggests that the hermaphroditic body's refusal to neatly conform to sexual binaries presents a wider cultural challenge to sexual boundaries—indeed, to the very notion of sex itself. This is accomplished by a curious double movement, where binaries are present both inside and outside the body at the level of morphology and at the level of culture. The intersexual body refuses to conform to the binary of sexual difference by which it could be easily categorized as "male" or "female." And yet, the means by which the cultural binary is challenged is the body's stubborn manifestation *of* a binary in which both male and female characteristics are legible at the surface of the body. Thus the body's stubborn insistence on a legible binary is precisely that which renders a categorical binary illegible.

Freud suggests that this gender ambiguous body has important implications for thinking sexed bodies, whether they be transgressively or normatively sexed. After positing science as the authority that can rectify popular opinion's misconceptions in matters of sex,

---

Freud explains why he wants to attend to the specificities of hermaphroditic bodies: "The importance of these abnormalities lies in the unexpected fact that they facilitate our understanding of normal development . . . [and] lead us to suppose that an originally bisexual physical disposition has, in the course of evolution, been modified into a unisexual one, leaving behind only a few traces of the sex that has become atrophied. It was tempting to extend this hypothesis to the mental sphere" (7).

What, exactly, is happening here? Freud grants that anatomical incidence of hermaphroditism is an "abnormality," a deviation from the normal, then asserts the "unexpected fact" that understanding this abnormality is a condition for understanding "normal development." This seems clear enough and squares with his later assessment of the biology of masculinity and femininity, even within the realm of the sexually "normal," as retaining the admixture of characteristics so prominent in the "abnormality" of hermaphroditism, so that "pure masculinity or femininity is not to be found either in a psychological or a biological sense. Every individual on the contrary displays a mixture of the character traits belonging to his own and the opposite sex" (86). The morphology of hermaphroditism is here the same *in kind* as "normal" morphology, differing only in the *degree* to which admixture is present. This is not to say that the difference between the normatively gendered and the hermaphrodite is insignificant, since the former has "his own" sex and the latter cannot. It does suggest, though, that the sex proper to any individual—the ability either to lay claim to ownership of a sex or to be claimed as the property of that sex—is itself a question of variation at the level of degree rather than of category.

What is most surprising in this passage is Freud's narration of his "temptation," which further radicalizes the propositions he sets forth. He plays with the idea that the physiology of the human species has developed from an originally bisexual morphology into a unisexual morphology, thus presenting—however briefly—the condition of intersexuality as the originary template for understanding sexual dimorphism in the species itself. This evolutionary metaphor can be read as having pernicious consequences, as it positions intersexual bodies as less developed, less evolved, than "unisexual" bodies, which have managed to "leave behind" the traces of the sex that they once retained. Bodily atrophy becomes the sign of phylogenic advancement. Yet, a more positive reading also presents itself, in which the intersexual body stands as the exemplary instantiation of sexual difference, both in the realm of morphology and in the realm of the psyche. For a moment, Freud offers the intersexual body as the condition that makes theorizing the universality of a "bisexual psychical disposition" possible at all. The extension of this hypothesis into the mental sphere, Freud offers, might explain "inversion in all of its varieties as the expression of a psychical hermaphroditism." What is proposed here is that intersexuality presents a productive disjunction between psyche and soma that can help us to understand both object choice and sexual identity, in cases of inversion, as well as, more startlingly, in "unisexual" bodies and psyches that take "normal" sexual objects.

But as soon as Freud narrates his temptation, he claims that it must be refused. However, the retraction is something less than a flat refusal, since Freud is so explicit in laying out the scope of what tempts him. The temptation to universalize his hypothesis is apparently more than Freud can resist, since he performs the extension even as he claims to refuse it. Freud regretfully concluded that the extension would not hold, dependent as it was on biological evidence that never materialized. That evidence—that "inverts," figured here as "psychical hermaphrodites," carry the somatic manifestations of hermaphroditism—could not be demonstrated. Thus Freud presents the "unexpected" universalizing turn, entertains it briefly by suggesting that "all that was required further to settle the question was that inversion should be regularly accompanied by the mental and somatic signs of hermaphroditism," then states that "this expectation was disappointed." The "evidence" was sought, on the one hand, in order to "settle the question" of the relation between inversion and hermaphroditism, and its absence clarifies the relation between inversion and somatic hermaphroditism: Freud finds no connection and concludes that they are "on the whole independent of each other." On the other hand, what remains *unsettled* is the question Freud raises as to the relationship between hermaphroditism and normal bisexual psychic disposition.

Freud's invocation of the categories of bisexual and unisexual in this context both clarifies and complicates matters. The use of the term *bisexual,* when it is oppositionally paired with a unisexual body, designates a body that displays both masculine and feminine characteristics (and the referent of *characteristics,* like the referent of *bisexuality,* is constantly shifting, alternately designating bodily appearance, the sexual apparatus (7), sex specific behaviors (8), and even the sexual instinct itself (6). In this sense, bisexuality becomes synonymous with hermaphroditism, and the use to which Freud is tempted to put hermaphroditism—his hope that an understanding of the hermaphroditic body might help us understand bisexuality— would appear to be frustrated by this conflation of terms, unless we are to understand that bisexuality simply *is* hermaphroditism. This last possibility finds support in Freud's choice of title for his discussion of hermaphroditism: "Bisexuality." Yet the discussion under consideration is but a brief detour (perversion?) in Freud's larger discussion of inversion. If bisexuality is simply hermaphroditism, this does not quite make explicit its relation to inversion. Like the examples of bisexuality Freud presents, the term cannot confine itself to one referent, but always works between registers. In outlining the relation between bisexuality and inversion, Freud refers to a second bisexuality that is not synonymous with somatic hermaphroditism, a "theory of bisexuality that has been expressed in its crudest form by a spokesman of the male inverts: 'a feminine brain in a masculine body'" (8).

According to this theory, bisexuality is always the appearance of masculinity alongside femininity, but the first type of bisexuality, the hermaphroditic type, is operative at the level of the body—male bodily attributes along with female bodily attributes. The second type, which Freud attributes to Karl Heinrich Ulrichs, removes the admixture of masculine and feminine from the realm of the strictly somatic. This model of bisexuality asserts that there is a coherent and unitary sex proper to the subject's body and another coherent and unitary sex proper to the subject's psyche. This, then, is an emphatic rejection of the notion of admixture that characterizes

Freud's bisexual body. Here each register, somatic or psychic, is capable of containing only one sexual possibility; thus sexual difference within the individual is safely contained within two distinct and unbreachable registers. Masculine and feminine are neatly split between the body and the psyche (or "brain"), and these categories are definitionally impermeable. Freud rejects this theory by suggesting that it unnecessarily "replaces the psychological problem with the anatomical one." That is, it displaces the question of sexual difference within the psyche onto the register of the body in a way that requires unsupportable conjecture, since "we are ignorant of what characterizes a feminine brain." For Freud, this characterization of bisexuality is insufficient in that it finds sexual difference incompossible within any given register and thus demands a consolidation of sexual signification within both soma and psyche in order for either to be sexually legible. The "crude" implication, Freud maintains, is that any admixture of masculine and feminine *within the same register* is socially and psychically unbearable. The sexual identifications that are possible in such a framework are circumscribed to such an extent that, practically speaking, we have returned to the realm of "popular opinion" in which a person must be either a man or a woman but never both. I will return to this metaphor of the "feminine brain in a masculine body" (and vice versa)—and the usefulness of Freud's critique of it—in later chapters, since it persists as a familiar trope in representations of transgender and transsexuality, although its phenomenological accuracy has been widely disputed in trans narratives.

Freud presents us with a body in which gender is divided between different registers, but the body is fractured at an even deeper level, since the physical body itself does not seem to exist as a simple and coherent whole for Freud. A notion of bodily unity that would depend on a body comprised of stable parts (both in the sense of nonchanging and selfsame and also easily identifiable) is hard to find in the Freud of *Three Essays*, insistent as he is on pointing out the ways in which bodies, whether hermaphroditic or unisexual, insist on signifying contrary to what we expect, whether we be "popular opinion," scientists, analysts, or theorists. We see Freud moving further away from a strictly biological or anatomical model of the body, focusing instead on the lability and plasticity of the erotogenic zones and detailing how these erotogenic zones give us a sense of bodily coherence. Freud lays out this alternative topography of the body in his discussion of infantile behavior and thumb sucking, in which he provides an expansive notion of what counts as an erotogenic zone: "any other part of the skin or mucous membrane can take over the functions of an erotogenic zone, and must therefore have the same aptitude in that direction. Thus the quality of the stimulus has more to do with producing the pleasurable feeling than has the nature of the body part concerned" (49). He has a great deal to say about the function of the mucous membrane of the mouth as an erotogenic zone, but he also designates the hand as an erotogenic zone (75) and claims that the skin is an erotogenic zone *par excellence* (35). Indeed, this ascription of erotogenicity can and does extend to every part of the body—to its surface, especially, but even to its very interiority. "I have been led," Freud says, somewhat boastfully, "to ascribe the quality of erotogenicity to all parts of the body and to all the internal organs" (50). Not only is everything capable of being a genital in this formulation, thus undermining the monolithic (or, at least, indexical) relation between genitals and sex, but the ability of the genitals to indicate sex is further undermined by Freud's comments about sex hormones and the transformative effects they had in mice: "It has become experimentally possible to transform a male into a female, and conversely a female into a male. In this process the psychosexual behavior of the animal alters in accordance with the somatic sexual characters and simultaneously with them" (81). In his speculative comments about hormones, Freud appears to be trying to strengthen the link between biology and sex or sexual identity: the biological change brought about by the introduction of sex hormones caused a concomitant change in the psychosexual behavior of the animal. The sexual behavior of the animal confirms its sex: the "heterosexual" behavior of the mouse (!) helps to determine its status as male or female. However, the move has the curious effect of *decoupling* the determination of sex from simple biological determinism: a change in hormonal level, which Freud takes care to distinguish from "spermatozoa or ova," produces an *actual male or an actual female*, regardless of genital morphology. The importance of spermatozoa and ova are not to be discounted, however. Even if they are unable to determine an individual's sex, they are, Freud tells us, determinative of masculinity and femininity: "'masculine' and 'feminine' are characterized by the presence of spermatozoa or ova respectively, and by the functions proceeding from them" (85). Taken together, these comments indicate that one can be a man without spermatozoa, but not masculine; one can be a woman without ova, but not feminine. After this diversion into the definitive role of biology in masculinity and femininity, Freud then assures us that neither can be found in a "pure" form either in a psychological or a biological sense, thus returning us to the realm of mixture and hermaphroditism, both psychologically and biologically.

Freud takes care to note that after the transformation of puberty "the erotogenic zones become subordinated to the primacy of the genital zone" (73). The same might be said of Freud's own theorizing, which, over time, becomes more consolidated and certain about the categories of sex, gender, and genitals. But there is a suspended state here in which Freud, however briefly, entertains the most radical notions of sex and gender. As Freud's thinking on the matter develops over time, the erotogenic zones do indeed become subordinated to the primacy of the genital zone in terms of their relative importance for his theorizing of masculinity and femininity. By the time of *Outline of Psychoanalysis* (1940), Freud is still considering bodies that display both male and female characteristics, but does not consider them to pose any serious challenge to the fundamental logic of binary sexual difference. A body is either male or female, and Freud asserts this as a "biological fact": "We are faced here by the great enigma of the biological fact of the duality of the sexes: it is an ultimate fact of our knowledge, it defies every attempt to trace it back to something else. Psycho-analysis has contributed nothing to clearing up this problem, which clearly falls wholly within the province of biology" (188). Perhaps we would do well to linger with Freud here in the initial, unsettled stage of his thinking on sex and biology—before the maturation of the theory—and consider some of the implications that might be drawn from it.

The ego is first and foremost a bodily ego; it is not merely a surface entity, but is itself the projection of a surface.
—SIGMUND FREUD, *THE EGO AND THE ID*, p. 26

In *The Ego and the Id*, Freud presents his famous assertion about
the bodily nature of the ego. Commentators have made much of
this sentence, and the brevity and ambiguity of the formulation
have led to much speculation about its consequences for theorizing
the nature of the ego and the nature of the body.[3] As we shall see,
some readers have suggested that Freud is shoring up the materiality of both the ego and the body here; others have claimed that it
is precisely the materiality of the body that is thrown into question
by this formulation. The first group of readers—those whose project is to claim for the body a concrete identity, self-sameness, and
irrefutable materiality—tends to read this passage as turning the
body and the ego into one indivisible unit, with the happy effect of
conferring an indissoluble materiality to both. The second group
tends to concentrate on the projection itself, asking after its mechanisms and material and noting the ways in which the visual register
is implicated in the construction of body and ego.

In the opening chapter of *The Threshold of the Visible World*,
"The Bodily Ego," Kaja Silverman asks how we should understand
Freud's claim that "from the very beginning and in its most profound sense, the ego is corporeal in nature" and how, in attempting to do so, we might understand "how gender, race, sexual preference and other culturally constructed and enforced distinctions
come into play at the level of the bodily ego."[4] Silverman turns first
to Lacan's theory of the mirror stage, in which Lacan more fully
elaborates the means through which the ego is constituted by and
as the projection of a surface. Lacan describes the infant held up
to a mirror by the mother and the infant's jubilation in seeing its
own reflection. As Silverman emphasizes, the infant's joy at being
presented with its own image is based on a complicated oscillation
between otherness and sameness: "On the one hand, the mirror
stage represents a *méconnaissance*, because the subject identifies

with what he or she is not. On the other hand, what he or she sees when looking into the mirror is literally his or her own image" (10–11). The infant recognizes him- or herself in the image of the being whose physical capacity outstrips his or her own. The impossibility of an absolute identity between image and the jubilant self that finds him- or herself in that image does not lessen the jubilation of the infant; the jubilance occasioned by a misrecognition fills the ego in a way that an "accurate" recognition never could. Silverman compares Lacan's account of the mirror stage with Henri Wallon's, in which what the infant recognizes in the mirror is not him- or herself, but a "love object" and, later, a "double or rival" (15). Wallon offers the anecdote of an infant who, when hearing his name, "looks to its mirror image rather than responding itself."

Silverman refers to this particular sort of identification through misrecognition as "identity-at-a-distance," a particularly elegant way of capturing the complicated interplay between interiority and exteriority, between sameness and difference, at the heart of our conceptions of both body and self. Although this formulation refers specifically to Wallon's account of the mirror stage, it can help us think the myriad ways in which the establishment of identity is always already marked by nonidentity or difference and contains distance at its very core. Silverman notes that this is true for Lacan, who "insists on the fictiveness and exteriority of the image which founds the ego" (10). If we take the liberty of widening the application of the formulation, we might conclude that, even more generally, there is a notion of distance built into *any* instance of identification. If that identification is with an idealized image, that image is always external to the subject simply by virtue of its location in the visual register, even as that image is internalized. And, too, symbolic identification, identification with an idealized subject position, is an impossible attempt to breach the gap between the particularity of any individual (failed) instantiation of a symbolic ideal and the ideal itself.

As we shall see, to think identity otherwise, as that which must exclude distance in order to be legible at all, is to repeat the scene of the infant before the mirror in an attempt to insist upon absolute coherence and wholeness. That coherence and wholeness, psychoanalysis insists, does not result in cultural legibility but, on the contrary, can only come at the price of representation itself. Plenitude and fullness, coherence and wholeness, are not only fictive states as far as subjectivity is concerned, but are the very conditions of being that are foreclosed by language and entry into the symbolic realm. Psychoanalysis offers a subject, fragmentary and incomplete, comprised of a body and a psyche. Not only do these two elements not add up to a coherent whole, neither body nor psyche can be properly thought as whole or complete.

The tripartite and fragmented structure of the psyche is by now familiar, but the psychoanalytic body, too, resists description as a unified whole. Charles Shepherdson calls the constitution of the body in psychoanalysis "that peculiar myth in which the little organism sets off in search of its body."[5] While this myth offers an exaggeratedly voluntaristic characterization of the situation, it does seem true that within psychoanalysis, one is not born a body, but becomes one. Lacan's mirror stage is an account of the way the infant, who had heretofore experienced his or her body in "bits and pieces," comes to identify with his visual imago, the idealized version of what he will eventually become. The temporal dislocation that attends the act is crucial: the infant feels himself to have a bodily coherence and mastery that he does not in fact possess at this stage of development. Bodily coherence is shown to be fictional in the sense that the infant assumes this coherence through an identification, an identification that is, like all forms of recognition, a misrecognition. There is a similarity between this account of phantasmatic bodily wholeness and Paul Schilder's: both assume that coherence is a function of the ego, rather than a reflection of the morphological configuration of the material body. The body that one "has" and the abilities or coherence that one attributes to it is a result of identification, which is always a fundamentally relational act. In Lacanian parlance, bodily coherence belongs to the realm of the Imaginary, not the realm of the Real.

As Silverman writes, within Lacan's schema, "the body does not exist even as a tenuous unity prior to its constitution through image, posture, and touch. Indeed, it cannot even be said to be 'in pieces,' since that implies that once assembled they would add up to a 'whole.' The physical indices through which 'difference' is ostensibly identified are consequently no more than insignificant elements within an incoherent conglomeration, devoid of both form and value" (22). I take that last sentence as a reminder that the desire to ground difference in body parts, to give the notion of identity an anchor in the realm of the irrefutably biological, will be frustrated from the outset by the picture we have of the body "prior to its constitution" through external forces: the raw stuff of the "literal body" (to use Silverman's phrase) simply does not provide a deep enough ground to plant a psychic identity.[6]

The body as it exists *for me*, the *corps propre*, only comes to be once the "literal body" assumes meaning through image, posture, and touch. And each of these examples of operations that constitute the body—image, posture, and touch—are predicated on distance. The externality of both image and touch would appear to be obvious, as would the distance necessary in the operations of identification and projection. But, as Schilder makes clear, even the "postural model" of the body, which would seem to be a wholly internal phenomenon, an internally discrete circuit, is itself built up through a series of images, identifications, and social relations.

SURFACE TENSION/SURFACE TRACTION

Bodily contours and morphology are not merely implicated in an irreducible tension between the psychic and the material but *are* that tension.

—JUDITH BUTLER, *BODIES THAT MATTER*, P. 66

Thus far, we have been examining representations of bodies primarily as surface. This figuration of bodies as surface is perhaps nowhere more apparent than in Didier Anzieu's work, in which he suggests that the effects of the models of depth and psychic interiority prevalent within psychoanalysis can just as easily be accounted for by a surface model. In *The Skin Ego* Anzieu takes Freud's formulation of the bodily ego as a starting point and postulates the ego as an envelope that contains the psyche in the same way the skin contains the body. *The Skin Ego* also owes much to Schilder's work: his definition of the skin ego is almost identical to Schilder's definition of the body image: it is "a mental image" that is both representative and constitutive of the self. Anzieu's text, like Freud's, frustrates an attempt to separate body and psyche into distinct and separate registers. Instead of viewing the skin as a metaphor for the psyche, he occasionally inverts this metaphor and suggests—in a somewhat startling formulation—that the psyche itself is a metaphor for the skin. "What if thought were as much an affair of the skin as of the brain?" he asks, and goes on to assert that the skin is indeed an "underlying base of human thought."[7]

Anzieu offers a systematic list of the ego's psychic functions: to maintain, contain, and protect the self; to act as a screen between self and world; to lend coherence to the self, etc. (Anzieu lists nine distinct functions, but stresses that the list is an open one.) He demonstrates that each of these functions can be assigned to the skin, that everything that holds true, psychically, for the ego can be read as a description of the structure and function of the skin (98–106). Though his reading emphasizes the comprehensiveness of the skin's functions—nearly every feature of bodily and psychic life can be located at is surface—the skin nevertheless resists characterization as a monolithic entity: "The skin is not a single organ but a whole set of different organs. Its anatomical, physiological and cultural complexity prefigures the complexity of the Ego on the psychical plane. Of all the sense organs, it is most vital . . . it alone combines the spatial and temporal dimensions" (14). Anzieu moves effortlessly back and forth between the materiality and the metaphoricity of skin, taking seriously Freud's suggestion that the skin is "the erotogenic zone *par excellence.*"

Anzieu asserts that "sexuality is accessible only to those who have acquired a minimum sense of basic security within their own skins" (39). This is a common enough synecdoche, in which familiarity or comfort at the level of the "skin" comes to stand in for a feeling of ease, comfort, or ownership in terms of the entire body. But how is it that we develop and maintain this feeling of ease within our own bodies, our own skins? And what are the consequences for embodiment and subjectivity when the relation between self and skin is not one of ease and euphoria but discomfort and dysphoria?

Radical as his notion of the skin ego is for rethinking both body and ego, Anzieu remains committed to the metaphor of the envelope, which at times threatens to reinstate the binary and hierarchized relation between body and psyche that he seems to want to upset. Anzieu emphasizes and appropriates the containment metaphors around which the Freudian schema is based: the body is the container that houses the psyche; the psyche is itself comprised of a surface envelope, a shell (consciousness) that surrounds and contains a kernel (the unconscious).[8] Anzieu is not alone in his advancement of this metaphor; this is perhaps one of the most common ways that Freud's commentators have conceptualized the relation of psyche and body.[9]

There are two problems with understanding the body as an envelope that houses the psyche, a covering for an internal "core." The first is that this psychic core becomes paradoxically both more solidified and completely evacuated as its contents become transferred, displaced to the surface of the body. Anzieu is committed to this formulation, opening his text with an elaboration of the body's function as a "dual support" of the psyche, in which the body is understood as comprised of a "biological body" and a "social body" (4). However, at crucial points, he seems to invert it entirely:

> By Skin Ego, I mean a mental image of which the Ego of the child makes use during the early phases of its development to represent itself as an Ego containing psychical contents, on the basis of its experience of the surface of the body. This corresponds to the moment at which the psychical Ego differentiates itself from the bodily Ego at the operative level while remaining confused with it at the figurative level.
>
> (40)

Though we are still within a model that thinks the relation between body and psyche as one of containment, the terms have inverted: traditional "envelope" metaphors for body give an "inside" of matter that is encased by a social envelope. Anzieu presents the "matter" as *outside*, as skin, that contains a nonmaterial psychic depth.

The second problem with this formulation of a material core overlaid with a psychic surface is its tendency to discount the surface as nonessential or unimportant or to rush past it in search of what "really" lies beneath it. As we shall see, Jay Prosser's use of surface causes him to always be looking behind or beneath the surface, where "surface" comes to stand in for a wild array of different things—the psyche, language, and even queer theory itself, and the core is thought as the body, materiality, and, most surprisingly, "the transsexual"—"The transsexual reveals queer theory's own limits: what lies beyond or beneath its favored terrain of gender performativity" (6). The model of surface, of covering, is seen as an occasion for an inquiry after what is behind or beneath that surface. Prosser wants to reveal the hidden and, presumably, disavowed materiality that lies beneath performativity, a materiality performativity (understood as synonymous with queer theory understood, ultimately, as synonymous with "Judith Butler") is trying to hide.

And, yet, this is not the *only* way to think this relation, as we will see in chapter 6. Elizabeth Grosz, for example, eschews metaphors of containment and models of depth in her discussions of the bodily ego, instead characterizing Freud's bodily ego as a play of surfaces. The body, for Grosz, is comprised of *inner* and *outer* surfaces, rather than an enclosing envelope: the ego is on the "inner" surface of the psyche and is a projection of the body's "outer" surface.[10] Grosz's emphasis on a surface model over and against a depth model is shared by authors coming from a number of different disciplines.[11]

This conception of the body as an envelope is where Anzieu's account of the bodily ego can be seen to diverge from the bodily ego as formulated by Paul Schilder. For what Schilder's body schema presents us with is the notion that the *body can and does exceed the confines of its own skin*. That is, the body is not an envelope for psyche, and the skin is not an envelope for the body: both body and psyche are characterized by their lability rather than their ability to contain.

Schilder's *The Image and Appearance of the Human Body* is an attempt to theorize just this relation between body and self. Schilder suggests the compossibility of an authentic and irrefutable "felt sense" of the body and the psychic mediation that connects that felt sense with our understanding of our own bodily materiality. Crudely summarized, Schilder's argument is as follows: we only have recourse to our bodies through a body image, a psychic representation of the body that is constructed over time. The body image is multiple (any person always has more than one), it is flexible (its configuration changes over time), it arises from our relations with other people, and its contours are only rarely identical to the contours of the body as it is perceived from the outside. Although Schilder's is the first book devoted to the subject, and he is often cited as having introduced the concept of the body image,[12] his theory owes much not only to Freud's notion of the bodily ego, which he takes as his starting point, but also to the works of early neurologists such as Henry Head. It is Head's "postural model" of the body, in fact, from which Schilder's body image is largely drawn. Indeed, Schilder often uses the terms *postural model, body image,* and *body schema* interchangeably.[13] Perhaps Schilder's most vital contribution to discussions of embodiment is his use of an interdisciplinary approach, his insistence from the outset that psychoanalysis, phenomenology, and neurology cannot and should not be conceived of as separate and distinct methods of inquiry into the question of embodiment.[14] It is this interdisciplinarity that allows him to take Freud's psychoanalytic concept of the bodily ego as a structure then informed by the findings of neurology and the approach of phenomenology.[15]

Silverman's presentation of Schilder's theory of the postural model of the body foregrounds the distance at its heart. Upon first consideration, nothing would appear to be more internal, or phenomenologically closer, to the subject than her bodily sensations. Far from being "biologically given," the body image, Silverman notes, "must be painstakingly built up" into the assemblage that we eventually come to recognize as a whole,[16] if only provisionally so. This process is never complete or final; the postural model exists less as a stable thing through space and time and more as a series of different models. Thus our sense of the body image, the postural model of the body, is a sedimented effect without a stable referent or predictable content, since it may be different in form and shape, moment to moment, through each new iteration.

It is the *constructedness* of the body image that Schilder wants to emphasize in his account, a construction that always takes place in a social world. The body image is always contextually situated, in relation to other bodies and to the world, and its construction is a social phenomenon: "The postural model of the body has to be built up. It is a creation and a construction and not a gift. *It is not a shape . . . but the production of a shape.* There is no doubt that this process of structuralization is only possible in close contact with experiences concerning the world" (113; emphasis mine). And elsewhere the image of the body is "not a structure, but a structuralization" (174). Here we see a clear echo of Freud's description of the bodily ego not as a surface, but the projection of a surface. In each case the important term is not the noun, but the verb; not the material, but the operation that gives it.

It would seem to be apparent that the body, in this account, is far from a simple biological given. Perhaps more subtly, the constituent parts of the body cannot be thought as biologically given prior to their assemblage. Even cutaneous sensation is not experienced without the intervention of psychic mediation. Silverman notes that, for Schilder, cutaneous sensation, "that element in the postural model of the body which would seem to evade psychic mediation," shows itself to be, like the specular image, built up from external stimuli: "Without social exchange, Schilder insists, it [the postural model] would never come into existence, since it can be defined only through the relationship between the body and the world of objects . . . it is only when the surface of our body comes into contact with other surfaces that we are even able to perceive it."[17] Touch is not external to, but constitutive of, the postural model of the body, whether it be the touch of external objects, or the touch of other human beings. Indeed, as Silverman points out, it is not only the touch of others that shapes our postural model but even "the interest others take in the different parts of our body" that is capable of shaping the body (126).[18] Silverman concludes that one of the most vital things that Schilder presents is the way that "an erotogenic zone is a feature of the bodily ego (14)," a reading that hinges on both Freud's account of the bodily ego and Laplanche's assessment of the significance of the openings of the body. Following Freud, Schilder highlights the disproportional significance played by the erotogenic zones and the openings of the body in the development of the body schema and articulates two different levels on which the development of the body image proceeds. "The building-up of the postural model of the body takes place on the physiological level by continual contact with the outside world. On the libidinous level it is built up on only by the interest we ourselves have in our body, but also by the interest other persons show in the different parts of our body. They may show their interest by actions or merely by words and attitudes" (137).

Schilder's move here, his inclusion of both touch and affect in the class of things that change, or create, the bodily schema establishes two things: first, the body schema's *origins* are relational, as is its function as a mediating entity between self and world (its *function* is relational). Second, this relationality, and its introduction of the social into the body/psyche circuit of the body schema, ensures that the body schema cannot be construed as an entirely voluntaristic project, somehow freely chosen by the subject. "There is no question," Schilder writes, "that our own activity is insufficient to build up the image of the body" (126).

The body schema is an image, a representation of the body, but it is also more than this. It is the perception, immediate and certain, that the body comprises a unit, but even here the body schema "is not a mere perception" and "is not mere representation" (11). Schilder is somewhat suspicious of the language of representation, insisting that "when we speak of pictures we simplify the facts" (176), and, following Head, emphasizes the *temporal* nature of the body schema. The postural model of the body changes over time, even from moment to moment; it is "in perpetual inner self-construction and self-destruction" (15–16). Perhaps even more crucially, the body schema's relationship to the past is an anaclitic one, where the coherence of the body is only established through reliance on a layer of accumulated memories whose support is then rendered invisible. Schilder opens *The Image and the Appearance of the Human Body* with Head's definition of bodily schemata:

> These [past impressions] may rise into consciousness as images, but more often, as in the case of special impressions, remain outside of central consciousness. Here they form organized models of ourselves, which may be termed "schemata." Such schemata modify the impressions produced by incoming sensory impulses in such a way that the final sensation of position, or of locality, rises into consciousness charged with a relation to something that has happened before. . . . Every recognizable change enters into consciousness already charged with relation to something that has happened before, just as on a taxi-meter the distance is represented to us already transformed into shillings and pence.
>
> (11–12)

What appears to be the immediate and unmediated sensation of the wholeness and coherence of the body turns out to be entirely reliant on the operation of memory. What finally delivers "the sensation of position, or of locality" to the body, and, importantly, to consciousness, is the relation between the "sensory impulse" and past impressions or memories, between a present feeling and *something that happened before*. The activity of the nerves, the sensory impulse of the body, is necessary but not sufficient for the production of the body schema, which relies for its coherence on a vast storehouse of past impressions, sensations, fantasies, and memories. Any bodily position only becomes psychically legible (and, thus *physically* legible) within the context of, and based on its resemblance to, its similarity to past physical positions. This translation is instantaneous, and there is neither any conscious translation necessary, nor any gap in time between the sensation and the translation.

Schilder insists that "changes in the body-image tend immediately to become changes in the body" (137). Within his formulation, then, the material body becomes something more plastic and labile than the body image. Even as it constantly cycles through its own production and destruction, even as it changes size, shape, behavior, and degree of coherence, the body image persists as the only means by which we apprehend our own bodies. Without the libidinal investment that can only be routed to the body through the mediating effect of the body image, the stuff of the body is reduced to "vague material" (166) without shape or form. And our relation to that "vague material" is often one of distance rather than proximity, where even the bodies of others may be more phenomenologically proximate to us than our own: "What is our own body and what is the body of others? . . . Our own body is not nearer to us than the outside world, at least in important parts" (234). What the function of the body image shows us is that the proximity between our own bodies and the world can be closer than the distance between the materiality of our bodies and our grasping of that body.

Schilder asks, "What is the physiological basis of the knowledge of our body?" His answer suggests that bodily materiality, even as we grant it, is not a simple matter: "Our discussion will show that we have to do with a complicated apparatus" (13). "We," as bodies, have to do with the "complicated apparatus" of the postural model of the body; it is fundamentally related to the questions of materiality and self. But, in some sense, Schilder is suggesting that we, as inquirers into the nature of the body, have to *make do* with the complicated apparatus of the body schema in lieu of any certainty about its physiological basis. An appeal to the "vague material" of the unmediated body is unable to settle the question of bodily materiality, since this "vague material" is always the precipitate of a psychic relation between body and world.

Indeed, the postural model of the body is itself not enough to guarantee any certainty about the various ways in which its materiality might be deployed. Schilder spends a great deal of time examining cases in which neurological impairment results in a disjunction between body image and the "literal body," between internal and external perceptions of the body. He is careful to note that these distortions of the body image, represented in their most extreme form in cases of anosognosia and hemiplegia, are "exaggerations" of the disjunction between the body and its representation that is present even in the "normal person" (81). "We are dealing, then, with general laws, which are of great importance for pathology as well as for the knowledge of our own body" (94). In discussing phantom limbs, Schilder takes pains to avoid relegating the phenomenon to pathology, insisting that "we" normal people have phantoms, too.

If the existence of the body schema asks us first to reconsider the question of the accessibility of the body's materiality, it next poses the questions: How is it that our bodies come to signify in excess of their material contours? What kind of body is this, and how is it understood and lived?

IMAGINARY MORPHOLOGIES

In laying out the structure of the morphological imaginary, Butler reads Freud's commentary on the questions of genital morphology and bodily coherence. She takes *On Narcissism* as a starting point, in which he defines erotogenicity: "Let us now, taking any part of the body, describe its activity of sending sexually exciting stimuli to the mind as its 'erotogenicity.'"[19] As we have seen, the attribution of erotogenicity to various body parts determines what "counts," both psychically and physically, as a body part and is directly related to our feelings of bodily coherence (or bodily disjunction). In her reading of Freud, Butler suggests that this notion of erotogenicity upsets the possibility of establishing a causal relationship between the material anatomy of a body part and its representation in the imaginary and replaces that causal thesis with a model that understands their appearance as temporally coincident: "If erotogenicity is produced through the conveying of a bodily activity through an idea, then the idea and the conveying are phenomenologically coincident. As a result, it would not be possible to speak about a body part that precedes and gives rise to an idea, for it is the idea that emerges simultaneously with the phenomenologically accessible body, indeed, that guarantees its accessibility" (59).

Butler rejects a paradigm of embodiment that thinks a material body overlaid with a layer of social/imaginary, encouraging us, rather, to consider the ways in which their emergence is, phenomenologically speaking, simultaneous. Though not causal, the relationship between flesh and idea(l) is both necessary and productive. Any part of the body, indeed, the body itself, has the same status as Schilder's body: it is only given, only accessible, through a mediating psychic structure. The structure of the "idea" thus corresponds to the structure of the body schema. And, like Schilder's body schema, the "idea" is capable of giving rise to properties that do not correspond indexically to the surface of the body, thus making accessible a body part whose ontological status in the material realm is less than certain: "These variable body surfaces or bodily egos may thus become sites of transfer for properties that no longer belong properly to any anatomy" (64).

Butler's morphological imaginary builds upon Schilder's schema in that she attends explicitly to the role of sexual difference in bodily representation. Our experience of the "fact" of anatomy is structured by a heterosexist symbolic whose operation is both ubiquitous and veiled. In the project of rethinking sexual difference and reconfiguring gender, the terrain of materiality is unlikely to produce the sorts of productive reconfigurations that might be possible within the imaginary domain. For if sexual difference pretends to deliver a certainty about the "truth" of identity at the level of anatomy, this "truth" arrives *only at the level of the imaginary*, which both governs the production of that anatomy and makes it available to the psyche.

From here we can dispense with two of the more persistent and widespread misunderstandings of Butler's theorization of the morphological imaginary (and her stance on materiality and embodiment in general). The first understands *imaginary* and *fantasy* as synonymous with imagination, hallucination, delusion, or conjecture and reads fantasy as that which is fundamentally opposed to materiality and reality (which are functionally synonymous). As Butler points out, fantasy must *not* be understood on the one hand as idle imagining or inconsequential daydream, which would figure the realm of fantasy as a free play infused with neither affect nor consequence. The stakes in the relation between fantasy and morphology, Butler insists, are high indeed: it is the location of subjectivity itself. On the other hand, to read fantasy as psychotic hallucination (or neurotic hysteria) is to overinvest it with affect. This characterization fails to account for the intertwining of the imaginary and social realms, obscuring the ways that the structure of fantasy *is* the structure of identification. As Butler remarks: "Fantasy in this sense is to be understood not as an activity *of* an already formed subject, but of the staging and dispersion of the subject into a variety of identificatory positions" (267n7). Fantasy is not something that the subject does, but rather something that enables the subject.

In broader terms, fantasy is often mischaracterized as a term opposed to reality, where the meaning of the latter term is thought to be self-evident, and its superiority to the realm of "mere" fantasy, obvious. This same structure is encountered in the second common misreading of Butler, the objection that Butler does not believe in materiality at all, or that her work is an aggressive attempt to strip bodies of their flesh and, consequently, subjects of their "reality." *Bodies That Matter* attempts to address the anxiety that dispensing with a causal relationship between body and psyche is necessarily to simply dispense with materiality altogether. She remarks that the caricature of this positing materiality as wholly an effect of the psyche

> would constitute a clearly untenable form of idealism. It must be possible to concede and affirm an array of "materialities" that pertain to the body, that which is signified by the domains of biology, anatomy, physiology, hormonal and chemical composition, illness, age, weight, metabolism, life and death. None of this can be denied. But the undeniability of these "materialities" in no way implies what it means to affirm them, indeed, what interpretive matrices condition, enable and limit that necessary affirmation. . . . [Materiality is] the "that without which" no psychic operation can proceed, but also . . . that on which and through which the psyche also operates.
>
> (66–67)

Butler's position on this matter is quite clear: she is not claiming that there is no such thing as materiality, but rather that when we claim bodies are material, the content of that claim remains vague and unclear. Not only does bodily materiality exist for Butler, she takes pains to insist that we must affirm that materiality, and that this affirmation is a fundamental condition of subjectivity.

How is it, then, that Butler's inquiry into the content and meaning of these "necessary affirmations" of subjectivity becomes construed as evidence of her unwillingness to take the body seriously?

THE MATERIAL FIGURE OF THE (R)EAL TRANSSEXUAL

Answering this question necessitates posing several others, namely: what is it that some queer and trans writers find liberating about the idea of substance? Why is bodily materiality appealed to for relief and redress, and how can the production of non-normatively sexed and gendered subjectivities be secured and sustained by this appeal? What is sought for queer and trans bodies and subjects in these appeals? What identities and solutions seem promised by bodily materiality and what identities and solutions does it prohibit?

In *Second Skins: The Body Narratives of Transsexuality*, Jay Prosser advances a theory of transsexual subjectivity that emphasizes the primacy of bodily materiality. Prosser wants to secure a bodily mooring for transsexual identity; he argues that the connection between transsexual subjectivity and transsexual embodiment has been loosened, or severed altogether, by queer theory's focus on the constructedness and discursiveness of bodies. In this sense *Second Skins* is representative of several attempts in trans studies to combat the historic neglect of transsexuality, particularly within feminist and queer theory. In regard to the political aims of such a project, Prosser and Butler would surely be in agreement; the political motivation behind Butler's inquiry into alternatively gendered embodiments does not differ significantly from Prosser's. They part company in the different means by which they attempt to reach the goal of theorizing a transsexual subjectivity.

Second Skins is emblematic of a trend in trans studies that appeals to bodily materiality in order to secure a firm foundation for both the specificity and difference of trans subjectivity. As we will see in chapter 3, many trans theorists conclude that a "real" materiality is the only thing that can give traction to the transgendered subject, to anchor his or her identity in both difference (the specificity of my transgendered body secures for me a coherent identity) and sameness (the materiality of my body extends subjecthood to me just as the materiality of your normatively gendered body extends subjecthood to you). *Second Skins* is both symptomatic of this larger trend and importantly unique in its theoretical engagements and investments and its suggestion that psychoanalysis, in particular, might be put to productive use in theorizing transsexual subjectivity.

Prosser attempts to locate "a substance to gendered body image" (6–7). This substance has three main attributes: 1. it is unequivocally material, 2. it provides incontestable evidence of the existence of "gendered realness," that is, it "gives the lie to social construction," and 3. it secures for transsexuality an identity grounded in sexual difference. I want to consider the possibility that Prosser asks the wrong question here, and suggest that the usefulness of the body image for theorizing gendered embodiment is precisely not that the body image is material, but that it allows for a resignification of materiality itself. For now, we will content ourselves with examining the explicitly psychoanalytic support that Prosser finds for his argument in favor of "gendered realness."

Prosser examines Butler's reading of Freud's bodily ego, concluding that her "rather eclectic" reading results in the deliteralization of sex. Prosser accuses Butler of playing fast and loose with the referent, where that referent is both "the body" of *The Ego and the Id* and, in a larger sense, the material body itself. Prosser charges that within Butler's reading of the Freudian bodily ego—a reading he considers to be "against the manifest sense" (42) of the text—the body is "square bracketed, demoted" (41) in order to allow her to conclude that the body springs from the ego. This, Prosser insists, is exactly contrary to Freud's point, which is that the ego springs from the body that, by virtue of its materiality, lends materiality to the ego. As support for his reading of Freud, and his quarrel with Butler, Prosser enlists Anzieu, whom he sees as battling the "desomatization" that has been the unfortunate byproduct of, alternately, Lacanian and post-Lacanian psychoanalysis (79, 242n13), poststructuralism (12–13), and queer theory (31–32). Prosser summarizes Anzieu's theorization of the skin ego thus:

> Anzieu emphasizes "the projection of a surface" as *derived from* bodily sensations" to represent the image of the body as derived from the feeling of the body. With a wonderfully uncomplicated literalism Anzieu renders Freud's "surface" as the skin. The body's physical surface or encasing provides the anaclitic support for the psychic apparatus: the ego, the sense of self, derives from the experience of the material skin. The body is not only commensurable with its "mental" projection but responsible for producing this projection. The body is crucially and materially formative of the self. Anzieu's means of demonstrating that all psychic structures stem from the body, the skin ego returns the ego to its bodily origins in Freud.
>
> (65)

Despite Prosser's appreciation for Anzieu's methodology, which he understands to be a "wonderfully uncomplicated literalism," it is clear that Anzieu works precisely at the juncture of the material and the phantasmatic and refuses to privilege the former over the latter. "The Skin Ego," he writes, "is a reality of the order of phantasy,"[20] where phantasy is seen as constituting the subject and as inseparable from "reality," just as in Butler's deployment of the term. Anzieu's reading of the Freudian bodily ego, in fact, concurs quite neatly with Butler's; he parses Freud's comment on the bodily ego exactly as Butler does, as establishing the body as "the projection of a surface": "The Ego is fundamentally a surface, to use Freud's expression (the surface of the psychical apparatus) and the projection of a surface (that of the body)" (136).

The desire for an "uncomplicated literalism" when sorting through these questions of body, materiality, and subjectivity is certainly understandable, particularly when so much is at stake. An uncomplicated resolution to the "question of the body"—and to the concomitant question of identity and subjectivity—would surely be a relief. Prosser's sees Butler's reading of Freud as symptomatic of a wider dismissal of materiality in favor of discursivity and views his own project as a call for a return to the simplicity of materiality. And yet, this call is a discursive operation that is deceptively complex. Any insistence on a bodily materiality outside and opposed to discourse about bodies is not, of course, located outside discourse: the call itself proceeds discursively. Butler elucidates this very dilemma:

> To posit a materiality outside of language is still to posit that materiality, and the materiality so posited will retain that positing as its constitutive condition. To posit a materiality outside of language, where that materiality is considered ontologically distinct from language, is to undermine the possibility that language might be able to indicate or correspond to that domain of radical alterity. Hence, the absolute distinction between language and materiality which was to secure the referential function of language undermines that function radically.
>
> (67–68)

Further complicating the picture is the fact that Prosser chooses to examine "the material figure of transition" and "the materiality of transsexual narratives." Though it is certainly possible to make claims about the relation between materiality and the figural, or materiality and narrative, it seems doubtful that that relation, in either case, is one of simple correspondence. The narrative and the figural are by their very nature inseparable from discursivity; it is unclear what it might mean to think these things outside language or, indeed, how the materiality of a narrative or a figure might correspond in shape or function to the materiality of flesh. And what kind of materiality is it whose purchase on "reality" is so tenuous as to be constantly threatened by the power of discourse to undermine or unseat it?

Prosser's position on bodily materiality is secured by a set of disavowals whereby transsexuals' relation to their "fleshy materiality" is uncomplicatedly and unproblematically positive and affirmative. It is easy to sympathize with the political aims of this strategy, yet it is fantastically strange that Prosser appeals to psychoanalysis to aid him here, because such an appeal fundamentally misunderstands what is arguably psychoanalytic theory's most important insight about the relation of the subject to his or her body. What Freud, Lacan, Schilder, Anzieu, Butler, and Silverman all suggest is that bodily assumption, and hence subject formation itself, is a constant and complex oscillation between narcissistic investment in one's own flesh and the "necessary self-division and self-estrangement" (to borrow a phrase from Butler) that is the very means by which our bodies are articulated. Prosser claims to be following Silverman in theorizing the relation between body and ego, stating that his "attempt to think transsexual embodiment here runs parallel to Silverman's chapter entitled 'The Bodily Ego,'"[21] but Silverman herself warns of the dangers of "naturalizing" the "psychic entity" of the ego.[22]

Founding a subjectivity on a bodily materiality that is ostensibly nondiscursive—whether that subjectivity is normatively or non-normatively gendered, whether that body is unisexual or bisexual—places the subject in a "domain of radical alterity" that aspires to be separate from, and uncontaminated by, the domain of language. And if that subject is also required to be an unbroken figure of plenitude, if any disjuncture at the level of the body or the psyche, or any disconnect between the two, must be disavowed or repudiated to secure subjectivity, then we are entering into psychoanalytic territory that is uncannily familiar. Prosser's emphatic insistence that the transsexual body is "unimpeachably real" ends up landing him squarely in the Real, that domain of plenitude and fullness that not only exists outside of language, but, indeed, is fundamentally incompossible with subjectivity itself. Psychoanalytically speaking, to be characterized by total plenitude and without lack is to be outside of language, outside of meaning, outside of the symbolic, outside of relation, outside of desire. It is a motionless and meaningless stasis equated with radical abjection and death—not a productive position from which to theorize subjectivity, trans or otherwise.

Prosser claims that transsexuals have an "investment of sex in the flesh" that is "undeniable." Here he would find no argument from Butler, who is quite explicit in her repeated insistence that the materiality of the body must be affirmed. Nor would his assertion be contested by Schilder, who suggests that narcissistic investment in the body is a precondition of livable embodiment: "We have to expect strong emotions concerning our own body. We love it. We are narcissistic" (15). Without that investment, our relationship to our bodies is one of depersonalized estrangement: my sense of the "mine-ness" of my own body—and, crucially, even my sense of its coherence—depends on this narcissistic investment.[23] Silverman, too, agrees that our bodily investments are undeniable.

To affirm a materiality—or, to be less abstract, to insist on the livability of one's own embodiment, particularly when that embodiment is culturally abject or socially despised—is to undertake a constant and always incomplete labor to reconfigure more than just the materiality of our own bodies. It is to strive to create and transform the lived meanings of those materialities. Or, as Butler concludes "The Lesbian Phallus and the Morphological Imaginary chapter of *Bodies That Matter*": "What is needed is not a new body part, as it were, but a displacement of the hegemonic symbolic of (heterosexist) sexual difference and the critical release of alternative imaginary schemas for constituting sites of erotogenic pleasure" (91).

2

THE SEXUAL SCHEMA

Transposition and Transgender in
Phenomenology of Perception

The body . . . is always something other than what it is, always
sexuality and at the same time freedom.
—MAURICE MERLEAU-PONTY,
PHENOMENOLOGY OF PERCEPTION

What I am all told overflows what I am for myself.
—MAURICE MERLEAU-PONTY,
THE VISIBLE AND THE INVISIBLE

PHENOMENOLOGY AND AMBIGUITY

In *Phenomenology of Perception* Merleau-Ponty makes but a single
reference to what might be called mixed-gender embodiment: "A
patient feels a second person implanted in his body. He is a man in
half his body, a woman in the other half" (88). This remark would
not seem to promise much for thinking about non-normative gender configurations. We are introduced to this person of indeterminate gender as a "patient," already marked by some indistinct
but defining sign of emotional or mental distress. That patient is
doubly confined within a binary system of gender. Even though this
patient is, phenomenologically speaking, both a man and a woman,

this gender configuration is not thought as some new third term that might exceed the binary of man and woman, but is conceived by Merleau-Ponty as a man, intact and entire, somehow fused with an also properly gendered woman, with the body divided down the middle neatly between them.[1] Despite this, I want to argue that, even given the dearth of attention to non-normative genders in this text, the phenomenological approach to the body that Merleau-Ponty offers in *Phenomenology of Perception* can be uniquely useful for understanding trans embodiment.[2]

Perhaps the most vital aspect of phenomenology is its insistence that the body is crucial for understanding subjectivity, rather than incidental to or a distraction from it. And one of the most important aspects of the body is its manifestation and apprehension of sexuality. Though Merleau-Ponty has been criticized for his masculinist approach, his insistence that sexuality is vital for understanding both the human body and subjectivity offers at least the promise of new ways of conceptualizing each that would seem to be aligned with feminism and trans studies.[3] That his work has not been much utilized in this way may speak to the strangely liminal position that gender and sexuality hold within his work: embodied yet not entirely physical, inescapable yet inchoate, both persistently present and impossible to locate.[4] In Merleau-Ponty's work there is something essentially *ambiguous* in sexuality. I suggest that this ambiguity need not be read, as it most often has been, as a phobic or hostile "avoidance" of sexual difference, but rather as a more purposeful confounding of that category.[5] There is something enabling in this philosophy of ambiguity; it is precisely the ambiguity attending sexuality that can become the means for understanding bodies, lives, and especially *relationality* outside the domains of male or female.

Merleau-Ponty describes that ambiguity through his explication of the sexual schema. Like the body schema, the sexual schema is a temporal affair and, like the body schema, the presentness of the sexual schema is inescapable and spans different temporalities, always pointing both to the past and to the future. This temporality of the sexual schema extends forward insofar as that which animates my body through desire depends upon those sensations, either compelling or painful, that I have previously experienced: my history shapes my desire. It also extends backward, as those experiences that I have previously had coalesce into a recognizable whole for me, to which I then give a narrative. My sexual desire, located always in this futural mode, thus meshes with my sexual history, located in my past, and creates a sexual self. The sexual schema both depends on my history and makes a history out of my past.

There is a danger of overstating the confluence of sexuality and identity, and this danger is particularly acute in relation to transpeople. Second-wave feminist receptions of transsexuality,[6] some recent biological theories about transsexuality,[7] and popular misconceptions of transsexuality all share this conflation of gender expression with sexual expression.[8] Historically, transsexuality has often been fantasized to be—and thus described as—a kind of hypersexualization; some trans writers' effort to disengage from the realm of sexuality stems from this historical conflation of transgenderism with sexuality. For example, Christine Jorgensen's autobiography, in which she claims to have no sexual feelings at all, can be read as a counterargument to the assertion that transsexuality is really "about" sexual desire rather than gender expression and that transformation of gender at the level of the body is only undertaken for the purposes of a closed circuit of sexual gratification.[9] The trans body thus becomes something akin to a fetish, and those aspects of bodily transition in particular or transgender experience in general that are motivated by a desire for a specific kind of gender presentation, rather than a specific kind of sexual expression, drop out of the model entirely.

But deemphasizing sexuality to avoid the perils of fetishization would seem to be accompanied by a different set of perils, for it is certainly an impoverished account of subjectivity that cannot make room for desire, and we might ask what sorts of contortions result when trans subjects are required to suppress or deny their sexuality. Might there be a way of avoiding the groundless conflation of transsexuality with sexual fetishism without denying trans subjects a sexuality altogether? Is there room in this picture for desire?

Merleau-Ponty opens his inquiry into the nature and experience of sexuality and its importance to embodiment by offering sexuality as a causal impetus for beloved objects in the world. "Let us try to see how a thing or a being begins to exist for us through desire or love" (154). This is not only an acknowledgment of the difficulty that we have, as embodied subjects, in recognizing other embodied subjects as subjects, the sometimes surprising efforts required, both rational and affective, for us to recognize that *this other who stands before me is like-me but not-me.* I only become bound to this other through "desire or love," and through that relation of desire or love the other comes to exist for me as a thing or being. But through a revisitation of Descartes and a tour through empiricism's correspondence problem, Merleau-Ponty comes to ask after the being of the self, the ontological solidity of *my* body, and not just the body of the other. What he eventually concludes is that I, too, am brought into being through desire or love. The beloved other comes to exist in my phenomenological field as such to the extent that she comes to exist *for me.* But I, too, come to exist *for myself* in this scenario, and only to the extent that either the other exists *for me* or I exist *for the other,* or perhaps both. Sexuality may be ambiguous, but it has an immensely generative power, a power that refuses to be distributed along familiar lines of heteronormative procreation. Indeed, this power to bring about the self is realized insofar as it refuses lines of procreation that would be either heteronormative on the one hand or autogenetic on the other. The former would require that the other and I are in some sense *for* a third and the latter would have me only *for myself.*

What might it mean to suggest that the body itself comes to be though desire? This claim underscores the degree to which our embodiment is intersubjective, a project that can only be undertaken in the presence and with the recognition of other embodied beings.[10] Merleau-Ponty's project must then be read as a radical unsettling of the Cartesian tradition that understands me to be a subject only to the extent that I am distinct and separate from others, where physical confirmation of that separateness can be found in the perfect boundedness of my body. These boundaries, Merleau-Ponty will suggest, are dissolved by sexuality. In this way, sexuality is more than just an affective response to a bodily event; there is, he claims "nothing to be said" about affectivity in this regard (155). This can be read as a reaction against aspects of the psychoanalytic model of sexuality, which he understands to be both determinative (bodily morphology determining psychic structures, anatomy is or as destiny) and programmatic (any somatic symptom lends itself to only one interpretation, that of sexual repression). Merleau-Ponty is writing specifically against Freud here, and I would argue that this section of the *Phenomenology* is offering the least interesting reading possible of Freud's theories of sexuality. For all his quarrel with psychoanalysis, Merleau-Ponty is in fact not rejecting understandings of either the mind *or* the body that psychoanalysis offers, but merely moving the capacities of the unconscious from the domain of the mind to the domain of the body and thus reconfiguring the imaginary topography of the subject rather than diminishing its capacity by doing away with the unconscious altogether. Unincorporated traumatic events from a "past that was never a present" (242) thus find both their retention and expression through a bodily, rather than a psychic, unconscious.[11]

Nevertheless, just as proprioception offers us a way of reading and understanding the body beyond the visible surface of its exterior, so too does sexuality make of the body a thing that is internality and externality folded one around the another. Indeed, internality and externality are themselves not perfectly bounded, and Merleau-Ponty describes sexuality in terms that precisely match a psychoanalytic, proprioceptive model of embodiment. The phenomenology of sexuality that Merleau-Ponty offers, its suffusion of the body entire and its transformation of the body into something whose erotogenic zones are almost entirely labile, maps almost perfectly onto the topography of sexuality that Freud lays out in *Three Essays on the Theory of Sexuality*.[12]

Sexuality is a matter not of seeing but of *sensing*, which takes place below and beyond the threshold of the visible: "The visible body is subtended by a sexual schema, which is strictly individual, emphasizing the erogenous areas, outlining a sexual physiognomy, and eliciting the gestures of the masculine body which is itself integrated into this emotional totality" (156). In this description, sex is not simply compared with or analogized to proprioception: sexuality *is* proprioceptive (and so, too, is sex, which we shall turn to in a moment). There is the visible body, the body for-itself as viewed by others, the material stuff of flesh that is animated and inhabited by a sexual schema. That sexual schema delivers to the subject a sexual physiognomy, just like the body schema delivers to her a bodily morphology. We might even say that the sexual schema in this moment exists prior to the bodily schema: Merleau-Ponty begins with a body, visible but vaguely defined, and then moves to a consideration of the sexual schema beneath it, only after which the physiognomy of the sexual regions of the body become delineated. It is only after that delineation wrought by desire that gender appears, first as a bodily fact ("the masculine body") and finally as an emotional one.

Merleau-Ponty's description of the visible body subtended by its sexual schema offers us two different kinds of gender. The presumptive masculinity of the ostensibly universal subject is unremarkably present, as it is throughout Merleau-Ponty's work. But there is a more nuanced and productive account of gender here as well, subtending Merleau-Ponty's more orthodox account of male bodies. Masculinity is specifically described as *gestural* rather than anatomical and the purpose of the body's materiality is finally to transmit this inchoate but expressive gesture. There is a double mimeticism at work here, whereby the gesture becomes the property of the body by virtue of being elicited *by the sexual schema itself*. This masculinity is also mimetic because it is citing, perhaps even soliciting, an other masculine body, a body located in some remote elsewhere yet proximate enough to function as a structuring ideal. What is perhaps most surprising in this account is its insistence that the sexual schema is neither *one*, that which might describe the presumptively masculine, nor *two*, that might encompass the excluded feminine and thus might be parsed between masculine and feminine or male and female. The sexual schema is instead, Merleau-Ponty writes, *strictly individual*. This theorization of bodily inhabitation is simultaneously dependent on the "individual," and thus grounded in particularity, but also insisting on relation, and as such cannot be attached to one singular region of physicality or even one singular mode of being. Merleau-Ponty suggests that a systematic and rigid notion of erotogenicity will not do, that it is not my morphology but rather my experiences and mental representations that fundamentally constitute which regions of my body will give me pleasure, and how.

Merleau-Ponty's is a view of sexuality that is fantastically ambiguous, so much so that it should come as little surprise that it has not been taken up as a model by more identitarian conceptions of sexual difference and sexual identity.[13] An insistence that phenomenological experiences of the body and the subject are individual rather than categorical situates the subject differently, temporally and socially. In terms of social organization, this insistence on particularity frustrates categorical summary; it means that neither sexual embodiment nor situatedness nor expression can be predicted by membership in any particular category of gender or sex. The implications of this disarticulation are more profound than the comparatively clearer decoupling of sexed identity (male or female), gendered identity (man or woman, femme, butch, or trans), and sexuality (lesbian, gay, bisexual, or heterosexual). Nor is this an articulation of the now familiar enough notion that feminine desire is by its nature unlocatable, diffuse, ambiguous (we might think of Irigaray again here). I am interested in arguing that an embodied response to desire is, through its radical particularity, unpredictable and impossible to map onto the morphology of the body. A woman's experience of sexuality may be tightly and intensely focused on a particular region of the body or it may be distributed throughout the body. So, too, might a man's. That is: we have zones of intensely erotic pleasure, but the relation between a body part and its erotogenic or sexual function is perhaps one of lightly tethered consonance rather than a rigidly shackled indexical mapping. And while a sexual physiognomy might be "outlined" by the erotogenic zones, the body's morphology is not determinative of the location or behavior of those zones, but, rather, is determined *by* them. Merleau-Ponty is insisting that sexuality is not located in the genitals, nor even in one specific erotogenic zone, but rather in one's intentionality toward the other and toward the world.

DESIRE AND TRANSPOSITION

Merleau-Ponty contends, in *Phenomenology of Perception*, that desire always puts me in relation with the world. Through desire, my body comes alive by being intentionally directed toward another, and I myself come into being through that desire. This does not mean that my desire is always gratified or that the existence of my desire alone is sufficient to secure a particular kind of relation to one beloved other or many or, indeed, any reciprocated relation at all to an other. Desire may be frustrated or unsatisfied or find—one could hardly call it a *choosing* since I am often unfree to choose either the inclination or expression of my desire—an object that is unattainable, structurally or otherwise. Desire in these moments may feel only like a constraint or an isolation. But withdrawing from desire, or attempting to stage its death, inevitably involves a truncation of one's own capacities to exist outside oneself. Desire involves, desire *is*, a being toward the other, and this necessarily conjoins me with, makes me part of, the world.

As we have seen, the organization of desire across different temporal modes and into a narrative coherence is sexuality. Sexuality, Merleau-Ponty writes, "is what causes man [*sic*] to have a history" (158). It is embodied and lived rather than excavated and analyzed. It is not only that which suffuses life; life is not possible without it.

> Sexuality is neither transcended in human life nor shown up at its centre by unconscious representations. It is at all times present there like an atmosphere. . . . From the part of the body which it especially occupies, sexuality spreads forth like an odour or like a sound. Here we encounter once more that general function of unspoken *transposition* which we have already recognized in the body during our investigation of the body image. When I move my hand towards a thing, I know implicitly that my arm unbends. When I move my eyes, I take account of their

movement, without being expressly conscious of the fact, and am thereby aware that the upheaval caused in my field of vision is only apparent. Similarly sexuality, without being the object of any intended act of consciousness, can underlie and guide specified forms of my experience. Taken in this way, as an ambiguous atmosphere, sexuality is co-extensive with life. In other words, ambiguity is of the essence of human existence.

(168–169; EMPHASIS MINE)

What we are asked to consider in this passage is sexuality, taken as a condition not of human *meaning*, as psychoanalysis would have it, nor of *identity*, as some strains of lesbian and gay studies would have it, but of *life itself*. And desire in this most resolutely physical sense is embodied but—importantly—not located. When Merleau-Ponty writes, "From the part of the body which it especially occupies, sexuality spreads forth," this may be read as something other than a phallic reference veiled by some coyness that forbids his naming the part. There is an important ambiguity secured with Merleau-Ponty's refusal to name the penis as an encampment of sexuality, an ambiguity that performs an unyoking of bodily parts from bodily pleasures. The join between desire and the body is the location of sexuality, and that join may be a penis, or some other phallus, or some other body part, or a region of the body that is not individuated into a part, or a bodily auxiliary that is not organically attached to the body. This passage asserts that the most important aspect of sexuality is not any particular part—not even the behavior of that part—but the "general function" which causes that part to be animated, the means through which it is brought into my bodily sense of myself and is incorporated into my self-understanding through a reaching out toward the world. Merleau-Ponty designates that function as *transposition*.

The engine of sexuality is transposition; we are offered transposition as a model for understanding what sexuality is for, does with, and brings to me. But what precisely is it? Merleau-Ponty at first makes an analogy between transposition and the ordering and use of the body that is the corporeal schema, suggesting an equivalence, or at least a strong resemblance, between transposition and the function of proprioception. Both are general in the sense that they take place below the level of conscious thought. Both function as conduit between bodily materiality and intention. But there is a difference in that proprioception emphasizes the relation between one part of my body and another part, the assemblage that constitutes my felt sense of my body as a whole. This sense is, of course, gained as I make contact with the world around me, but it is at its core a consciousness that is of and in my body. Transposition describes a slightly different phenomenon, a sense of self that is not additive or cumulative, but a function that emphasizes a shifting from one mode of being or bodily inhabitation to another, involving something like a substitution.

This is a substitution that relates to my material being, and is in some sense an intermediary for it, but cannot be reduced to a function of materiality as such. It is assuredly not a linguistic substitution, for Merleau-Ponty designates this transposition as "unspoken" and emphasizes, just as he does in his discussion of proprioception, the unthought and nearly reflexive nature of my relationship to the sexual schema. In the quoted passage, transposition describes a kind of chiasmic crossing that transforms both body and desire as each comes to stand in the other's place, and with that displacement becomes confused with its other. Transposition describes the process by which the desire that houses itself in my body *becomes* my body itself—not held proximately by thought, but felt and experienced (as opposed to only referred to) through and as the body. If I can be said to have desire, this is only so to the extent that I find it as my body. Simultaneously, my body, in its desire, *becomes* desire itself. The flesh of it is felt only as an animated leaning, intentional in the sense that the desire animating it has an object—it is desire to the extent that it is desire *of*—but also intentional in that my sense of it coalesces around a purposeful being toward this desired object. My body becomes a leaning or a yearning, a propulsive force that negates any sense of my body as solid or still, or indeed as *mine*, in that this sensation owns me more than I own it.

We are given an eye and a hand in this passage, offered a description of one kind but two expressions of desire, the desiring look and a desire that motivates the reach of a hand. In the desiring look, the eye that comes to rest on an object finds there a still point, an anchor that grounds vision itself and transforms it so that what is, factually speaking, a blurring upheaval in the visual field is sensed as an unremarkable shift of focus through this process of transposition.[14] My look has an object, and I trust that object to ground my look and thus know that the world itself is not turning, that the "upheaval" that occurs when I turn my head and look at something is both occasioned by that desired object and quieted by it. This experience, though entirely mundane and unremarkable, is a decentering of the self that happens because I turn toward another, and yet that other magically restores me to myself by persisting as the focused and sustained object of my look. The reach, too, is something that is simultaneously disorienting, dizzying, decentering, *and* consolidating, purposeful, incorporative. When I am thirsty, I move toward the glass on the table, unbend my arm, grasp the glass, move it up to my lips and drink. This is not a matter of cognition, but of changing my comportment, my embodiment, my bodily being so that it encompasses the object of my desire and interacts with it. My body comes into concert not only with those objects in the world toward which my desire is intended but also with itself in that moment—it becomes purposefulness. The transpositional paradox comes when my arm, which allows me to take hold of the glass, fades from my experience even and only through the act of the reach. In reaching, the arm itself tends to recede from view or disappear as both an object of consciousness and a phenomenological presence. The object of desire supplants the self as center.

Is the scenario different if our body impels us toward another subject rather than an object? What is my experience of my own body if, rather than thirst making me reach for a glass of water, desire causes me to reach toward another person? Instead of reaching toward a *what* that is an object, I am reaching toward a *who*, another subject, and this renders the situation both similar and different. When I reach for the other, I do not feel *my arm* but an intensification of both the proximity and the absence of the one for whom I am reaching. My sensation can in some sense feel itself to be located in that other, and my arm, unbent and reaching out, is no longer the location of my sensation but rather becomes the gesture through which I am toward the other. The arm is the conduit of desire, but not the seat of its sensation. My body is the vehicle that puts me into compelling and sometimes heady proximity to the objects of my desire in this way, and, in the case of sexual desire, my body comes alive through being intentionally directed toward another.

This then is the substance of the transposition which, according to Merleau-Ponty, animates my body in desire: my sensation becomes more ambiguous and diffuse even as it intensifies because I am suddenly spread out as a sensing subject, located both in my body and that toward which my body bends. The locus of my sensation seems to shift, and my arm, if I reach out, is experienced phenomenologically less in its function as *my arm* and more in its function as *toward you*. This dispersal and transposition need not be read as diminishing either the sensation or the body part in question, but might instead be a way of understanding how in sexuality I am dispossessed of my body and delivered to it at once. A sexual transposition also involves a displacement of the body as a coherent amalgam of conscious thinking, which is surely obvious enough. But this transposition, even as it is the intensification of bodily pleasures, also involves a dissolution of the body as material ground, as phenomenological center of its own world. That center, suddenly, is shared. So self and other together comprise not only the joined unit of my affective life but also the phenomenological pivot of sensory apprehension of the world.

But if I am found in the other, so too am I lost there. The "me" that is conjoined with the world in this way is already displaced, disassembled. Phenomenology would suggest, and psychoanalysis would agree, that the object of desire is never a person whole and entire, but a fixation on this particular part or that—or a number of parts in succession. There is already at the heart of sexuality something disassembled about the body as an object of desire and also as the vehicle of my desire, to the extent that various areas of my body may be differentially called forth through my desire, that the intensity of my sexual feeling would manifest more intensely in some regions than in others. We unmake the other even as we create them as an object of our desire.

What significance might this notion of transposition have for transpeople? This phenomenon of transposition is no less true for transpeople than it is for normatively gendered people. Transposition, in the case of transpeople, is also the process in which sensations become animated through the body and the body becomes animated by sensation. Desire is experienced bodily through a series of substitutions or reconfigurations that are also present, though perhaps less marked, in normatively gendered people.

What happens, in particular if I am a transperson reaching toward that other?

Or if it is a transperson toward whom I reach?

SEX AND TRANSCENDENCE

Existence is indeterminate in itself, by reason of its fundamental structure, and in so far as it is the very process whereby the hitherto meaningless takes on meaning, whereby what had merely a sexual significance assumes a more general one, chance is transformed into reason; in so far as it is the act of taking up a *de facto* situation. We shall give the name "transcendence" to this act in which existence takes up, to its own account, and transforms such a situation. Precisely because it is transcendence, existence never utterly outruns anything, for in that case the tension which is essential to it would disappear.

(169)

When it is misconstrued as pathology, transsexuality has most often been characterized as a mental disturbance in which a person fantasizes hirself to have the genitals of the sex to which sie does not belong. It is on the basis of this fantasy, whereby a misrecognition of one's own body is understood to signal a break from reality, that transsexuality has been characterized as a psychosis rather than a neurosis. As this logic would have it, the materiality of the body is the arbiter of reality; the presence of, say, the transman's phallus is a hallucination if he has not had bottom surgery and merely "ersatz" if he has.

But phenomenology, as we have seen, is a realm in which one's own perceptions retain pride of place as a means of determining truth. My own phenomenological mode of embodiment—of bodily configuration or comportment—is itself understood as constituting a truth. This does not mean that I construct the truth, whole cloth, from the cloister of my own experience, nor does it provide hallucination with the stamp of legitimacy. What it means is that my experience of my body, my sense of its extension and efficacy, the ways that I endeavor to make a habitable thing of it, and the use I make of it—or, in the throes of desire, perhaps the use that it makes of me—are my necessary relation to whatever materiality I am. The sexual schema is rather a way of becoming uncloistered in and through the body, in that it delivers my own body to me through the movement of my body toward another. Thus, through desire, my body is no longer a conglomeration of its various parts in their expressions as "inner phenomena," but is suddenly the vehicle through which I am compelled into relation with the world, where it is finally only that relation that gives me a body.

Merleau-Ponty suggests that sexuality is transformed into something of a more "general" significance and seems then to be suggesting that sexuality itself, or the baser realm that it may occupy, is transcended, and we are delivered into some more rarified realm. The merely sexual is meaningless; it is only once the sexual achieves a more general significance that it achieves meaning. But it is also true that Merleau-Ponty uses sexuality as the exemplar of transcendence; *transcendence* is the name he gives to the relation between self and world that is sexuality. He wants to claim both that sexuality only means something once it means something greater than itself and, at the same time, that sexuality need not point to some more momentous aspect of existence to be significant because sexuality is itself coextensive with existence: "There is interfusion between sexuality and existence, which means that existence permeates sexuality and *vice versa*, so that it is impossible to determine, in a given decision or action, the proportion of sexual to other motivations" (169). This confusion is not incidental. Merleau-Ponty's paradoxical conclusions regarding the status of sexuality—does it matter or does it not?—mirrors the status of sexuality itself, which is constantly "interfused" with existence.

Sexuality offers itself as one means by which a transformation from ideality to particularity becomes possible. We might even say that sexuality is the means by which Merleau-Ponty most thoroughly revises our inherited Cartesian presumptions about body and world. It is through sexuality that the body—and thus the *self*—is transformed from a thing that is concerned with itself to a thing that is concerned with others. Sexuality as a mutual project offers another person's body to me as an object of desire, as "not just a body, but a body brought to life by consciousness" (167), and my body in turn is visible and vulnerable to the other in this same way. Sexuality then becomes relation, not in the sense that all relations are at their heart sexual, nor that sexual relations are about the masquerade of one thing for another (as bad readings of Freud would have it), but that sexuality is always offering my embodied existence as held in this inescapable and tensile paradox: I am for me and I am for the other, and each of these modes of existence realizes itself in my body. Sexuality is one among only a handful of ways I can experience both these modes simultaneously, and can be the means by which the distinction between myself and another can dissolve, enacting the confusion that will become transcendence.

"IN THE FULL FLESH"

Mom, I seen him in the full flesh. I seen it. I know he's a man. Problem done. Now let's go to bed.

—LANA TISDALE, *BOYS DON'T CRY*

The 1999 film *Boys Don't Cry* is based on the story of Brandon Teena, a young Nebraska man who is killed when he is discovered to be transgendered.[15] There is a scene in the film where Lana Tisdale, Brandon Teena's lover, is confronted by two of her friends,

John Lotter and Tom Nissen. They have heard rumors that Brandon is not really a man but in fact a woman only pretending to be a man, and have come to Lana's house looking for Brandon with plans to forcibly strip him and thus lay bare his "true" identity. This assault is undertaken to punish and humiliate Brandon, and the wrong that Brandon is being punished for is not just misrepresenting his gender, but misrepresenting it *to Lana*. Forcibly stripping Brandon is only part of their aim—it is not enough that they see Brandon's nakedness, what they then want is for Lana to see it. They do not want merely to satisfy their own suspicion that Brandon has no penis and is therefore in their minds not male; they also want to force Lana to look at Brandon's naked body in their presence, so that the nature of the assault sets Lana up as the arbiter of Brandon's gender.

Thus humiliation is conceived by Lotter and Nissen as the way to "protect" Lana from being duped by Brandon and his presentation of the "wrong" gender. Lana's response to this is to protect Brandon: she attempts to stop Lotter and Nissen's assault by telling them—"I seen it": "I seen him in the full flesh. I seen it. I know he's a man. Problem done." How ought we read that claim, "I seen it?" Is it just an untruth offered by Lana as a form of protection to spare Brandon the violence that threatens him at this point in the film, a violence that will kill him by its end? I want to ask whether Lana's statement might be understood as something other than an instrumental lie. The "it" that she has seen is unspecified; Lotter and Nissen and perhaps the audience understand her to be referring to a penis, but she will not name the part as such. In declaring "I know he's a man," she is pointing not only to Brandon's own conviction but also to her understanding of him and his gender; her utterance serves to confirm Brandon's masculinity and his sense of himself as male even in the face of the assault by asserting that she shares that sense. That knowledge of his masculinity is emphatically embodied as well as ambiguous. She knows him to be a man because she has "seen him in the full flesh," a statement of embodiment rather than the naming of a body part, an ambiguity that enables both Brandon's gender identification and Lana's recognition of that gender.

There is a dual ambiguity contained in Lana's statement, situated in the relationship between materiality and flesh and also surrounding perception itself. The "full flesh" does more work than simply acting as a veil for the phallic reference, and "flesh" does a great deal of theoretical work. I want to suggest that the work done by that use of the word *flesh* in Lana's utterance can be explicated by considering its meaning in the phenomenological vernacular and that Lana's description of flesh has useful concordance with *flesh* in the Merleau-Pontian sense of that word, what he describes as a carnal relation with the world. It can name an aspect of embodiment that is not quite the body or a dimension of the world that is not quite quantifiable.

Merleau-Ponty considers perception to be a relational structure, where those relations do not map neatly onto the relation between subject and object. He attempts to frustrate this distinction between subject and object, between the seer and seen, between inside and outside, by according relation a primacy that had previously been reserved for the object itself. His final, unfinished work, *The Visible and the Invisible,* can be read as an attempt to show the ways in which familiar philosophical distinctions—and even familiar experiential ones—between subject and object, between the hand that touches and the hand that is touched, between our visible, bodily being and those aspects of ourselves that are not visible, are undermined by the importance of the relations between these categories. If the physical body can be thought as a discrete and bounded entity, capable of being distinctly set apart from the ground that is its world, this identification is less a matter of disconnection or differentiation and more a product of relation. A body becomes so by virtue of its interaction with what surrounds it, not because it is composed of a stuff that is radically foreign to its surroundings.

How are we to understand the relation between body and world and our perceptions of those relations? We are certain of our perceptions of the world, we are sure that they "belong" to us, and we are sure that they show us the world as it "truly" is. And yet, a reliance on perception to confirm our certainly about what we know of the world can be misleading in that it cannot always account for those nameless structures that are true to experience but foreign to an objective assessment of that experience. If I stand in the middle of the road and survey it as it stretches before me, I see that it differs in width as it approaches the horizon, but "the road close-up is not 'more true': the close, the far off, the horizon in their indescribable contrast form a system, and it is their relationship with the total field that is the perceptual truth" (22). In this way perception points toward a network of relations rather than confirming the material "truth" of any single element in that network or system. In considering perception in this way, "every distinction between the true and the false, between methodic knowledge and phantasms, between science and the imagination, is ruined" (26).

This conclusion might seem at first to difficult to support, since it is one thing to claim that our perceptions of the world are inescapably perspectival and another to claim that this collapses distinctions between true and false, between methodic knowledge and phantasms. In the case of the body, the distinction that Merleau-Ponty wishes to challenge would seem to be the very distinction that allows the body to be thought as a bounded and legible entity. Ultimately, the act of perception ruins any clean division between the body and the world in which that body is situated, and if my body can still be understood as mine, it cannot be thought as more proximate to me than the world through which my body moves: "What I 'am' I am only at a distance, yonder, in this body, this personage, these thoughts, which I push before myself and which are only my least remote distances; and conversely I adhere to this world which is not me as closely as to myself, in a sense it is the only the prolongation of my body" (57).

How is it possible to understand the world as something capable of being as close to me as I am to myself, as something that is felt and functions as an extension of my body? This is an account of ontological truth that refuses to give primacy to either the perceiver who registers perceptions of the world or the world as a material fact over and against our perceptions of it. The truth of being exists somewhere in between these two registers, between what appears (the visible) and that which cannot be captured by flat and factual assertions about the appearances of the world (the invisible). The way in which Merleau-Ponty offers the category of the phantasmatic is significant in its restructuring of the relation between the visible, the invisible, and bodily being. We might expect the phantasmatic to be paired with "materiality," thus presenting an opposition (even if a collapsing one) between the phantasmatic and the invisible and that which is visible, material, and substantive. The phantasmatic is instead paired with "methodic knowledge," suggesting a relation of opposition between the phantasmatic and what we can know, rather than the more familiar opposition between the phantasmatic and what we can see. If the phantasmatic can be described as something (or, more properly, some nonthing) that escapes our attempts to grasp or survey it, it would seem that the aspect of the phantasmatic that retreats from our perception is not the solidity of its materiality, but the solidity of our own knowledge of it. Merleau-Ponty reconfigures the phantasmatic, transforming it from a register characterized by a lack of materiality into a register characterized by an ungraspability. The phantasmatic may or may not be material. It is not necessarily invisible, but it is indefinable, rendering the phantasmatic as that which cannot be encompassed by our knowledge of it, rather than that which cannot be perceptually grasped. There exists a certain borderlessness to the phantasmatic; a methodical attempt to survey it, as we would any commonplace object, always fails to fully encompass it and can neither give a thorough account of its material dimensions nor translate that material into meaning.

This failure of perception to account for the totality of a thing is, of course, true of any object in the world toward which perception might be intended. Every object is shot through with an infinite number of possible appearances that no single act of perception can encompass and no series of perceptions can exhaust. Even a perception in which we have all faith, a perception that seems to deliver a truth about the object, cannot encompass the reality of that object, because "'reality' does not belong definitely to any particular perception. . . . In this sense it lies *always further on*" (40-41). Perceptual faith cannot help us locate the reality of the object—it is not even able to finally decide on its *own* location, seeming sometimes to emanate from the presence of the object and sometimes to be located in the body of the perceiver, and the incompossibility of these two positions (my perception cannot be both in the thing itself and in me) leaves the question of the location of perception undecidable. Yet perception is not impoverished by its inability to deliver the whole of any object; perception always gives us something less than this whole, but also something more through the multitude of connections it makes between the perceiver and the thing perceived. For Merleau-Ponty, perception is not a passive activity whose aim is to capture a quantifiable measurement of the world through recording and measuring the qualia of any particular object within it. Perception produces our relations with other objects and subjects, and these relations are, finally, the location of the object's meaning. The perceptual truth of the object becomes the creation of its meaning, a meaning that is produced rather than found.

What consequences might this theory of perceptual truth have for thinking gender variance? First and most obviously, it suggests a lack of accord between the object as it is delivered by our perception and the "reality" of the thing perceived, a reality that always lies "further on" than any objective perception. What one might read from the contours of the body is something less than the truth of that body's sex, which cannot be located in an external observation of the body, but exists instead in that relation between the material and the ideal, between the perceiver and the perceived, between the material particularity of any one body and the network of forces and contexts that shape the material and the meaning of that body. The perceptual truth of the body is not necessarily what we see, and the traditional binary of sexual difference might have less purchase on the body's truth than other ways of apprehending its lived reality. Or, to turn again to the film, Brandon's sex "close up" is not more true than Brandon's sex "far away," just as "the road close up is not more true than the road far away."

The category of the "flesh" also offers a way of thinking embodiment that takes seriously the productive capacities of its psychic investments and understands the phenomenological experience of the body to be as vital as an objective assessment of the body's corporeality. Merleau-Ponty offers a theorization of flesh in which it is not reducible to the material and is a product of relations between myself, the other, and the world. Of course, the term is often employed as if its referent were clear and obvious: *flesh* is understood as bodily substance.[16] This has been true in discussions of the transgendered body in particular: Jay Prosser describes the body's "fleshy materiality," making no distinction between these two terms. It is simple, it is visible, it is material, and, in both of these instances, the term is deployed to dispel the cloud of linguistic abstraction that is thought to attend discussions of the body. More colloquially, the term *flesh* is used to describe a mode of being allied with visibility and presence and often indicates a certain relational component to that being. To say that one is present "in the flesh" connotes being present to or for someone else, an observing or other entity differentiated from the self and for whom the flesh becomes a display, a guarantor of the embodied presence of personhood. (The phrases *in the flesh* and *in person* are practically interchangeable—the former acts as a guarantor of the latter.)

Merleau-Ponty's definition of flesh shares with the colloquial, everyday deployment of the term the notion of relation, but is both more restricted (my flesh and my person are not the same thing) and more expansive (my flesh need not be coterminous with my body, but can extend into the world, which itself has a flesh). He asks, "Do we have a body—that is, not a permanent object of thought, but a flesh that suffers when it is wounded, hands that touch?" (137).

In working to differentiate body from flesh, Merleau-Ponty opposes them, attributing to the one the characteristics of object and to the other the characteristics of a subject. The first distinguishing property of flesh is *that it suffers*; it is only secondarily important that it has "hands that touch." This is not quite a distinction between passivity and activity—suffering may be as active an engagement with the other as touching. (Recall that the body is active when it "opens itself to others," including opening itself to the possibility of being wounded by the other.) It does, however, draw a distinction between the body as it is seen, as object, and the body as it is felt and phenomenologically experienced. And herein lies the greatest difference between Merleau-Ponty's explication of flesh and flesh thought as merely the material stuff of the body.

Flesh is that which, by virtue of psychic investment and worldly engagement, we form our bodies into, rather than the stuff that forms them.

To become flesh is to enter the world and engage with it so fully that the distinction between one's body and the world ceases to have meaning. It is to inhabit one's body, to "to exist within it, to emigrate into it, to be seduced, captivated, alienated by the phantom, so that the seer and the visible reciprocate one another and we no longer know which sees and which is seen . . . " (139). Flesh is the world's seduction of the body and the body's incorporation of the world into itself.

Merleau-Ponty continues:

> It is this Visibility, this generality of the Sensible in itself, this anonymity innate to Myself that we have previously called flesh, and one knows there is no name in traditional philosophy to designate it. . . . The flesh is not matter, is not mind, is not substance. To designate it, we should need the old term "element," in the sense it was used to speak of water, air, earth, and fire, that is, in the sense of a *general thing*, midway between the spatio-emporal individual and the idea, a sort of incarnate principle that brings a style of being wherever there is a fragment of being. . . . Flesh is an ultimate notion . . . it is not the union or compound of two substances, but thinkable by itself.
>
> (139–140)

Merleau-Ponty insists that flesh is not a singular substance, but neither is it the "union or compound of two substances, but thinkable by itself." Flesh designates a certain unlocatabilility of the body, neither the substance of the thing nor a pure ideality, but constructed somewhere between these two. When Merleau-Ponty asks "is my body a thing, is it an idea?" he answers that "it is neither, being the measurement of the things. We will therefore have to recognize an ideality that is not alien to the flesh, that gives it its axes, its depth, its dimensions" (152). The body itself is, finally, a mixture or amalgam of substance and ideal located somewhere between its objectively quantifiable materiality and its phantasmatic extensions into the world. Merleau-Ponty suggests a mode of bodily inhabitation through which we allow ourselves to be seduced by the phantasmatic aspects of the body, suggests that we give ourselves over to the world in affirming the flesh that is not-quite-the-body and thereby find a more deeply rooted and expansive engagement with the other and the world.

Flesh then is a thing that is thinkable, but a thing that has not been thought. Flesh is neither matter nor mind, but partakes of both these things and yet cannot be described as a mixture of them. It is forged through our relations with others, in all their phenomenological particularity, yet is itself "a general thing." What, then, might we take from this theorization of the flesh to help us understand transgendered embodiment? Merleau-Ponty's description of flesh sounds in several crucial aspects like a description of transgenderism or transsexuality: a region of being in which the subject is not quite unitary and not quite the combination of two different things. An identity that is not secured by the specificity of the materiality of the body, nor by a particular mental quality, but is something involving both. It can be thought by itself, yet has been unnameable. Neither a singular substance nor a union of two substances. In both, too, the question of relation is primary. To feel one's own flesh, or to act as witness to another's, is to unsettle the question of subject and object, of material and phantasmatic, in the service of a more livable embodiment.

2

HOMOERRATICS

3.1. Lila, Mr. December. *Photograph by Ace Morgan*

3

BOYS OF THE LEX

Transgender and Social Construction

TOWARD A HOMOERRATIC OF QUEER CULTURE

San Francisco, historically and practically the epicenter of North American queer culture, has exactly one lesbian bar.[1] There are, of course, plenty of opportunities for lesbians to meet and frolic throughout the city, and on most nights of the week one can easily find a club or bar hosting a women's night or, barring that, some other lesbian-friendly space. But San Francisco's only seven-days-a-week self-proclaimed "dyke bar" is the Lexington Club. The club regularly advertises in local newspapers as "a totally *gay* club where every night is ladies' night." The Lex, as it is affectionately termed by its patrons, sold a calendar for the year 2002 titled "'Boys' of the Lex," which features individual photos of the club staff—bartenders, barbacks, door boys, bookkeepers, and Ace Morgan, the calendar's photographer—and each of these "boys" reads as transgressively masculine.

Morgan's photograph of Mr. December shows Lila, the founder and owner of the bar (figure 3.1). She stands next to Armon, a seated man whose cheeks are covered with shaving lather, and holds his goatee in one hand and a straight razor poised carefully next to his face in the other. The photograph is set not in the Lexington Club but in the Eagle Tavern, a local leathermen's bar, which is attested by the groups of burly daddies that populate the background of the photograph and by the baseball cap emblazoned with the bar's logo that Armon (an Eagle bartender) is wearing. The circulation of masculinity within the photograph is a complex one; Lila "reads" as female, but it is her masculinity that is foregrounded, both literally and figuratively, against the male bodies in the background. Armon's position is not quite submissive—he looks directly into the lens with a sly smile—yet his bearded and masculine face is vulnerably close to the razor that hovers in front of it. Lila is in charge of the scene, not only of the man she is about to shave but also, in some more expansive sense, of the scene of masculinity as it is played out in the leathermen's bar. The photograph cites the stereotype of the butch lesbian as castrating woman, threatening masculinity with a knife at the ready.[2] Yet the postures of the men in the background are relaxed and friendly, and the sense of danger in the tableau of the foregrounded figures is softened by the stance of the two bodies in relation to one another, which is more tender than aggressive. The butch lesbian is not assaulting masculinity but homoerotically engaging with it.

The photograph represents a kind of masculine homoerotic, though the common understanding of homoeroticism or homosexuality as "love of the same" is insufficient for understanding how this eroticism depends on difference and alterity, at the level of sex, of gender, and of bodies. For if this is an erotics of similarity, it is a similarity that is crucially circuited through difference. We might assume that all the subjects in the photograph are "of" the same gender (and we may or may not be right), yet they are clearly not of the same sex, and the photograph's erotic power is generated by this difference within sameness. The locations and intersections of difference and identity become difficult to parse: the calendar uses an image of a gay leathermen's bar to promote the Lexington Club, "a totally *gay* club" (which reads as a tongue-in-cheek assertion of a gayness that is not quite lesbian and not quite male homosexuality) "where every night is ladies' night" (where those "ladies" are all identified as boys). In this context *homoerotic* is an unhelpfully flat adjective that cannot quite keep up with the libidinous and identificatory refractions produced by the image. The display of the photograph and its contextual use might better be called *homoerratic*: a libidinal economy of sameness whose participants nevertheless wander or stray from their customary or expected courses in unpredictable and surprising ways and whose energy depends on the very unfixability of those erotic identifications and exchanges.

If the Lexington Club is where the women are, it is also where the boys are, and for the boys of the Lex, this seems to be one and the same category. Bre, the cover boy of the calendar, is perched on a rooftop overlooking San Francisco's Mission District (figure 3.2) and is eating a layer cake that reads, in piped-on frosting, "my cake." Is there some sense in which being one of "the 'boys' of San Francisco's only fulltime lesbo bar" (as the photograph's caption reads) is an instance of being able to have one's cake and eat it too? What understandings of sex and gender, of bodies and relation, make such identifications possible?

I would suggest that this calendar, as an artifact of queer sexual culture, offers a corrective to one of the more persistent critiques in gender, and especially transgender, studies: that queer theory, with its valorization of flux, instability, and all things postmodern, ignores or minimizes the implications of gender as it is lived in "real life." This call for a return to "real" gender, as opposed to gender as it is merely "theorized," draws a distinction between gender as it is conceptualized and gender as it is lived, where the latter is thought to somehow expose the former as either hopelessly utopian conjecture or—worse—bent on dissolving the reality of gender as it is embodied. This division, which posits the materiality of the body as a stable ground against the wild proliferations of a supposedly disembodied and disengaged theorizing, has the effect of flattening out "theory" to the point of caricature.

To theorize gender, to ask after the ways in which bodies inhabit different sexes and genders and what social structuring make those inhabitations possible, is not to suggest that any of those categories are incidental or meaningless. How we embody gender *is* how we

3.2. Bre, coverboy, "Boys of the Lex," 2002. *Photograph by Ace Morgan*

theorize gender and to suggest otherwise is to misunderstand both theorization and embodiment. To offer the category of real gender in an attempt to discipline what are perceived as the excesses of theoretical gender is to domesticate gender as it is lived and to deny its considerable complexity, which often outpaces our language to describe it. It is undeniable that queering gender is not only theoretical work. But it is also surely the case that those everyday instances of embodying transgressive gender that might at first seem far removed from academic discourse are performed with a complexity and a self-awareness that are rendered invisible if we understand them as simply opposed to a theorizing that is unnecessarily complicated and complicating. What the boys of the Lex demonstrate is that gender as it is lived and embodied is, in some powerful sense, always already theorized. When a distinction is made between the theorizing and the performance of gender expression, we might do well to ask who or what such a distinction serves.

Within the emerging field of transgender studies, many writers have suggested that queer theory's most profound legacy has been the advancement of social construction as a way to understand gender and embodiment. Although some writers understand transgenderism as evidence of the social constructedness of bodies, a growing number contend that transgenderism presents a challenge to the theory of social construction, that the materiality of the transgendered body exposes social construction as a fiction, and a dangerous one.

Trans writers have articulated at least three objections to social construction: it is simple where gendered embodiment is complex, it is inattentive to or dismissive of the reality of bodily materiality, and it offers no room for bodily resignification or resistance. I want to contend that each of these objections hinges on a fundamental misreading of social construction's meaning and the use to which it has been put in theorizing gender.

In *Trans Liberation: Beyond Pink or Blue* Leslie Feinberg argues that transgendered people have been rendered historically invisible by a culture that abhors gender difference. Feinberg suggests that theory has a role to play in helping mobilize social change because it can "counsel action," yet Sie also suspects that the category is general in a way that removes it from "real life." "History is the record of past experience. Theory is the generalization of that experience. It's that simple."[3] If history, theory, and their relation are "simple" things, so for Feinberg is the idea theory uses to explain gender: social construction. Sie states: "I do not hold the view that gender is simply a social construct—one of two languages that we learn by rote from early age. To me, gender is the poetry each of us makes out of the language we are taught."[4] Social construction, in this view, is something *simple*, an adjective that wants to modify both *social* and *construction*. The social realm that produces gender oversimplifies it by legislating only two possible choices, and social construction's unsatisfying simplicity is related to the role of theory as a "generalization of experience": neither is able to account for experiences that deviate significantly from the norm. The transmission of this insufficiently general experience is also seen as simple, that which is transmitted by rote to passive subjects. Social construction becomes something akin to a grammar lesson, and the active work of living a gender is seen as a poetic opposition to a strict grammar of gender as legislated somehow from above.

I will return to the implications of this linguistic metaphor, noting here only that Feinberg's analogy to language in hir rejection of social construction posits an active subject who exists—and embodies gender—outside the constriction of the social realm. A similar, if perhaps more emphatic, objection to social construction comes from Jamison Green, who writes that "thanks to the feminist critique, we can now say 'gender is a social construction,' as if we are above it all."[5] Green does not specify whose critique—indeed, whose feminism—this might be and offers us a picture of social construction as that which is unconnected to lived gender, something that obscures, or even threatens, the stakes of gender, a gender that ostensibly exists for subjects and bodies outside simplistic "constructions." Social construction sets gender apart from the bodies that live it, hovering above, behind, or below a transgendered subject whose experiences of gender are unconstrained by any of its constructions.

These writers see social construction as simple and lived gender as complex. Conversely, some trans writers take the opposite approach, chastising social constructionism for obscuring the simple, material fact of bodies with linguistic abstraction and complexity. In Jay Prosser's account, the materiality of the transsexual body "gives the lie to social construction," where a dysphoric relation to the body asserts a truth—again, a simple truth—over and against the abstruse tangle of complicated theories of gender.[6] Jason Cromwell, another author who writes on FTM (female-to-male) identity, questions the connection often made in trans studies between bodily dysphoria and the certainty of the body itself: "If I have the wrong body, whose body do I have and where is my body?"[7] But if the certainty of bodily dysphoria is for Cromwell unable to deliver an ontological certainty about bodies, it does produce a body unmarked by social construction, a body that exists in defiance of, and resistance to, theories about the body. "The phenomenological body," he writes, "is a site of resistance to sex and gender ideologies . . . for transpeople."[8] In both cases social construction is viewed as false because the prescriptions that determine normative gender fail to "take"—the resistance of the transgendered body to materialize a normative gender is seen as a failure of that construction. Social construction is consequently seen as a mechanism capable of producing only normatively gendered bodies, while non-normative gender configurations presumably exist outside the realm of "gender ideologies" altogether. In this view, transpeople undermine gender completely because of the material specificity of their differently gendered bodies.

This premise that the materiality of the transgendered body renders transgendered people outside or beyond gender leads to the assertion that what characterizes transgenderism, along with a specific kind of embodiment, is a specific kind of *agency*, and it is on this issue of agency that critiques of social constructionism are most assertively advanced. Social constructionism is seen as a force whose purpose is to limit, alternately, the ability of transpeople to self-define or their claims to an "authentic" embodiment or the very possibility of transgenderism itself. Green contends that social construction renders the agency of transgendered people invisible: "I believe gender belongs to each individual, to do with as he or she pleases: it is not possible for an 'objective' observer to paste gender on another person."[9] Cromwell contends that "transpeople . . . are not like other people. Rather than allowing society to dictate who and what they are, they define themselves."[10] Kate Bornstein says that "those of us who are questioning gender ought to be able to name ourselves apart from the troublesome institutions" that determine gender.[11] Social construction is presented as the powerful force that inhibits such attempts at self-definition and agency, and Green suggests that it imperils gender itself, stating that we must "attempt to wrest gender loose from the grip of social constructionism."[12] In her *Invisible Lives: The Erasure of Transsexual and Transgendered People*, Viviane Namaste goes even further, claiming that, because of its commitment to social constructionism, "queer theory as it is currently practiced needs to be rejected for both theoretical and political reasons."[13]

Social construction is thus viewed as too simple to have any relevance to transgenderism yet so powerful that it threatens not only transpeople but gender itself. One wonders exactly what it is that is passing for social construction in these conversations. It would be difficult to find a proponent of social construction who claims that it is a simple process, or that its effects are inconsequential, or that it places us—normatively gendered and transgendered alike—somehow "above it all," as Green contends. Perhaps this is why social construction circulates in many articles about transgenderism, both popular and academic, without reference to the history of its use or to any individual authors who have used it, and why writers attacking social construction seem to be referring to many different theories and ideas, all of which get grouped under one rubric.

SOCIAL CONSTRUCTION AND BODILY HISTORY

Some clarifications would seem to be in order. Social construction is not the same as a social constriction, or social role, or social control, or cultural expectation. It does not mean not real or unimportant. Social construction is not synonymous with performativity or queer theory, though it is importantly connected to both. To claim that the body is socially constructed is not to claim that it is not real, that it is not made of flesh, or that its materiality is insignificant. To claim that sex is a social construct is not to claim that it is irrelevant, or invariant, or incapable of being embodied or reworked. To claim that our experiences of our sexed and gendered bodies are socially constructed is not to claim that our experiences are fictive, or inessential, or less important than our theorizing about sexed and gendered bodies.

What, then, is meant when we say that the body is a social construct? It means that our bodies are always shaped by the social world in which we are inescapably situated. This cultural shaping happens at the conceptual level, in that what we are able to imagine about what our bodies are or may become—even to decide what "counts" as a body and what does not—is structured by the history of how bodies have been socially understood, by what bodies have been. But that imagining is not only a conceptual act, not "merely" a theoretical undertaking; the same social forces that constitute a body as culturally legible or illegible also shape the very feelings of embodiment that would seem to be most personal, most individual, and most immune to regulatory injunction. What we feel about our bodies is just as "constructed" as what we think about them, and the power of social construction as a model of understanding embodiment stems from its insistence that these categories are not separate but always intertwined.

Social construction must not be construed oppositionally to a "felt sense" of bodily being, for one can contend both that a body is socially constructed and that its felt sense is undeniable. What social construction offers is a way to understand *how* that felt sense arises, in all its historical and cultural variations, with all its urgency and immediacy, and to ask what it is, finally, that is delivered by that felt sense. This tension between the historicity of the body and the immediacy of its felt sense is the precise location of bodily being, and mapping this tension is the work of transgender studies and theories of social construction alike. Cromwell suggests that theorizing transgenderism requires a middle course between essentialism and constructionism, asserting that neither alone can "account for individual experiences. Both sides of the coin contribute to the whole. Rather than viewing bodies, sexes, genders, and sexualities as either essentialist (nature) or constructionist (nurture) and flipping the coin periodically to explain the behaviors of persons, both theories must be taken into account. People do feel that aspects of their being are essential (natural), yet they also know that what they feel is due in part to how the dominant society constructs (nurtures) ideologies seen as pertinent to being an embodied, sexed, gendered, and sexual being."[14] Cromwell is trying to offer a middle position, supplementing constructionism with an affirmation of the felt sense of the body that, he suggests, can be secured only through recourse to essentialism. Yet his last sentence is not a description of a compromise between essentialism and constructionism but is, in fact, a description of social construction. Claiming that the body *feels* natural is not the same as claiming that it *is* natural.

There is perhaps no discipline or school of thought that has considered this terrain more thoroughly than phenomenology. Maurice Merleau-Ponty's phenomenological work on embodiment, in particular, makes productive use of this tension. People do indeed feel that aspects of their being (in this case, their bodies) are natural and essential and that unexamined feeling is itself essential to embodiment. I do not need to consider the history of the body, or even the personal history of my own body, to inhabit it phenomenologically. Moving through life as an embodied subject—eating, writing, sleeping, walking to the store—does not depend on a constant consideration and evaluation of the forces that have shaped and continue to shape my body. Indeed, bodily life would grind to a halt were such awareness required; our proprioceptive relationship to the body is, of necessity, unexamined during daily life. The phenomenological body presents itself as simply *there*, as unproblematically available to me. Yet this simple givenness is a fiction, albeit a necessary one. Anything that I might do with my body, any action that I perform with it, any way that I inhabit it acquires legibility only in the context of all my body's previous actions, positions, and modes of being.

The social aspects of my body, that sedimented history of which it is composed, do not disappear even if the ease of my proprioceptive possession of my body renders its social aspects invisible. The force of my conviction about the certainty of my own body paradoxically obscures the social realm and the formative role it plays in making embodiment legible. The social realm might seem to disappear or fade away, but its effects do not, even when they are unattended to, even when they "pass" as natural. The body is always *subtended by its history*. The body is felt as an immediate reality, situated in the spatial "here" and the temporal "now," and the presentness of our bodies to us—and of the things our bodies deliver to us—feels absolute. Yet as a perceived and perceiving entity, the body depends on a substratum of history, even if that history is invisible in the more mundane course of everyday life. "Perception," Edmund Husserl writes, "is related only to the *present*. But this *present* is always meant as having an endless *past* behind it and an open *future* before it."[15]

How are we to understand that obscured history and its relation to the bodies that it subtends? Michel Foucault states in the introduction to *The Use of Pleasure* that his project in *The History of Sexuality* has been to uncover and write a "history of truth." That truth is excavated and read through a history of bodies, viewed as sites of power and resistance. Bodies can only be understood, only become legible, through their historically contingent specificity. A body does not exist as a naturally given phenomenon for Foucault; the "natural" body is produced through subjection, a social construct masquerading as a natural entity.[16] Understanding bodies is necessary if we are to understand power because bodies are both produced by and bear the evidence of a power that is nonlocalized and dispersed; it is recognizable only through its effects, which are often bodily effects. If we must understand bodies to understand power, it is conversely true that we must understand power to understand bodies. Discipline, for example, is a kind of power that cannot be reduced to the institutions or apparatuses through which it flows, although its effects can be seen in and on the bodies it regulates. The disciplinary regimes that produce bodies as sexed and gendered may be visible in certain institutions, or particular medical technologies, or instances of bodily violence, but discipline itself is none of these things. Foucault writes that "'discipline' may be identified neither with an institution nor with an apparatus; it is a type of power, a modality for its exercise, comprising a whole set of instruments, techniques, procedures, levels of application, targets; it is a 'physics' or an 'anatomy' of power, a technology."[17]

An example of disciplinary power's nonlocalized effects, one with particular resonance to transpeople, might be gendered restrooms.[18] Restrooms are precarious terrain for the genderqueer, and the decision as to which door to enter is not always an easy or obvious one, particularly for butches or FTMs at an early stage of transition. If a butch chooses the women's room, the "proper" choice for the sex to which sie is assumed to belong if sie is not able to "pass," sie risks stares, hostile commentary, or getting chased right out by women alarmed that a "man" has entered (either mistakenly or with predaceous intent). If sie enters the men's room and fails to pass, sie risks worse. Segregated restrooms are obvious instantiations of the binary gender system, but cannot be said to *be* that system. The power to enforce a gender binary is not located in any one particular restroom or in the women and men who might police that territory against the genderqueer; it is instead dispersed through an entire matrix of "instruments, techniques, procedures, levels of application, targets." If this power cannot be localized or identified, this does not lessen its effects or force, a force that increases in proportion to the extent that a single instantiation of that power becomes ontologized. Consider, for instance, those stylized stick-figure silhouettes on restroom doors: they do not merely refer to gender but are perfectly abstracted icons *of* gender, depicting no activity or action other than ontology and differentiation, or perhaps ontology through differentiation.

A reading of gender, then, that focuses exclusively on the agency of the individual misses this entire matrix of power in which gender takes shape. The fact that power is always implicated in embodiment, but varies in the degree to which that implication is made manifest, is overlooked by Cromwell and Green in their descriptions of the interactions between gender as it is socially understood and gender as it is lived, and this oversight leads to one difficulty with Cromwell's description of sociality:

> According to performative theory, gender is a "routine, methodical, and recurring accomplishment" by members of society who thus express masculinity or femininity. That people "do gender" in the presence of others (West and Zimmerman 1987:126) may have some validity. Even when alone, however, people have and manifest a gender. If gender were only important in social situations, then transpeople would not know that their gender is different than what societies dictate they should be according to their bodies. Transpeople do not take off gender as though it were clothing. Contrary to Butler's statement about there being "no gender identity behind the expressions of gender" (25), gender and gendered identity are, and feel, basic to beingness.[19]

This last observation that gender and gendered identity feel "basic to beingness" would seem to be vital. But Cromwell's understanding of the social world is a curious one here. Not only does there exist for Cromwell an "outside" to the social, all one need do to access it is shut the door to one's room. But "social" does not, of course, mean in the room with other people, and conflating the two reduces the social so narrowly as to render the category entirely useless. I may shut the world out, but this does not make it go away, nor does my own constriction of focus make its effects any less real. Equally problematic is Cromwell's assessment of Butler's theory of performativity—that gender is freely chosen and just as easily discarded, that it is merely playful theatricality. The misreading is a common one, though Butler herself has been very clear that this is a fundamental misunderstanding of her position. The idea that "one woke in the morning, perused the closet or some more open space for the gender of choice, donned that gender for the day, and then restored the garment to its place at night" would require "a willful and instrumental subject, one who decides *on* its gender, is clearly not its gender from the start and fails to realize that its existence is already decided *by* gender. Certainly, such a theory would restore a figure of a choosing subject—humanist—at the center of a project whose emphasis on construction seems to be quite opposed to such a notion."[20]

It is here where the divide between social constructionism and the theories advanced by trans writers is difficult to bridge. For it is exactly such a choosing subject that many trans writers are championing, a subject to whom gender "belongs," in Green's words, to "do with as he or she pleases." If it is true, as Cromwell asserts, that transpeople are uniquely able to "define themselves," what sort of theory of subjectivity is being offered here, and how is it capable of bringing into being fully autonomous subjects whose agency is so unbounded that it exceeds the social realm itself?

THE GRAMMAR OF GENDER

In these accounts, the transgendered subject can be distinguished from the normatively gendered subject by the specificity of hir embodiment and by hir ability to self-define apart from the oppressive social structures that determine gender. But this call for an autonomous subject who freely chooses hir gender is complicated by the way language circulates within that call. To define oneself is a linguistic act, and even if that act of self-definition is offered in opposition to mandates of identity that feel somehow imposed from above, this does not place that project of self-definition outside either the linguistic or the social realm. If gender labels could be easily rejected or "torn off," as Bornstein suggests, there would be no way to account for their power or their persistence. Any argument asserting the importance of self-definition for transpeople must already recognize the power of language and of naming in the process of subject formation.

Language is figured as that which is able to deliver a stable and coherent identity to transpeople, but also that which obscures it. Green writes that "gender studies are focused on the social differences between persons with (presumably) male and female bodies. This is not really talking about gender, but about sociology and politics. . . . When are we going to really talk about gender? Not until we learn to separate gender from the language we have traditionally used to describe it."[21] Green's frustration with the inability of gender studies to "really talk about gender" is at its core a frustration with language itself. This frustration is understandable: gender, in this view, is something that exists apart from politics, apart from sociology and theory, something that must be separated from language in order to be seen clearly, and the labor of elucidating that which escapes language through the use of language itself is a formidable and frustrating task indeed.

For Green, gender is located at the bodily level, yet is not reducible to the body. Green defines gender as the internal conviction—ostensibly produced with no interference from the social realm—that one is either male or female. But "male" and "female" are social categories, and the very fact that an internal conviction can deliver such a powerful certainty about one's individual sense of belonging to, or being alienated from, either category attests to the inseparability of one's own experience of gender and the larger social classifications that determine it. Gender is a bodily phenomenon, yet in the case of transsexuals it is unyoked from the morphology of the body with which it is in conflict. Green emphasizes the internal feeling of dysphoria that attends transsexuality, suggesting that it is this feeling that is central to transsexuals' senses of themselves. The implications of basing subjectivity on a feeling of dysphoria are not altogether benign and would seem to construct that subjectivity in absolute negativity, opposed to both bodily morphology and conventional categories of gender.

In this account, the felt sense of the body delivers a certainty about identity, and though that felt sense might arise from a complicated nexus of body and psyche, the feeling itself is described as simple—the conviction that one is either a man or a woman—and as powerful and incontestable evidence of a coherent identity. Yet this feeling is unlocatable (it does not arise from or correspond to the morphology of the body) and is incontestable (it is not subject to question or doubt but presents itself as a "natural" fact). The felt sense of identity can, by virtue of its unlocatability, be said to arrive from elsewhere; the embodied subject can neither control nor reform it. He cannot name its origin or dispute what it asserts; he can only submit to it. In the case of gender dysphoria, a felt sense of identity carries with it an alienness, an otherness that determines its origins and its trajectory even as it presents itself as the most internal of phenomena. It would seem problematic to suggest that such a subject possesses an absolute agency to determine his or her gender identity if the conviction about that identity hinges on a feeling that is impossible to resist and compels submission rather than conferring any sort of mastery.

Green is surely right that bodily feeling is deeply personal and vital to subjectivity, no matter how that subject's gender is configured. Were bodily feeling able to deliver a certainty about either the body or the identity of the self apart from the body, it would be able to do so only *because it is structured like language*. We will explore the mechanisms and consequences of the parallel structures of gender and language in chapter 7

We have seen that some trans writers have suggested a return to the "real" of the body in thinking transgenderism and that trans-gendered subjectivity hinges on a certain kind of linguistic agency. Some of the troubling consequences of this approach to think-ing transsubjectivity can be seen in the works of several critics of transgenderism who see the phenomenon as evidence that the real of the body is resistant to ideologies of gender and that transgen-derism is defined by a series of linguistic acts.[22] Bernice Hausman understands "the demand for sex change," which takes the form of "hormonal treatment and plastic genital surgery," to be "the most important indicator of transsexual subjectivity."[23] Haus-man is able to advance this claim through her neatly tautologi-cal definition of *transsexual*: she limits the scope of her argument to those persons who have undergone sex reassignment surgeries, which excludes most female-to-male transsexuals, transsexuals who undergo partial surgeries or no surgeries at all, transsexuals whose only bodily interventions are hormonal, and—perhaps most important—transgendered people. Thus "demand" for sex change surgery is the most important indicator of transsexual subjectivity because the category transsexual includes only those people who demand sex change, rather than encompassing all people who feel themselves to be members of a sex that their bodily morpholo-gies do not manifest. Hausman mentions transgenderism briefly in her epilogue, noting that the "broadening of [medical] diagnos-tic criteria may also have encouraged the development of 'trans-genderism' as an optional position for those subjects experiencing 'gender dysphoria'" (130), indicating that transgenderism, like transsexuality, is a medically created condition, even if its "suf-ferers" do not choose any medical intervention at the bodily level. Transgenderism, in this account, is a limbo of sorts, an "optional" position for those who desire, but cannot obtain, sex reassignment surgery: transgendered people are merely pretranssexuals. Haus-man is skeptical of the claim that some transpeople may not desire bodily intervention, taking this as evidence of the power of the body's materiality:

If there are subjects willing to live with partial sex change (usually hormonal, without surgery), this may be an indication that the attempts at technological sex change do not achieve the changes desired. This would be precisely because the body does not accommodate all of the procedures of "sex change"; the body, in other words, resists making "gender" real. . . . What we must do is rethink the body as the site for sexual signification. Theorizing the body means taking it seriously as a material structure that exceeds the power of language to inscribe its functions.

(199–200)

In Hausman's version of transsexuality, then, we are faced with an autonomous subject whose "demand" through language brings himself, and his social world, into being. This autonomous subject is yoked to a body that, paradoxically enough, is vulnerable neither to the power of language nor to any ideologies of gender, a body that stubbornly manifests a sex that is fundamentally unalterable. Hausman suggests that medical professionals created the very idea of gender to legitimate sex reassignment surgeries for transsexuals. Gender becomes the logic by which a transsexual can claim an (false) identity as a member of a sex that his or her body does not manifest. Medical professionals script the narrative that transsexuals must follow to gain access to medical treatment and "be" a sex, and the idea of gender—understood as the notion that a sexual identity might be unmoored from the bodily markers of sexual difference—is what makes this transition from "authentic" to "simulated" sex possible. It is in this sense that transsexuals are, Hausman writes, "the dupes of gender" (140). Because of the category of gender, transsexuals mistakenly suppose that the category of sex is a malleable one, and they themselves become the putative evidence of this malleability. Yet if transsexuals are taken in by the ruse of gender, it is a ruse offered by the medical establishment in response to the demands of transsexuals themselves. Hausman offers a model of transsexual subjectivity in which they are "dupes" and also possess an agency so total that their desires legislate an ideology of gender that threatens to destroy sexual difference. Hausman dismisses the notion of gender performativity, regarding it as "playing at" sex over and against the bodily markers of real sex, yet her theory of the transsexual demand is strikingly performative:

> Demanding sex change is therefore part of what constructs the subject as a transsexual: it is the mechanism through which transsexuals come to identify themselves under the sign of transsexualism and construct themselves as its subjects. Because of this, we can trace transsexuals' agency through their doctors' discourses, as the demand for sex change was instantiated as the primary symptom (and sign) of the transsexual. . . . The demand for sex change became the most significant symptom of transsexualism, its irrefutable sign.
>
> (110–111)

This focus on the demand as constituting transsexuality is taken from Catherine Millot, for whom "transsexuality involves an appeal, and especially a demand, addressed to the Other."[24] Reading the demand for sex change as the "irrefutable sign" of transsexual identity and understanding that identity to be formed by the narratives that transsexuals offer to their doctors for access to medical services transforms it from a bodily phenomenon into a linguistic one; it is not the surgery that "makes" the transsexual but the demand itself. The demand magically imbues the transsexual with identity and subjectivity, and this is a linguistic act that never misfires, never fails. Hausman's presentation of the transsexual subject shows the dangers of understanding absolute agency as the hallmark of subjectivity. To present the transsexual as a figure of absolute agency in this way is to take the idea of the choosing subject to its most extreme extension. Her agency is so total that every desire becomes a demand, and her relation to gender cannot be properly described as a choice, since she is able to bring the category of gender itself into being. In fact, contrary to Hausman's report, transsexuals understand the medical and social histories that they report to their doctors as highly scripted and compelled, a set of necessary fictions into which they fit their experiences in order to be recognized as transsexual. Hausman reverses that formulation and reads those discourses as evidence of transsexuals' agency; official medical discourse is understood as an extension of the will of transsexuals themselves. The poverty of the willful agent model for understanding transsexuality and transgenderism is brought into relief by this caricature of the all-powerful subject, which derives from a wild misreading of the power relations that determine sex and gender. This subject possesses a firm sense of identity unbroken by any rupture or dissonance, one who freely chooses a satisfying configuration of gender and sex with which to identify or, failing that, reconfigures the very structures of sex and gender. All her demands are met, and her control over her identifications and circumstances is both total and effortless, meeting with no resistance from social structures or cultural prohibitions. Such a subject does not so much reside in the social world as create a fully formed one around herself.

The description of transsexuals as people able to exert absolute control over their doctors, their bodies, and the categories of sex and gender stands in stark relief to their own descriptions of their exhausting, unsatisfying, and often unsuccessful attempts to negotiate the medical and legal systems through which sex change is officially conferred.[25] Hausman acknowledges this gap in her preface, which states that her book is about identity, but "is not, however, about people," a remarkable claim for a text so distressed about the ways in which constructions, both social and "literal," enact an erasure of the real.[26] The real of the body, in Hausman's account, is the only brake on the monstrous power of transsexual subjectivity, a body whose materiality both foils transsexuals' attempts to reconfigure their identities and resists even the notion of "gender identity" itself, asserting its subordination to the real of already sexed morphology. It is unclear whether this description of bodily materiality can be interpreted as anything other than biological determinism of the most pernicious sort. It is finally this "real" that most concerns Hausman, and, though their political aims are fundamentally opposed, she shares this concern with some trans theorists. Like them, she insists that "what we must do is rethink the body as the site for sexual signification. Theorizing the body means taking it seriously as a material structure that exceeds the power of language to inscribe its functions" (200). This claim echoes Cromwell's understanding of the material body as "a site of resistance to sex and gender ideologies" and Green's demand that we leave language behind in order that we may "really" talk about gender.

TRANSCENDING THE REAL THING

Since the injunction that we do comes from so many quarters, let us endeavor to take the body seriously in just this way, to see what might result. It is easy enough to grant that the body is a material structure; this much has never been disputed. If we are to understand the real body as opposed to linguistic inscription, it is in some important sense resistant to description, since description always inscribes that which it seeks to identify through naming. This resistance to signification would extend outward, protecting the body from the meddlesome speculations of philosophers and theorists, and also inward, defying our own efforts to make sense of our situatedness within it. The materiality of this body is immune to construction or transformation and to attempts to alter it from its natural and given state. What sort of truth does this body contain? What the "real" body tells us—or, rather, what it silently displays, without benefit of language—is nothing. Considered only as a blunt materiality, severed from any psychic investments, it has no meaning at all. This body is mute and impenetrable, a fleshy monad that is only "Real" in the Lacanian sense of that word, foreclosed from language, symbolization, and meaning. It is a body that belongs to no one, in the sense that what it describes is unrecognizable as a phenomenologically lived body and hardly recognizable as human. It is unclear what is served in revering this body or what ideal of embodiment it offers in return; no one could claim ownership of such a body—and who would want to?

It has been argued that "treating the body as a manipulable thing suggests there are no psychic investments in it that require consideration."[27] This is exactly wrong. Manipulation is what transforms psychic investments into bodily, lived investment; manipulation *is* investment. The psychic investments that we have in our bodies are not safeguarded or amplified by reverentially cordoning off its materiality into a realm untroubled by the messy tangles of inscription and meaning.

Though this real body would seem to have little relation to the phenomenologically lived body, the process by which we are asked to strip it of both its history and psychic investment is remarkably similar to the phenomenological reduction. Husserl considered phenomenology to be a method for understanding things as they are and not merely as they appear to be. Husserl's famous declaration "to the things themselves!" was a call to establish an absolute certainty about existence. This certainty can be achieved through what he termed the phenomenological reduction or *epoché*, an attitude toward the world that consists of suspending judgments about it, a bracketing off of what we know to determine how that knowledge comes about and to guarantee a correspondence between our knowledge of objects and those objects themselves. This bracketing, or reduction, is characterized by "the rigorous abstention from all knowledge claims involving transcendence and the consequent restriction of the critique of knowledge to claims concerning the domain of immanence."[28] Transcendence is the process of inference by which we gather impressions and perceptions of the object toward which our consciousness is intended and impute to that object an existence in the world beyond our perceptions. The "problem" of transcendence is one of correspondence; we have no way of knowing if our perceptions of an object correspond with the object itself, hence we "infer," rather than experience, an object that transcends our perceptions (59). Husserl says that we must suspend our "natural" attitude toward the world, in which the possibility of knowing the objects within it is taken for granted and the world and its objects appear as given, in order to replace it with a "philosophical attitude" that is a "reflection on the relation between the object and our knowledge of it" (16). Yet the phenomenological reduction is a means rather than an end, not a stopping point but a philosophical attitude that attempts to establish a ground for the possibility of knowledge. It is not meant to supplant our natural attitude toward the world—one cannot move "suspended" through the world—but rather to "win a new region of being, a region of individual being."[29] Maurice Natanson describes the *epoché* as "psychological breath-holding" whose purpose is redemptive: Husserl is attempting to redeem the belief that undergirds the natural attitude toward the world and provide it with a firm and certain foundation. In this way it is less radical than linguistic idealism, since "with the performance of epoché the real world does not change in any way, nor does the phenomenologist."[30] Through the reduction, the world is *for me*; "I possess in myself an essential individuality, self-contained, and holding well together in itself, to which all real and objectively possible experience and knowledge belongs."[31] This mode of being, sometimes termed "phenomenological idealism," posits a being who, through a systematically implemented isolation from the world, restricts itself to that of which it has radical certitude; the ego contracts the world until it contains only the ego itself. Husserl stresses that the world as it exists outside the ego may still exist: "I do not deny this 'world' as though I were a sophist, I do not doubt that it is there as though I were a skeptic; but I use the phenomenological epoché which completely bars me from using any judgment that concerns spatio-temporal existence."[32] As Natanson suggests, what we take for granted in our inhabitation of the natural attitude is not so much the existence of the world we inhabit but that that world is the same world others inhabit, that we all perceive the world in the same way. Embedded in the natural attitude is the assumption that the world is the same for others as it is for us.[33]

The phenomenological reduction is thus useful as a tool for understanding how our natural attitude toward the world contains problematic presuppositions and allows us to view the world apart from the clouding hindrance of those suppositions. Through the evacuation from the ego of perspectives different from my own, the phenomenological approach secures the world as a site of difference, a difference prohibited by the natural attitude's unquestioned assumption that "the world" has the same referent for any given subject. "The 'I' of the person must be released from the 'we' that binds it. Phenomenological reduction is a movement from the 'I' as a communally grounded reality to the ego as a source of what is ultimately the individual's *own*, his 'ownness,' in Husserl's language."[34] Yet as Natanson notes, the phenomenological reduction cannot be a tool for thinking intersubjectivity, and Husserl himself was frustrated by the "problem of intersubjectivity" (195). Any communication or genuine interaction with others, rather than a disinterested contemplation of them, requires a withdrawal from the philosophical attitude and a reentry into the natural mode of being. This is Merleau-Ponty's primary critique of the phenomenological reduction, and his insistence that the natural and philosophical attitudes toward the world (indeed, that body and psyche or subject and world) can never be cleanly split caused him to conclude that "the most important lesson which the reduction teaches us is the impossibility of a complete reduction."[35] Indeed, Merleau-Ponty seems to be gently admonishing Husserl for his faith in the reduction when he writes that "the world is not what I think, but what I live through" (xvi–xvii).

The operation of the phenomenological reduction produces a body strikingly similar to the "real" body proposed by some trans theorists in its isolation from historicity and lack of situatedness within a social world, but that body differs in two important respects. The first is the different notion of "real," where for trans theorists "real" is equated with what is actual, what is materially given, that which resists theorizing and whose existence for the subject is beyond question. In phenomenological language, "real" means something quite different from this. "If there are worlds or real things at all, the empirical motivations which constitute them must be able to reach into my experience, and that of every single ego."[36] This implies not so much that the object is one thing for many people but that it is many things for many people. A real object is a "complex of all of its possible appearances," containing within it the possibility of its own being for and from the perspective of any individual person (251). In this sense, what constitutes something as real is not its materiality but a horizon of possibility, an openness to all the different experiences that it represents to any given person.

On its face, this might appear to be philosophical speculation of the worst sort, precisely the dismissal of the real world against which critics of theoretical and philosophical approaches to gender warn us. This view, however, misses the purpose toward which such speculative endeavors aim. The phenomenological project is not an attempt to do away with the real world, but rather to question our suppositions about that world so that we might see it more clearly and utterly. This is the second distinction between the real body thought as a nonsocial material thing and the real body that phenomenology offers; the former is real to the extent that it confirms what we already know (about materiality, about gender, about itself) and the latter is real to the extent that it points toward its own capacity to exceed what we suppose about it. To be real, in this sense, is to hold one's body and one's self open to the possibilities of what one *cannot* know or anticipate in advance. It is to be situated at materiality's threshold of possibility rather than caught within a materiality that is at its core constricted, constrictive, and determining.

It could be protested that we have not "really" talked about gender yet, that we have responded to that call by offering only more linguistic abstraction and speculation, and this objection might not be altogether without merit. Perhaps we might conclude by returning to the boys of the Lex, to see if they might help lead us back to real gender. In the beginning of this chapter I asked what understandings of gender, bodies, and their relation make an identification as a boy of the Lex possible. It is undeniably true that each of these boys has a real body, and each of them manifests a real gender, although neither of these categories can be simply determined by the other. All of them identify as boys in some way, though the degree to which this name captures their identities varies for each of them. Some of these boys consider themselves to be women, some of them relate themselves to that category only marginally, and some do not consider themselves women at all. Defenders of the notion of real bodily sex might respond that though "woman" might be a social category and thus lend itself to reconfiguration or resignification, the category of female is surely a biological one, and if the boys are not women they can safely be identified as female by virtue of their bodily morphology. But can we understand these boys to be female bodied? We might risk yet another departure from real gender in moving to the realm of representation (though is not gender always in some sense read through its representations?) to consider the photographs of their bodies. Some of the boys photographed in the calendar display the bodily markers of what is conventionally thought to signify female: a swell of the hip or a chest that is not entirely flat. But none of them are feminine, and some of them do indeed read as male bodied. What might it mean to insist that these bodies are "really" female, to contend that they contain a truth about the identity of these boys that their gender presentations or identifications can never refute? What is served by insisting that their bodies make these boys women, even if those bodies are coded as more male than female—a coding legible to their friends, lovers, random passersby, themselves—other than the most rigidly deterministic and conservative notions of proper categories of sex and gender? It is not the notion of a women's space that might be uncontaminated by masculinity, for the Lexington Club is full of not only boys who may or may not be women but femmes who do identify as women and who, as Butler puts it, "prefer that their girls be boys," or, perhaps, want their "boys to be girls,"[37] and a growing number of boys who may or may not be women and who like their girls to be boys—an increasingly visible butch-on-butch, or trans-on-trans, homoerratic. Though it cannot fail to have meaning, the body's morphology does not in any of these instances script either identification or desire, and those who understand bodily morphology to be constitutive of a truth that exceeds ideologies of gender would do well to take seriously some of the ways in which gender is currently being lived.

4.1. Mud, 2005. *Photograph by Lily Rodriguez*

4

TRANSFEMINISM AND THE FUTURE OF GENDER

TRANS/GENDER/WOMEN'S STUDIES

What is the relationship between women's studies, feminism, and the study of transgenderism and other non-normative genders? In asking after the place —or lack of place—of transgender studies within the rubric of women's studies, I want to suggest that feminism, particularly but not exclusively in its institutionalized form, has not been able to keep pace with non-normative genders as they are thought, embodied, and lived. Recent contestations around the term *transgender* echo some of the same concerns about referentiality and identity that have surfaced in the past through the circulation of the terms *queer* and *woman* within feminist discourses.

In this chapter I want to suggest that, if it is to reemerge as a vital discipline, women's studies must become more responsive to emerging genders. Genders beyond the binary of male and female are neither fictive nor futural, but are presently embodied and lived, and the discipline of women's studies has not yet taken account of this. Until women's studies demonstrates a more serious engagement with trans studies, it cannot hope to fully assess the present state of gender as it is lived, nor will it be able to imagine many of its possible futures. It is equally true that trans studies needs feminism. Trans studies in its current, nascent state is often dominated by a liberal individualist notion of subjectivity, in which a postgender subject possesses absolute agency and is able to craft hir gender with perfect felicity. Without the systemic understanding that women's studies provides of the structures of gender—and the relations of power that underlie those structures—trans studies is unable to understand gender as a historical category and cannot provide an account of how the present state of gender emerged. This is especially necessary when discussing violence against transpeople, which cannot be made sense of using an entirely individual and voluntaristic theory of gender.

In the spirit of these larger concerns I would like to consider three sets of photographs that particularize and complicate the relation between trans identity and feminism in both its institutionalized and popular forms. One of these sets gives us an image, and a narrative, of trans subjectivity offered in conformity with the popular view that transgender populations and lesbian and feminist populations—and, by extension, transgender issues and concerns of lesbians and feminists—are not only different but mutually exclusive. The public view of trans and lesbian feminist communities as divided, and transfolks themselves as the agents of this division, has a mutually reinforcing relationship with the way that transgenderism does or does not merit attention in the academy. Encounters between trans and feminism are increasingly happening outside the academy, where the public voice of feminism is seen as a direct product of institutionalized women's studies programs.

Trans studies does not of yet have anything like a stable foothold within the academy. The amount of academic work on trans issues is increasing, but, institutionally speaking, "transgender studies" is not always a legible category.[1] This may be due to its defiance of categories more broadly, though it would hardly be singular in this respect, since the same might be said of several different kinds of area studies. Or it might be because there is still little consensus about the place of the study of gender within the university, still less agreement about the place of sexuality, and transgenderism seems to imply that both of these things are at issue, and in provocative ways. Some of the work on trans studies being produced today emerges out of the social sciences: anthropology, sociology, history. But much current work on trans issues emerges from the humanities, and some of this work is housed in women's studies departments. In some ways this would seem to be a "natural" alliance: women's studies would seem to offer a rich array of tools, already in place within an institutional setting, to examine gender, its production, perpetuation, and transgression, and the ways embodiment, identity, and social structures are shaped by those productions. Women's studies has also offered a place in the academy where discussion of bodies and difference, and an interrogation of the way power figures and disfigures bodies differently, can take place.

However, trans teaching and scholarship have not always received a warm welcome within the domain of women's studies. One might read this absence as a temporal fact, evidence only of the pace of institutional change, and conclude that inclusion at the level of both scholarship and curriculum is surely forthcoming. This view would suggest that transgenderism is merely the latest in a long line of identities whose existence has posed a challenge to women's studies and its own various moments of presumptive universalism and that women's studies as a discipline will reckon with the identities and concerns of transpeople, just as it has with the work of women of color, lesbians, sex radicals, and queers. Leaving aside the question whether this has been achieved—whether these other marginal identities have actually been successfully addressed by or integrated into women's studies or found their own unassimilated home there—there are reasons to believe that a developmental model of the growth of women's studies can neither predict the shape of women's studies departments in the future nor describe the trajectory of trans studies within the academy.

There is a different way to understand the reluctance of women's studies to respond to trans studies. In some ways trans studies is singular in the difficulty it presents to such a program—a difficulty that becomes manifest if, instead of understanding trans studies to be offering yet another subject position to be subsumed under the category of "woman," we understand the task of trans studies to be the breaking apart of this category, particularly if that breaking requires a new articulation of the relation between sex and gender, between male and female. Indeed, the specificity of trans as a kind of subjectivity uniquely suited to pose a challenge to fixed taxonomies of gender meets resistance in the specificity of women's studies as a discipline whose very essence depends upon gender to conform to just such a fixed taxonomy. The category of "woman," even if it is understood to be intersectional and historically contingent, must offer a certain persistence and coherence if it is to be not only the object of study but the foundation of a discipline, and a subject formation that describes a position of referential resistance might not be easily incorporated into such a schema. Such a subject, however, would prove useful to the extent that that subject embodied and literalized a position perpetually *outside* the referential system of gender. I would argue that the trans subject has been just such a subject for women's studies, necessarily proximate but inassimilable, able to enact and secure gender as a binary system only to the extent that sie is exiled from it. The transgendered subject is the constitutive outside of binary gender.

Wendy Brown points out that the definitional instability that attends all disciplines is especially acute in women's studies, and that its institutional specificity inheres in the fact that its task is not quite to provide particular tools or methodologies—impossible given its interdisciplinary founding and scope—but rather to function as a discipline on the basis of its description of a particular kind of subject: women. This leads to one of the "very real conundrums currently faced by those of us in women's studies." Brown continues:

Women's studies as a contemporary institution, however, may be politically and theoretically incoherent, as well as tacitly conservative; incoherent because by definition it circumscribes uncircumscribable "women" as an object of study, and conservative because it must resist all objections to such circumscription if it is to sustain that object of study as its *raison d'etre.* Hence the persistent theory wars, race wars, and sex wars notoriously ravaging women's studies in the 80s.[2]

Brown offers a context for current crises in women's studies by suggesting that those crises may themselves be necessary for the perpetuation of the field itself. She points out that while women's studies demonstrates an ever expanding attention to different adjectival permutations of its subject, its perpetuation as a discipline depends on an ever tightening focus on that subject, which leads to an unsustainable paradox:

> There is something about women's studies, though, and perhaps about any field organized by social identity rather than by genre of inquiry, that is especially vulnerable to losing its raison d'etre when the coherence or boundedness of its object of study is challenged. Thus, paradoxically, sustaining gender as a critical self-reflexive category rather than a normative or nominal one, and sustaining women's studies as an intellectually radical site rather than a regulatory one—in short, refusing to allow gender and women's studies to be disciplined—are concerns and refusals at odds with affirming women's studies *as* a coherent field of study.
>
> (23–24)

If there are no methodologies here, only subjects, then the only way to expand the reach of a discipline is to increase the range of subjects it represents, an expansion that often happens in an additive way. There are thus two models of additive subjectivity at work in the variant of women's studies that Brown's critique describes: first, an addition of unrecognized (for they could hardly be said to be "new") subject positions to a universal that had not previously included them (women of color are also women, lesbian women are also women, disabled women are also women) and, second, the admission that those other aspects of subjectivity are also vital to personhood.[3] Brown argues that the "additive" model of subjectivity championed by women's studies in its attempts to reckon with difference is insufficient in three ways. First, it operates under the mistaken assumption that power functions primarily as a force of subjugation, ignoring the productive capacities of power, the fact that it does not just oppress subjects, but fundamentally makes them. Furthermore, power cannot be understood to operate the same way in making race, class, or sexuality; different kinds of power, operating according to different norms and having different aims, are operative in each instance. Finally, a subject conceived as "intersectional," as cleanly joined layers or partitions of identity demarcated along separate axes of interpellation, bears little relation to any kind of lived subjectivity:

> As so many feminist, postcolonial, queer, and critical race theorists have noted in recent years, it is impossible to extract the race from gender, or the gender from sexuality, or the masculinity from colonialism. To treat various modalities of subject formation as additive in any of the ways suggested by the terms above is to elide the way subjects are brought into being through subjectifying discourses, a production that is historically complex, contingent, and occurs through formation that do not honor analytically distinct identity categories.
>
> (24)

If it is true that mainstream women's studies has a historical and sustained commitment to an additive model of identity, and also true that the discipline has an equally entrenched belief that sustaining identity requires privileging the truth of "experience" as an inevitably gendered cornerstone of feminist epistemology, then women's studies offers a description of subjectivity that would seem particularly poorly suited to understanding trans subjects.

If there is a certain ossification of identity necessary to the continuation of women's studies as a discipline, might there still be some less circumscribed home for trans work within the academy? And is there a way trans studies might negotiate some of the more vexing difficulties of women's studies, such as the cultivation of a space that can bear a certain degree of gender nominalism, without lapsing into normativity?

Riki Wilchins has suggested that "trans-identity is not a natural fact. Rather, it is the political category we are forced to occupy when we do certain things with our bodies."[4] This insight offers trans identity as something akin to an act, but also as something that is not reducible to a question of choice. Moreover, it might suggest that transgender studies is more closely aligned with lesbian and gay studies than women's studies, despite the fact that trans is an identity based on gender rather than on sexuality. However, some of the same difficulties that attend the confluence of trans studies and women's studies also mark the relation between trans studies and gay and lesbian studies. In discussing the current state of trans studies in relation to lesbian and gay studies and politics, Susan Stryker makes a similar point to Brown's in describing the hope she sustained in the mid 1990s that queer theory might offer a radically progressive, even revolutionary, model for understanding gender and sexuality within academia. Stryker's current sense is that this hope was never quite realized:

> While queer studies remains the most hospitable place to undertake transgender work, all too often *queer* remains a code word for "gay" or "lesbian," and all too often transgender phenomena are misapprehended though a lens that privileges sexual orientation and sexual identity as the primary means of differing from heteronormativity. Most disturbingly, "transgender" increasingly functions as the site in which to contain all gender trouble, thereby helping secure both homosexuality and heterosexuality as stable and normative categories of personhood. This has damaging, isolative political corollaries. It is the same developmental logic that transformed an antiassimiliationist "queer" politics into a more palatable LGBT civil rights movement, with T reduced to merely another (easily detached) genre of sexual identity rather than perceived, like race or class, as something that cuts across existing sexualities, revealing in often unexpected ways the means through which all identities achieve their specificities.[5]

Just as the term *gender* often functions as a descriptor that promises to unsettle some of the difficulties with *sex* (determinist, binary, natural, etc.), but means only and exactly "sex," Stryker understands *queer* to now function as a term whose lack of referentiality is no longer the mark of an anti-identitarian politics, no longer the name for a deviation from a norm that might regulate either gender *or* sexuality, but as a code for "lesbian or gay." There is similarity between Stryker's and Brown's critique of additive identity politics, though it is interesting to note that Stryker finds some cause for hope in using *gender* as a vector that might "cut across existing sexualities."

Not all proponents of trans studies would agree with this characterization of the object or aim of trans studies as a radical disruption of familiar ways of gender and subject production, and there has been a fair amount of criticism from some who understand this way of perceiving (or, indeed, *doing)* trans studies to be a denial of transgendered subjectivity.[6] Figured thus, trans studies would seem to be in rather close accord with other challenges to the stability of the subject, namely, postmodernism and its iteration within sexuality studies, queer theory. Indeed, some trans theorists understand postmodernism to be uniquely useful to trans studies. Stephen Whittle suggests that it is precisely the postmodern decentering of the subject and its insistence on "a multiplicity of voices" that has allowed the voices of transpeople to enter discourses on gender. In her essay "The Empire Strikes Back," a foundational text for trans studies, Sandy Stone agrees with the necessity of "heteroglossic" accounts of gender and offers the still more radical position that transpeople destroy utterly the reliance on "experience," and the nomenclatures and categories it ostensibly confers, undergirding feminism and institutionalized women's studies.[7]

Those categories are changing, and this is true within the gender binary as well as outside it, even if many changes in gendered identification or self-description may easily escape our notice. For at least two decades there has been much discussion and hand-wringing about the increase in the number of young women who will not call themselves feminists. But there has been another generational shift slightly to the side of this one in the register of gendered self-description. For example, a majority of the people who take my classes do not identify as such. That is, among the more or less feminine, more or less normatively gendered women whom I have had as students in women's studies classes, I would venture that a large percentage of them, perhaps nearly half, do not call themselves women, nor do they describe each other with that term. They use the word *female* instead. It goes beyond the scope of this chapter to ask why that might be the case, but many interesting and important questions might be asked here: Is it possible that the legacy of institutionalized women's studies has been to decrease the number of female subjects willing to, in the words of Denise Riley, *be* that name?[8] Is it an instance of liberation to refuse "woman," or a sign of something less celebratory? Is there something about the seeming indisputability of the category of "female" that is more comfortable or manageable than the category of "woman"? If "woman" is understood to be a cultural achievement, does this enhance the possibility of its failure, and does that risk of failure evoke a disidentification? This trend seems to suggest that, both inside the binary and outside of it, women's studies has not yet met even the rather low bar of descriptive positivism in terms of both sex and gender.

"LGB FAKE-T"

The strongest affiliation of trans studies is with lesbian and gay studies. This connection is sometimes made under the sign of coalition, of similar terms and struggles, but can sometimes symptomatize a certain confusion about what transgenderism is and what its relation to gay or lesbian identity might be. Trans writer Dean Spade has coined the term *LGB fake-T* in reference to the ways trans is often assumed under the aegis of lesbian and gay studies without any attention to its difference and specificity.[9] This conflation is sometimes made because of the suspicion that gender *means* sexuality, that gender here is merely a cover story for not only sex but sexuality as well. Sometimes gender comes to stand in for sexuality, and sometimes sexuality is actually standing in for gender.

The recent marriage debates, for example, have been framed by the press and lesbian and gay advocates alike as a *gay* issue rather than a *gender* issue, though sexual conduct is only implicitly rather than explicitly addressed, as it was in *Bowers v. Hardwick* or *Lawrence v. Texas*. One could just as easily imagine that the marriage debate might have coalesced around issues of gender and gender freedom; it certainly seems true that it has done so for the religious right's opposition to gay marriage. Those slogans are, of course, infused with loathing of queer sexuality and the "abomination" of sodomy, though the ubiquitous slogan "marriage is between a man and a woman" imagines itself to be a corrective to improper *gendering* as much as it does wayward sexuality. Similarly, what are primarily *gender* issues are misread as *gay* issues. Recent newspaper headlines reporting on trans issues reflect this conflation: "Transsexual Ousted from Shelter Shower for Sexual Orientation" and "Nuances of Gay Identities Reflected in New Language: 'Homosexual' Is Passé in a 'Boi's' Life."[10] That last title enunciates the anxiety, or perhaps scorn, that *homosexual* as a signifier is being overthrown in favor of this newfangled term *boi,* momentarily forgetting the fact that *homosexual* never *was* a signifier of gender in the way that *boi* is and that the "nuance" of the identity reflected by this word is precisely not the marker of sexual identity that *gay* would be, but a nuance of gender. Further, the anxiety that the bois are about to overthrow the homosexuals might be assuaged with the observation that, for all we know, this boi might indeed be a homosexual boy who likes other bois. We err when we assume that these descriptors must be mutually exclusive by rendering the boi presumptively heterosexual and by rendering the homosexual presumptively gender normative.

The transwoman referred to in the headline was assaulted and dragged out of a public restroom not because of her sexual orientation but because of her gender presentation. There was no sexual activity in that restroom; the prohibited "activity" was the presentation of her gender. Like most people who harass or assault transpeople in public restrooms, including the police, the denizens of this women's restroom decided that this person was not sufficiently feminine to lay claim to space in that restroom, and the dispro-

portionate response of the attack points to one of the more pernicious consequences of these conflations. The confusion of sexual
and gender identity is grounded in the false presumption that gender transgression both conceals and reveals something about sexual
transgression, a something that is perceived to be threatening.

The intersection between transgression and violence here is both
sobering and widespread, both frequently remarked upon and also
covered over. The film version of *The Celluloid Closet*, for example, concludes its argument that lesbian and gay people have long
been the subjects of onscreen violence with a montage of scenes
from Hollywood cinema in which gay and lesbian characters meet
with violence or death. Though it understands itself to be cycling
through representations of homophobic violence in cinema, a closer
look reveals that many of these characters are trans, and the punish-
ments enacted and repeated onscreen are visited on characters who
are transgressing gender norms rather than sexual ones. Parsing
gender from sex from sexuality in this way is obviously a fraught
enterprise, and I do not want to exaggerate the gulf between them.
Gender and sexuality are inevitably, if unpredictably, bound. But
this does not mean that they are the same thing, and the assertion
of their fungibility has dire consequences for transpeople.

PUTTING AWAY THE KNIVES

One of these conflations is now vexing discussions of transpeople
in the popular press. A 2006 article in the *New York Times*, one in
a series on FTM transmen the *Times* ran intermittently for several
years, begins by offering a conflation between gender and sexuality
along these same lines. However, the article ends up postulating
not a collapse between trans and lesbian communities, but rather
suggesting their antagonism.[11] The relation between lesbian and
trans communities is described as an all-out war, a "conflict" that
"has raged at some women's colleges." The parties to this war,
the article asserts, are intractably divided. The article briefly mentions the Michigan Women's Music Festival as one particularly visible site of this conflict. The founder and producer of the festival,

Lisa Vogel, has maintained a policy barring all transpeople (both MTFs and FTMs) from the women's-only space since 1991, the year when Nancy Jean Burkholder was ejected from the festival for being trans. This policy has been protested by transpeople and their allies, who oppose the ban not because they reject the idea of separatist space, but rather on the grounds that transwomen *are* women and thus must be included in women's space.[12] One former producer of the festival who supports the ban is cited in the article as saying, "'by turning yourselves into men, don't you realize you're going over to the other side?'"

Stryker's observation that all gender trouble has now become consolidated under the sign of trans and that members of the gay and lesbian community, through that containment, are able to represent themselves to the public as ever more similar to heterosexuals, and thus safer, is exemplified in the premises and conclusions of the *Times* article. There is an incendiary rhetoric mobilized, whereby the discrimination and violence faced by transpeople are asserted as emanating from lesbians, and that aggression in turn is figured as the defensive response of a community whose existence is threatened. The article opens with a quotation from one of the characters on Showtime's lesbian soap opera *The L Word*; she is dismayed that another character on the show has come out as trans, is adopting the name Max, and is about to start taking testosterone. She responds to the news with regret: "It just saddens me to see so many of our strong butch women giving up their womanhood to be a man." The article reports that a furor erupted on lesbian blogs after Max's transition and cites one blogger who called for the murder of the character by "testosterone overdose." That the suggested virtual murder of a fictive transman at the hands of lesbians opens the *Times* story is quite chilling. It soon becomes clear that the story is not about transmen at all, but is instead a story about the response of angry lesbians to the peril that transmen represent to their communities. But the anger and specter of violence behind it are offered with a kind of preemptive logic; it is implied that the lesbian anger that leads to online murderousness is in some way justified, a communitywide strategy of self-defense in response to the threat that transmen pose to the categories of woman, lesbian, and butch.

This at first begs to be dismissed as merely a recycling of the most threadbare of clichés: the angry, manhating lesbian. I would like to suggest two things, however, that point toward something still more unsettling at work. Lurking behind the rage at transmen, and the rhetoric of war and self-defense that peppers the article, is the baseless but pervasive suspicion that transpeople are dangerous, and dangerous in way that violates women in particular. This suspicion becomes transmogrified into fantasies of trans predation, where transpeople are compared to rapists or claimed to embody a threat, sometimes particular and sometimes vague and unspecified, to nontrans women.

Questions of violence and violation have circulated in sometimes telling ways in popular coverage of transgenderism for many years.[13] Indeed, violence is offered as an essential feature of trans identity. The *Times* article contends that the FTM trans movement "has gained momentum only in the last 10 years, in part because of increasingly sophisticated surgical options, the availability of the Internet's instant support network, and the emotions raised by the 1999 movie *Boys Don't Cry*, based on the true story of the murder of Brandon Teena, a young Nebraska woman who chose to live as a man." One could dispute this chronology with relative ease— FTM transgenderism has, of course, been an important issue inside and outside lesbian communities even before the *Times* started covering it. But what is being offered with this chronology is an origin story of sorts, and, for the *Times*, the birth of transgenderism can be dated with some precision to a particularly performative speech act. In 1998 Kate Bornstein wrote an opinion piece for the *Times* called "Her Son/Daughter" in which she referred to the "transgender movement." The editors balked at this phrase. Bornstein, when she asked why, was told that if they printed the phrase *transgender movement* it meant that there *was* such a thing.[14]

It is certainly true that transmen have received increased media attention in recent years. But the most disturbing thing about this chronology is that it locates the birth of the movement in the moment of a transman's death and the "emotions raised" by that death. Thus the origin story of the transgender movement is crafted as a reverse Stonewall, where the founding moment of violence does not rally the community and the public against discrimination and harassment, but instead marks the first instance in a chain of endlessly repeated stagings of that death. Stonewall as a founding myth gains its power from the claim that the queers and queens fought back.[15] Citing *Boys Don't Cry* as a founding myth would seem to insist the fatal opposite: that Brandon could not fight back then, that those like Brandon cannot fight back now, and it implies that those on the other side of the barriers, so to speak, are lesbians.[16]

There is a second kind of violence here, in addition to the preemptive violence against transmen who supposedly represent a threat to lesbianism. This second violence is a disfiguration of the category of butch, which undergoes a disciplinary feminizing in order to make it conceptually distinct from transgenderism. Butches who choose to transition, for example, are described as "giving up their womanhood." The outrageous claim that butches have an unambiguous and possessive relationship to their own "womanhood" is necessitated by the claim that they are different from transfolks. Since a butch and a transman might look alike in terms of gender, might have equally masculine gender presentation, that "attachment to womanhood," vaguely defined and not necessarily accompanied by any visible femininity, would be the only thing that might distinguish them. The category mistake here insists that butches are resolutely women in order to outline the parameters of butch identity in contrast to transmen. To wit: transmen loathe their breasts, but butches do not. Transmen attack and reject their bodies, but butches celebrate theirs. Transmen want to pass as men in public, while butches want to be recognized as women. Transmen think of themselves in masculine terms and prefer masculine pronouns, while butches reject masculine pronouns, male roles, and male ego ideals. Transmen want male privilege, but butches reject male privilege. Transmen hate themselves, butches honor themselves. If this seems to be a portrait of butchness that is both highly motivated and staggeringly inaccurate, it is no coincidence. This line of protest is identical to the "feminist" reaction against butch/femme identities and sex roles all-too-familiar from decades past. The argument is exactly the same, save only that transmen are now cast in the role of the villain previously played by butches.

This is itself staging the death of the butch, precisely to save her from the contaminatingly dysphoric masculinity of the transman. Before laying the blame for the death of butchness at the doorstep of transguys, it seems important to pause and recall that hand-wringing about the death of "real" butchness, mourning the end of its era or grieving over the loss of butches has been a constant accompaniment to butchness itself. Butchness as a style of queer masculinity is in part constructed by the model of nostalgic where-have-they-all-gone scarcity.

The *New York Times* article criticizes transition in precisely this mode and effects a denigration of transmen through the valorization of butchness. Butchness is held up as a desirable ideal in opposition to trans, whereas previously, before the current trans debates, it was butchness and butches themselves who were castigated for these same reasons, for getting too close to an unacceptable limit of masculinity or maleness. It appears that the line has moved, that transmen are now the new limit case of masculinity as opposed to butches, who are now held up as a lesbian ideal. This tendency has been noted and criticized extensively in trans theory, perhaps most notably by Judith Halberstam. Halberstam notes that this assigning of gender transgression to trans bodies and marking (or unmarking) all other bodies as normative happens in trans theory and transphobic theory alike and wants, along with Stryker, to complicate "models that assign gender deviance only to transsexual bodies and gender normativity to all other bodies"(153).[17]

The sort of rhetoric Halberstam identifies has the effect of constructing the lesbian community as more palatable to heterosexuals, as Gayle Rubin points out in "Thinking Sex," and it is particularly apparent in popular discourse. First, it distances lesbians, who are then presumptively gender normative, from transgendered people. Furthermore, it suggests that, if gender normative lesbians are just as uncomfortable with the strange universe of gender change as heterosexuals are, the readers of the *New York Times* need not linger too long in considering their own homophobia or transphobia.

The violence circulating in discussions of transition, even in feminist responses attempting to be awake to it, continues to happen in several different registers. Transition is framed as if it were akin to a death or as if the post-transition subject will with hir emergence enact the death of the pretransition subject. Transition is further figured as murderous in discussions of the procedures of FTM transition, which are sometimes described as self-mutilation or, more hyperbolically, "violence against women." But there is something about these discussions of "self-mutilation" that very quickly end with the knife pointed the other way. Bernice Hausman has suggested that the bodily interventions of transition are violence toward the self, and violence toward the self is evidence of the incompatibility of trans theory and feminism, because "feminists precisely understand their gender investments by attacking the social system, and not their own bodies, as the origin of the problem of dysphoric sexed embodiment."[18] Lesbian writer Alix Dobkin, who frequently refers to FTMs as "mutilated women," ends one of her pieces against transgenderism with the sentence "let's put away the knives," making clear that in her view lesbians are somehow now the target of that violence rather than transmen themselves.[19]

Lesbianism in these exchanges becomes refashioned in conformity with the shape of heteronormative relations. Lesbianism is about family, where transgenderism is about *breaking up the family*. Lesbianism is about community—virtual (viewers of *The L Word*), online (bloggers), educational (women's colleges), and political (women's spaces), where transgenderism is about *exile from community*. Lesbianism is about safety (domesticity, separatism), where transgenderism is about *danger* (to self, from transition, or to others, by *invading* women's space). Note that there is scarcely any mention of the trans communities that these men join if and when they leave the lesbian community. Or, indeed, of lesbian and queer communities that refashion themselves in positive ways to retain and maintain kinship and connection with their trans members. The space outside the lesbian community is figured as a space of utter isolation and disconnection. The article moves through a number of options for transmen, starting from the blogosphere murder and moving to the less fatal but perhaps no less definitive solution of exile. A quotation from a graduate of Mills College (read: professionally trained feminist) frames the rhetorical question this way: "'When do we kick you out? When you change your name to Bob? When you start taking hormones? When you grow a mustache? When you have a double mastectomy?" According to this logic, lesbian communities can and must reject transpeople: it is not a matter of *if* transmen will be exiled from lesbian communities, it is only a matter of *when* and *how*.

WAVE OF MUTILATION?

The *New York Times* article is accompanied by two pictures of Shane Caya, a transman discussed in the article. The first is a shot of Shane, his ex-partner Natasha, and their three-year-old child. All three are smiling as Shane lifts the young child into the air. The second depicts Shane from the waist up, without a shirt on. He sports a head of short, salt-and-pepper hair, an upper arm covered with tattoos, and a muscular, well-sculpted male chest. The caption on the photo reads:

Shane Caya displays his mastectomy scars.

The caption shocks, not because of its tone—fairly matter-of-fact, really—but because of the mismatch between what it reports and what the reader first sees, which is simply a male body. No matter how normal-looking Shane's chest is, what it is made to show, according to the caption, is not his masculinity, but a violence done to femininity in order to achieve that masculinity. The caption sees missing breasts, rather than a male chest, and we the readers are asked to read his body for evidence, to search the photograph for the scars that trace the lower contour of Shane's pectorals—the "tell" that would ostensibly give the lie to that maleness. This is, by now, a familiar mode in photographs that accompany media coverage of transfolks. A photograph of a "normal-looking" transperson will be shown next to a caption or sidebar that announces either their trans status or their surgical status, functioning as the "reveal" that offers the transperson's portrait as a game of spot-the-missing-gender. In this case, the second photograph is positioned underneath the first, as if it were negating or undermining the picture of familial happiness above it. There is a triple shaming in this portrayal, for Shane is both recalled into femininity with the invocation of his former breasts and named as the agent of his own castration. The photographic strategy of framing transition as that which ends familial happiness is also enacted at the level of narrative; Shane and his partner break up, we are told, because of his transition.

These sorts of photographic strategies serve, finally, to rearticulate the *difference* of transpeople, their irreducible dissimilarity from both the lesbians they are understood to have been and the men they are now wanting to become. The article seems to take some pains to reassure us that even if transsexuals walk among us, we will always be able to pick them out. That rhetoric mimes a different kind of war where cultural anxiety about difference is mobilized to fuel a war on terror in which we are told always to be alert because potential terrorists could be hidden among us. In each kind of war, danger is embodied as difference masquerading as sameness, precisely the affront the lesbians in the article locate in the bodies of transmen. And, in each kind of war, preemptive violence is offered as the only weapon effective against such an enemy.

Insisting that this is a picture of Shane's *scars* rather than Shane's *pecs* offers his chest as "the horror of nothing to see." This last, of course, was Freud's assessment of the child's apprehension of female genitals, which comparison with the penis renders not just nothing but a horrible nothing. Indeed, much of the anxiety and anger in discussions both popular and academic about FTM transition centers around the loss of the breasts from top surgery, so much so that the focus on breasts and their fate during transition is becoming an analog to the centrality of the penis in popular discussions about transwomen. The preoccupation with transmen's bodies extends beyond the physical presence of the scars resulting from top surgery to the question of what it is, exactly, that those scars signify. The excessive concern for the breasts, the desire to "save" them or to save the "young women" who are considering top surgery from "mutilating" their breasts and themselves in this way, understands transition to be a transaction whereby the transman purchases the nonmaterial privileges of the phallus at the price of the material flesh of the breasts. Thus an ostensibly feminist concern offers a disingenuous grieving for the removed breasts as a symbol of the transman's relinquished femininity, though I would venture that those breasts were rarely affirmed or avowed as such when they were still a part of that transman's body.

If public fascination with transpeople often becomes consolidated into a fixation with "the" surgery, which in MTFs is misunderstood to be castration, the focus in people's discussions of FTMs becomes top surgery, again misunderstood as a kind of castration, or reverse castration. The breasts become the absolute signifiers of femininity—offering a positive confirmation of sex, even when clothed or covered, in a way female genitalia do not. The fixation on the breast is displayed in the *Times* article, which has nearly nothing to say about bottom surgery, making only one mention of an "ersatz penis." And while this might have the refreshing effect of not reducing gender and sexuality to genital morphology, so often the case when trans appears in the popular press, that fascination is not banished but finds itself attached to a new part. In commenting about people's fascination with her penis and *the* surgery, Riki Wilchins offers, in a remark that characteristically insists on both her trans specificity *and* her feminism: "Transexual women are unerringly described as 'cutting off their dicks.' No one ever formulates this act as gaining a cunt—not even lesbians, feminists, or transgender women" (193).

THE MAKING OF A MAN

I'd like by way of comparison with the photograph that appears at the beginning of this chapter to turn to a series of photographs taken by Jana Marcus and displayed in a show called "Transfigurations: The Making of a Man." The insistence on "making" here resonates with the language of becoming that Judith Butler sees as the legacy of a certain strain in feminism now being continued by trans theorists: "In some ways, it is Kate Bornstein who is now carrying the legacy of Simone de Beauvoir: If one is not born a woman, but rather becomes one, then becoming is the vehicle for gender itself."[20] I want to suggest that these photographs portray their transitioning subject quite differently from the *Times* photographs, thereby offering us an altogether different narrative about the making of gender.

The series consists of three black and white photographs of a young transman named Aidan. The first photograph shows Aidan seated, looking relaxed and somewhat pensive. His arms are folded loosely over his chest. He is wearing a T-shirt that says, in letters that are only partially discernible, AMBIGUOUS. The second photograph shows a shirtless Aidan with a bound chest. In the third, Aidan is unwrapping the gauze and gazing down at his chest and the results of a very recent top surgery inscribed there. This series and the photo from the *Times* each depict shirtless transmen, but their content, framing, and stance toward both their subjects and their viewers are quite different.

The Aidan series is striking for a number of reasons, but particularly interesting is the way it portrays and literalizes gender as a matter of the relation between inside and out, between self and viewer, between the visible and the invisible. The triptych of Aidan's chest—clothed, bound, naked—offers us a progression from total concealment to naked revelation. This contrast between outside and inside is ubiquitous in trans writing, where inside often stands in for a certain immaterial truth of gender, and outside for a false and unwanted fleshly covering. From Jay Prosser's *Second Skins* to Jamison Green's *Becoming a Visible Man* to Max Wolf Valerio's *The Testosterone Files*, transition for transmen has been described as a process of transforming the body so that its visible signifiers of gender come into accord with the internal invisible sense of gender. This model reflects the lives of transpeople more generally in that transition is not a sudden leap across a precipice into a wholly unknown gender. To insist that Aidan was resolutely female prior to surgery would seem inaccurate at best and interpretively violent at worst. External bodily change here becomes the sign of internal continuity and persistence.

In the case of this image, the photograph shows Aidan without a shirt, chest bound. His arms are lifted above his head, his head is turned slightly to the left, his eyes are closed. That binding produces an almost perfectly flat contour, as the curve of both breasts is compressed by the binding. But we are able to *see through* this binding, which is made of Saran Wrap or a similar material. The effect is the presentation of a bodily modification that can only do its work as a gender modification when covered or concealed, a covering or concealing that is nevertheless made almost magically transparent to the viewer. The photograph thus offers a remarkable reversal of relations between inside and out that become entwined; Aidan's internal self-image of the chest as a flat, masculine plane becomes externalized and enabled through the binding, which itself disappears, leaving only its effects behind. We are offered a certain identification with Aidan in this act of looking, an identification that is perhaps intensified with the quotation that accompanies the photograph, in which he describes the pain of binding and the bodily dilemma he faces:

> Depending on what I'm wearing I can look like a guy. I wear big clothes to cover my body, but I don't feel very confident. If I'm wearing a jacket it covers my chest and I tend to pass more, but in the summer I tend to wear t-shirts and need to bind my breasts. In order to look flat-chested I have to tie the binding so it's fairly painful and intense. People use ace bandages, saran wrap or anything that will hold you in tight. If I bind too tight, I can't breathe. Now I wear a sports bra cause I'm just not willing to be in pain anymore. I've been struggling with this for a number of years, and now it's just getting worse. I just want to be comfortable in my body. Soon I'll have chest surgery.

The taxonomies that we saw earlier would have transmen and butches as separate kinds of beings, with the former fleeing the body and the latter at home in it. Aidan's description, though, might come from a butch or a transman with equal ease.

After surgery, Aidan has this to say about his new chest:

I'm sure surgery was right for me. I've wanted to take my transition one step at a time. . . . Chest surgery had become an immediate need for me because the breast thing was just getting worse and worse. I felt like if the only thing I did was chest surgery, I would feel a lot better about myself. I would be able to wear shirts that fit and look the way I want them to. My chest is very concave where my breasts used to be, but I love that it's flat. I have to wait a couple months to lift weights, so my chest won't look the way I want it to for a long time. But my physical transition has started, and soon I'll take testosterone. Yesterday it was windy outside and my shirt pressed firmly against my chest and for the first time I wasn't conscious of my breasts . . . it felt amazing!"

The last photograph is indeed one in which *Aidan shows his mastectomy scars*. But that description seems much more apt here than for the *Times* photograph, and its effect is exactly the reverse. Aidan faces the camera squarely, again shirtless, again shown from the waist up, but whereas in the first photograph his eyes met ours, and in the second his eyes were closed and his head averted, in the third he looks down at his chest. His hands open up a large piece of cloth that circles his chest, though the material this time is opaque, perhaps made of gauze, and seems to reference both binder and bandage. He gazes down at his chest and the quite prominent post-surgical scars there, still new and healing. Whereas in the previous photograph, the camera was given a view of Aidan's chest from which he averted his eyes, in this final photograph the camera, Aidan, and the viewer are all focused on the new topography of his chest. We are invited to look *with* him rather than *at* him.

Aidan does not yet report that he is utterly at home in his chest or in his body. He indicates that he sees his new chest as the *beginning* of male embodiment—"my physical transition has started . . . my chest won't look the way I want it to for a long time"—that top surgery is the start of this process, rather than its culmination. Again, transition is shown as a process of embodiment, a continual becoming, rather than one act that begins and ends with a surgery.

And this structure of being and becoming exceeds a simple dichotomy of inside and outside. Aidan reports the exhilaration of being outside after surgery, feeling his shirt pressed flat against his chest by the wind, and not having to feel conscious about his breasts. It is significant that this is not a purely internal consciousness of self. His uncomfortable awareness and disavowal of his breasts grows stronger over time as a result of failing to pass, as other people, perhaps reading him as gender ambiguous, examine the chest of a presurgery Aidan, and read the breasts visible beneath the shirt as confirmation of femaleness. This external misrecognition leads to an extreme feeling of consciousness of that particular part and self-consciousness about its presentation, which becomes impossible to separate from Aidan's consciousness of himself. Thus his internal sense of discomfort with his external appearance may not be a simple misalignment or mismatch, but an internal sense of dysphoria that becomes amplified as it circuits from his body to the gaze of an external world that is brutally hostile to gender ambiguity to become internalized and incorporated as a part of his gendered sense of self.

TRANSGENDER MASCULINITY

The trans position is often described by lesbian feminist critics as a capitulation to gender normativity that is both an abandonment and a selling out of lesbian sisterhood. The critique would have us understand that there is, in the abandonment of the solidarity of "woman," a profoundly unethical relation to one's lesbian "sisters." But it seems crucial to consider what ethical stance is taken when someone insists that the only position for a transman that is not a betrayal of lesbianism or feminism is to bear his pain and his discomfort rather than considering having his breasts removed. If his passing is understood as some sort of betrayal, what is it, precisely that has been betrayed? What is our response if failure to pass makes him the target of violence or otherwise endangers him? What would it mean to insist that Aidan must not modify his body in order that he bear the visible marker of a "womanhood" with which he has no identificatory relation? Consider the lesbian feminist demand that a transman suffer in his body as confirmation of his femininity rather than transition. If, for example, a transman's desire to feel comfortable in his own body is objected to on the grounds of lesbian solidarity, should we not ask why it is transmen's bodies that must be mobilized in particular, why the bodies of the gender transgressive among us are forced to differentially bear the weight of and responsibility for that solidarity? Might it be that the lesbian desire for masculinity—the sexual longing of a lesbian for masculinity embodied in someone who is not male—can still incite crisis in the lesbian community?[21] And is lesbian reassurance that this desire does not make them straight—their need to be reassured about their own *lesbianism*—purchased at the price of the safety and bodily habitability of transmen and also butches and other masculine women?

Sameness, then, becomes the spur that causes some lesbians to reject trans identified people in their communities. I would suggest a different kind of sameness is at work when transmen find themselves and each other through communities of gendered commonality. Griffin Hansbury convincingly argues that transmasculinity can best be understood not as fidelity to any single ideal of gendered embodiment, or conformity to a singular fantasy of the uniformly male body, but rather as a range of masculine bodily expressions and feelings.[22] His emendation of the totalizing concept of community with the language of the spectrum allows masculinity to be understood as a *way* of being (more or less masculine) rather than a *kind* of being (transmen versus nontransmen), less a fixed ontology of transgenderism and more a performative account of transgenderism. That is, Hansbury helps us understand that transmasculinity is not the injunction to be any one single or simple kind of subject, fit neatly into one self-identical category, and moves away from a notion of one single trans identity to introduce us to the growing diversity of experience that travels under the sign of trans.

Hansbury's account provides a useful counterpoint to the *Times*'s depiction of transmen and their partners in two respects. First, it makes powerfully clear that transpeople do indeed have communities—that far from being the figures of abject isolation described by the

Times, they are people whose lives are shared, and often with one another. Second: whereas the *Times* article understands transmen as the agents who disrupt or destroy their intimate relationships so as to be trans, Hansbury gives us a different perspective in which it is the lesbian partners of transmen who choose to end their relationship rather than the transmen. It is surely true that both scenarios are possible, that sometimes it will be the transman who will leave a relationship and sometimes it will be the lesbian partner. It is also true that such relationships can be viable and do not necessarily end. But Hansbury helpfully reminds us that, when such couples do part, transpeople are not always the agents of division, that their experience can be one of extreme vulnerability and abandonment rather than the comparatively cavalier dismissal of relation in favor of identity the *Times* describes.

It seems possible that the consolidation of sameness, the drive toward a certain uniformity, does not entirely drop out within Hansbury's discourse but instead displaces itself onto a different register. I am interested in the critical and political stakes of this question, which seems to be emerging, in a number of different forms, in current discussions of trans issues. Is it possible that the moment "sameness" is abandoned as a normative ideal governing identity it resurfaces as a normative ideal governing *relation?* It seems undeniably true that the transmasculine community is something more capacious than a consolidated unity, but I wonder if this diversity of expressions of transmasculinity covers over a more subtle and fundamental form of sameness if identity is something achieved by removing the self from relation and evacuating the self of difference. That is, if we are to understand transmen as "self-made" (to echo the title of Henry Rubin's book on FTM identity), is there some way in which identity becomes understood as the product of sameness, the self-generated precipitate of an entirely internal process? And, to the extent that it does form itself in relation, does a transmasculine identity emerge only insofar as it displays a similarity, a resemblance to other masculinities?

There are times in Hansbury's article when identity is described as if it were an attribute or property of the individual, a paradigm familiar from some trans writing in which the social power of the

"I am" is invoked to counter the erasures and invisibilities that transpeople face. At other times, Hansbury usefully supplements this model with a model that understands gendered identity as an achievement of relation, something formed through the invocation of and interaction with community. Within Hansbury's article and within the transmasculine community he describes, each of these transmasculine identities—woodworker, transman, genderqueer, man—emerges and becomes legible only in relation to *each other* and gain their meaning and coherence from its ordered relation to similar, but not identical, positions on the spectrum of masculinity. Indeed, the very notion of the spectrum depends on this relation; the spectrum itself is, in a sense, nothing but the visible trace of the bond between proximate but bounded categories of gender. Hansbury offers us scenes of affirmation—at the True Spirit conference, in therapy and groups, in conversation, in happy dogpiles—in which the expression and discovery of identity is something that happens in relation with, in the company of, in solidarity with, other transmasculine folk. This notion of gendered identity as a project undertaken in the company of and solidarity with like others is a familiar legacy from feminism. But if the legacy of feminism can be read in the transmasculine community, the status of the feminine here is harder to read.

I am tempted to read these relations among men, transmen, and genderqueers as circuits of sameness, which complicate and queer the common conception that the most valued and idealized form of masculinity in trans circles is the straight bio male. And one possibility seems to be the radical and unsettling potential of homoerotic or homosocial bonds of masculinity within transmasculine communities, and the possibility that an already queer masculinity is located at the heart of transmasculinity. Moreover, I want to turn to the status of the feminine, the female, and the lesbian in these accounts and ask if these homosocial bonds might form a closed circuit of identity that runs the risk of eliding or evading difference rather than engaging with it.

Hansbury offers this description of the formation of the transmasculine subject and emphasizes the too-often-overlooked fact that transguys and butches might be, from the outside, indistinguishable:

[The genderqueer] must find a way to turn down the volume on the many voices that exert their desires; they must tune in to their own inner self-perception. What makes a Genderqueer boi different from a butch dyke? Physically, there is often no difference. Again, it is all about self-interpretation. The boi; or guy; perceives himself, and wishes to be perceived, as a transmasculine boi. That's a much taller order than that of the Woodworker or Transman who asks to be seen as a man.

(259)

Hansbury turns our attention to those aspects of gender that are internal rather than observable, the *felt sense* that confirms our gendered sense of self. Within this account the genderqueer's task is to find a way "to turn down the volume on the many voices that exert their desires; and tune in to their own inner self-perception." These voices emanate variously from the transmasculine community (who wants the genderqueer to transition), the lesbian community (who wants the genderqueer to remain "female"), and "the non-trans world" (whose wants remain unspecified but may be safely assumed hostile if not annihilatory). It seems significant that the only other thing that characterizes these voices, in addition to the fact that they are unwelcome, is their desire, which is not just passively present, but actively exerting itself on the genderqueer boi—a press that has to be actively resisted.

The location of these scripts, too, is uncertain. They are identified as external and social, somehow separate or separable from the thoughts, feelings, desires, and identity of the transman himself. But the suggestion that the genderqueer can "turn down the volume" on them would seem to indicate that they have been internalized at least to the extent that the genderqueer can quiet or stifle them. Or perhaps this is an internalization and an externalization happening at once: the press of a desire that would contradict or threaten a consolidated sense of identity is externalized to the extent that it is understood as coming from elsewhere, emanating through the voices of other people, other communities. But as soon as these threatening desires are externalized, read, and responded to as if they came from outside the self, they are simultaneously internalized, brought under the control of a self that could turn them down at will. What might it mean to understand the genderqueer's or, for that matter, the transman's task as turning down or tuning out the polyglot voices the world directs toward him?

As a method of resisting pervasive homophobia and transphobia, this would seem not only strategic but, to some degree, necessary. We might ask, however, whether this turn inward, this shutting out of the world, might have unforeseen consequences for either the consolidation of identity or the possibility of relation? Does it necessitate that we understand desire and identity, inside and outside, self and other, in ways that are mutually threatening? If the goal is to achieve a stable and enduring sense of self-identity, is there room for a transmasculine subject to encounter the other's desire without evacuating or annihilating it? Or feeling evacuated or annihilated by it in turn? Indeed, is there room for transmasculine desire, or is he required to surrender any claim on that desire in return for a stable and legible identity?

It reads as significant that the structural positions occupied by the feminine in this text are quite limited. The feminine others that appear here—the lesbian partner of the butch who forbids transition and the homo- and transphobic straight-identified partner of the woodworker—are figures of denial and negation. There is little space here for crafting identity alongside difference rather than in reaction to it. Does the voice of the other, particularly the feminine other, always only say no, replace a true identity with the proscription of a false one, hinder transition or threaten to leave because of it? The figure of the lesbian partner who issues the ultimatum "It's T or me" is the perfect figure of exactly this choice, in which interaction across difference comes only at the expense of a "true" identity, where *being* and *having* foreclose one another, where identity is purchased only at the cost of desire. The figure of the forbidding feminine partner puts the transmasculine subject in the position of either being (transmasculine) or having (a partner), but not both.

Hansbury goes on to complicate this zero-sum game of identity and desire, however: "Again, it is all about self-interpretation. The boi; or guy; perceives himself, and wishes to be perceived, as a transmasculine boi. That's a much taller order than that of the Woodworker or Transman who asks to be seen as a man." This seems on its face like a contradiction—how can identity be "all about self-interpretation" and yet require this petition of unnamed and unknown others? But I would suggest that much work is being done by this request, in the moment that the woodworker or transman "asks to be seen" as a man.

What Hansbury describes here is a perfect reversal of the theory of interpellation as described by Louis Althusser in "Ideology and Ideological State Apparatuses"[23] and subsequently taken up by Butler to describe the process of gendering. Interpellation is an account about the formation of identity in which the world issues forth a series of names and categories, calls to which I must respond in order to emerge as a subject. The usefulness of interpellation here for this discussion, it seems to me, is that it offers a way to understand the complex operations of naming and the relations between self and world, self and other, that our categories of naming and identity want to broker. It helps us account for the ways in which we find ourselves labeled, named, and identified prior to any deciding on our part, and why those labels can prove so resistant to our own strategies of revision and recuperation, a fact to which most transpeople can likely attest. I claim my name and am claimed by it at once, or am claimed by categories of identity that then determine how I will be perceived and received in the social world. And throughout these processes of naming, of categorization, the operation of gender is not merely an adjectival appendage to my subjectivity, but a precondition of its achievement. Interpellation explains the ways in which my identity has a social life that exceeds my own, that even my "own" identity, in all its particularity, depends on the names I am called, the ways I am recognized, by others.

In Hansbury's account, the scene of social intelligibility is reversed. It is not that the world flings a name at me, a name that fails to fully capture who I am, to which I am nevertheless obliged to respond. It is that the "I"[33] of Hansbury's report emerges outside that naming in order to dictate its terms, to assure that the category with which I am saddled meshes seamlessly with the particularity that I am. It is not the world which calls me into being, but rather

I who dictate the terms of my being to the wider world in which I am situated. This request "to be seen as" is something other than a lament about invisibility or the impossibility of ever being truly and deeply recognized beneath or beyond the categories and labels where one takes up residence or that take up residence in us. To ask to be seen *as* something asserts both an equivalence and an incommensurability at once, rather than asserting one at the expense of the other. Butler reminds us of this structure, pointing out that, when she sings "You make me feel like a natural woman," Aretha Franklin invokes the distance, the gap between her particularity, the supposed naturalness of the category, and the insistence that the two are reducible.[24] In Butler's account, what mediates between them, what bridges this gap, is desire.

Hansbury thus places us at this important and confounding juncture in subjectivity, where the language of categorization inevitably installs a gap between who I feel myself to be and the category by which I am named. He points to exactly this gap with his assertion that "I am not comfortable labeling myself as just a man. For me, it's too limiting." He is describing a tension between the certainty of the man he knows himself to be and the social recognition that can confirm or withhold that certainty. The request *to be seen as something* involves a temporal reversal: that I first know myself to be a man and therefore ask you to see me as such. But those forces of recognition are just as vital in forming our perceptions of ourselves as any purely internal felt sense. I would even suggest that it is impossible to conceive a *purely internal* felt sense of gender, that the social structures of gender are always attending and informing that felt sense.

The inevitably social structure of even our most intimate and personal apprehension of gender would seem to be confirmed by the fact that even the most interior felt sense of gender seems to be confirming the social binary by which gender becomes legible. That is, Hansbury feels like *a man* and not some obscure and private gender for which there is no name or common cultural point of reference. And if it is the case, as it seems to be with transmen, that the normative gender configurations of the social world conspire to give the lie to that internal felt sense, when the world says "you are a man"—or withholds that determination—based on outward appearance, then it seems true that survival depends on an understanding of self that exceeds the normative constraints of the category *and* that this more capacious self-understanding is not by itself sufficient to assure recognition. To assert that transmasculinity hinges on self-interpretation, individual and self-reflexive acts of identification, is not yet to address how these identifications might be materialized or become visible in the world or what nexus of relations underlies those materializations and visibilities.

How, then, might we think these two contradictory modes of identity side by side: on the one hand, the fully autonomous subject possessing a gender that springs whole from an internally felt sense of self and, on the other, the subject making the request of the other, hoping to be conferred the properly gendered name that the normative gender configurations of the social world conspire to withhold? And are they compossible modes of address, the self-assured agency enabling the assertion of "I am" and the vulnerability embodied in the request "to be seen as"? To ask to be *seen as* a man, even to demand to be seen as such, seems a quite different operation and understanding of the creation and deployment of a gendered identity than a paradigm that understands it to be the willed and willful creation of a fully autonomous subject. To what extent does the latter category rely on a fantasy of a gender springing whole from an internally felt sense of the self? And who is imagined to be on the receiving end of such a request? Is it the case that the request to be seen can only be offered in its vulnerability and answered from a place of deep recognition by another transmasculine person? Can the call and response of request and recognition only play out within a scene of "deep horizontal comradeship" (the phrase is Benedict Anderson's) with other masculine subjects? In what ways does the most satisfying answer to that call come from another man? Does the question require the disavowal, or double disavowal, of the feminine other? And how might desire help us to understand the way in which bonds of recognition and reciprocity are shaped not only between one masculinity and another but also between masculine and feminine?

Let us return to the pair Hansbury offers us as figures of sameness and difference in relation, the genderqueer boi and the butch dyke. Hansbury steadfastly refuses to map the difference between these two categories onto bodily differences. Faced with a masculine body that nevertheless might not quite "pass" as male, we would not be able to determine through bodily cues alone whether this person might be a butch dyke or a genderqueer boy. Hansbury demonstrates that the importance of the body for establishing a gendered subjectivity has less to do with its morphological configurations and more to do with how flesh might be signified and resignified, where this resignification will sometimes involve visible changes to the body and sometimes will not. The body, comportment, or even degree of masculinity is not sufficient to determine identity along the transmasculine spectrum, and the body's anatomy is less crucial here than the way the body is phenomenologically inhabited.

And yet, in the case of the butch dyke and the genderqueer boi, is it truly only a matter of self-identification that divides them? Hansbury insists that "it's all about self interpretation," and I want to press a bit on this conclusion. If the difference between a butch dyke and a transmasculine boi is not located in the body, is there another important distinction to be drawn? At the level of language alone, we seem to be offered a distinction between sexual orientation and gender identity: when we describe someone as a dyke, or identify that way ourselves, we are announcing something about perversion and desire. The first thing we seem to know about a dyke is that she desires, before we know enough to say who or what she desires or even if she is recognizable to herself or others as "she." The first thing we know about a transmasculine boi is his gender—boy—before we know the complicated sets of avowal and disavowal that give rise to that gender. As subject positions, *dyke* would seem to describe a habit of desire, and *boy* a habit of embodiment. And yet, to understand *dyke* and *boy* as circumscribing separate modalities of being and having is to miss the nuances of both. To say "dyke" is to already be saying something about gender, and the press of perverse desire(s) in "boi" might be read in a number of different directions.

It certainly seems important to acknowledge that models of homosexuality can prove and have proven insufficient in understanding transgender issues and to ask, as Hansbury does, what might be gained when we insist upon the distinction between gender identity and sexual orientation. I believe it is equally important for us to look toward what gets lost or falls away with that distinction between perverse forms of desire and perverse expressions of gender. On one hand, it certainly seems evident, as many commentators have noted, that gay bashing and other forms of homophobic violence are used precisely to police *gender* boundaries. Insisting on the radical separability and separateness of sexual orientation and gender identity overlooks the ways in which these two categories are mutually implicated, even when they are not mutually constituting. That is, even when the trajectory of one's desire cannot be predicted *by* one's gender, it surely is the case that my desire is experienced *through* my gender and that a strict parsing runs the risk of impoverishing both categories.

MUD

I'd like to conclude by considering Lily Rodgriguez's 2005 photograph *Mud* as a representation of trans bodies and subjectivities that captures some of the complex and indeed joyous dynamic between queer and/or trans masculinities that Hansbury describes. *Mud* breaks with the still, composed framing of portraiture in several ways, most obviously in that there are two subjects in the frame instead of one, suggesting that we are already in the territory of relation, difference, and engagement with the other, rather than contained within the monadic confines of solitary identity represented by the conventions of portraiture. Indeed, spectatorship is at issue in the photograph, but this spectatorship is more obliquely presented than the locked gaze between a sitting subject and an unseen camera. Within the frame of the photograph, a pair of fuzzily discernible shoes stand in the background, indicating that relations here are not simply dyadic but at least triangular. In this scene spectatorship is bound with identification is bound with desire, and some "I" is probably looking on, to borrow from Freud. The horizontally splayed tangle of the bodies of these two people refuses to be quite captured temporally (the figures are blurred with movement) or spatially (the stretch of each of their bodies exceeds the frame). The photograph is centered on the point of contact between their two bodies, and they are engaged in a struggle that reads as agonistic, playful, and erotic in equal parts. It is not easy to discern whether these two figures are pushing each other away or drawing each other near or attempting both at the same time. We witness an engagement of masculinity with masculinity which refuses to reduce to sameness. One of these figures bears a scar on hir bare chest, and the chest of the other figure is bound by a sports bra. A bodily difference, to be sure, but what kind of knowing do we believe to be delivered by that difference? Does it announce a difference of gender identity? Of sexual identity? Of class? Of access to surgery? Of age? Of politics? I would suggest that we cannot possibly know the answer and that this undecidability of what conclusions we can and cannot, should and should not, draw from the bodily markers of masculinity can help us open up a space where we might ethically engage otherness without the fear of mutual annihilation. Feminists have learned—and championed—these distinctions in the realms of race, of class, of sexuality, of ability. Why, then, does this aporia stubbornly and surprisingly remain in the realm of gender?

3

TRANSCENDING SEXUAL DIFFERENCE

AN ETHICS OF TRANSSEXUAL DIFFERENCE

Luce Irigaray and the Place of Sexual Undecidability

AGAINST SEXUAL HYLOMORPHISM

Luce Irigaray raises a number of questions in "Place, Interval" about place, sexual difference, and the body as it is given through relation.[1] I want to ask whether a nonheteronormative reading of body and relation is possible within the logic of Irigaray's work in *An Ethics of Sexual Difference* and, if so, what room might be made for sexual relationships that fall outside the scope of the strictly heterosexual or bodily and identificatory configurations that cannot be understood as strictly male or female. I want to follow Irigaray in insisting on the importance of a theory of place and relation to such questions and to depart from her by moving toward a number of points at which such an intervention might begin, a queer reading of Irigaray in which bodies, boundaries, and relations of sexual difference need not exclude the sexually different or the differently sexed.

Irigaray's reading of Aristotle in "Place, Interval," like her readings of other philosophers, is primarily concerned with relation, with self and other, where *self* is figured as the masculine subject of philosophy and *other* as its elided feminine. Central to her reading of Aristotle is an inquiry into the place of that relation between self and other. Woman, Irigaray will argue, is allied with place in the same way that she is allied with matter against the masculinity of form, and, in several crucial ways, place resembles form but is not reducible to it. This is at first a surprising strategy, a reversal of the ways in which matter has been historically allied with the feminine and form with the masculine. Irigaray proceeds quite differently here, and her reading of form and boundedness, rather than matter, as feminine nevertheless places its anchor in the sexual specificity of the body. Irigaray's reading hinges on the fact that matter in Aristotle's account is both density *and indeterminacy*, and the view of matter that we are given in *Physics* IV understands it to be fundamentally without form or shape. In "Place, Interval," Irigaray reads form in Aristotle as a description of the feminine, as a description of place.

As we shall see, there is an impossibility of place for the feminine: place is what the feminine is for the masculine, but what the masculine can never be for the feminine or, indeed, what the feminine can never quite be for herself. Irigaray ingeniously reverses this and reads the feminine as the container, that which houses the masculine and functions as the fixed external boundary for his moving center. The problematic, as Irigaray poses it, is for the feminine to find or to become a place for herself and thus find herself in place, and this is accomplished so that she may become place for the masculine. The means by which she accomplishes this, a reclaiming of the skin, reads at first as a strategy that might be deployed as successfully by the masculine as by the feminine, a means of finding body and place, but there are important ways in which a "corporeal surveying" of the outermost layer of the body, the skin—or indeed, of the body *as* that which is bounded by its skin—might even confound the familiar divisions between masculine and feminine as they are articulated here.

In my reading of Irigaray's reading of Aristotle, I want to make two claims about place, the first, following Irigaray, having to do with the place of self and the second, departing from her, having to do with the place of relation. Thinking seriously about the external contours of the bodily boundary, as Irigaray suggests that we do with "skin," can help us understand how a body—especially a female body—might find its own place and thus be able to move from its own place toward relation with others.[2] The second claim I want to make is about that relation to others. Irigaray has offered sexual difference as "the major philosophical issue of our age,"[3] and she turns to Aristotle to theorize relations across sexual difference, asking how bodily and sexual relations might bridge the interval of sexual difference. I want to suggest that even with Irigaray's often dazzling conceptual reversals, interventions by which her own text comes to be folded around Aristotle's like a skin, in "Place, Interval" the question of sexual difference ends at an impasse. This impasse stems from a fundamentally *hylomorphic* understanding of sexual difference: a conviction that male and female, like matter and form, must always be ontologically conjoined.

Is it possible that Irigaray's notion of sexual difference and her insights into the ways in which sexual difference is crucially generative might be of use in an account of sexual difference that aims to challenge gender and sexual heteronormativity? What would it look like if the divide of sexual difference were not fixed in the place it now occupies, marked as the boundary between "male" and "female"? Were that boundary not mapped onto the body in strictly determinative ways, we might be able to theorize sexual difference between women, between men, or between bodies and psyches who do not find easy home or place in either of these categories. A queer reading of the place of sexual difference, then, might be able to answer my second question by way of the first.

WHERE IS PLACE?

Midway through the *Physics*, Aristotle turns to the question of place, explaining that we must have a thorough understanding of place if we are to understand both existence and motion, "both because all suppose that things which exist are *somewhere* (the non-existent is nowhere—where is the goat-stag or the sphinx?), and because 'motion' in its most general and primary sense is a change of place."[4] Contrary to the hope that place will be sufficient to give things a solid anchor in existence, we find that place is reckoned only through relation. The place of things, and thus the "thing" of place, is only found through other things. According to Aristotle, "the existence of place is held to be obvious from the fact of mutual replacement. Where water now is, there, in turn, when the water has gone out as from a vessel, air is present. When therefore another body occupies this same place, the place is thought to be different from all the bodies which come to be in it and replace one another" (208b, l.1).

When Aristotle first introduces us to place in the beginning of *Physics* IV, he does so indirectly. We are led to infer place not from any direct experience with or of it, but because of the loss of a body or object, its displacement (or destruction) by another object. "The existence of place is held to be obvious from the fact of mutual replacement." Place is the nonmaterial residue of two different, separate bodies. The question of place is from the outset already a question of relation, of mobility, of replacement, of bodies, place reveals itself through a succession of different bodies, one supplanting the other in the same space—water then air—and the relation of these different bodies is mutual only to the extent that it is mutually exclusive: place stands as a testament to the fact that the two bodies cannot share the same space. Place is the marker of the bounded and separate identity of the two bodies, and only by virtue of this does space become transmogrified into place. Place is the space where two bodies can never coexist, the space that they cannot ever share.

Place then is testament to a lack of relation, of the progression from water to air, where neither leaves the trace of itself, leaves no mark that it was housed or held there. Place is place to the extent that it is different from either of these, water or air, and neither leaves any trace. Place persists emptily and is established through a network of relations of mutual exclusivity. Place exists to the extent that it is demarcated and separate from the things that inhabit it, and it persists to the extent that the things that inhabit it, in this first instance, at least, are different from one another and pass through it leaving no part of themselves in it.

Aristotle, then, seems to be offering place as a relation, or non-relation, of mutual exclusivity, at least at first. Place develops as the text continues, however, becoming the location where relation happens and eventually becoming that very relation. Place is eventually established as *only* relation, only established by the proximity of the two bodies who share it, neither of which is quite place. "Place," writes Aristotle, "is the boundary of the containing body at which it is in contact with the contained body." We are still presented with two separate substances, neither partaking of the other, but are now offered a place that is entirely comprised of the touch between them. Aristotle eventually concludes that "the innermost motionless boundary of what contains is place" (212a, l.20). That is, an object, a body, moves within the context of a fixed and bounded something that does not move. And that fixed and bounded something is not merely a space of contact, but is itself another body, a body that is necessary for the establishment of place but is not reducible to it, is not the same as place itself: "If then a body has another body outside it and containing it, it is in place, and if not, not" (212a, l.32). Place would then be the plane of contact between the body that encapsulates and the body that is held.

Here we may note the problematic that Aristotle touches upon briefly and Irigaray dwells upon at some length: if place is the *innermost* boundary of the body containing, this leaves the external layer of that body without its own place, outside of place. In order to see if the outermost surface of the containing body, the feminine body, might become housed in itself, or cast a place around itself, Irigaray suggests that we read this external boundary as skin: "But each of us (male or female) has a place—this place that envelops only his or her body, the first envelope of our bodies, the corporeal identity, the boundary, that which delineates us from other bodies. Form and configuration also determine one's size and all that makes one body unsubstitutable by another. Could this be called a corporeal *surveying*?"[5]

We will return to this question of corporeal surveying: what exactly is it? Is it a scopic activity? A tactile one? What are the proper, and improper, objects for such a survey?[6] Here we will note Irigaray's claim that to become place for the man, woman must be place for herself. Like Aristotle, she introduces us to place by showing us the existence of place prior to relation, a radical boundedness into which the other does not—cannot—move. We have the place of the self established as the place of the body and the place of the body understood as its outermost boundary, its envelope, its skin. In the Aristotelian model, however, place does not yet encompass the outermost boundary of this body. The task as Irigaray describes it is to transform the skin into something that also contains, to feel the skin as its own bounding envelope so that the body might house itself. The body must perform that bounding function for itself before it can properly house the masculine. The first step toward relation between feminine and masculine, Irigaray suggests, is for woman to find and claim her body as a discrete and separate entity.

I will return in a moment to the collapse of feminine and woman here and see if it might not be possible to coax those two categories apart, in order to give them a relation to one another other than simply sameness. It is important to understand this relational bind that Irigaray describes, that woman's own emergence as a discrete entity cannot come before her encounter with the other but rather only emerges in relation to this other who is proximate to her, installed inside of her, away from whom she needs to retract to the outermost extensions of her body and being in order that she might return with something like place to offer him. In order to find the place that each of us, female and male alike, *is*, the feminine retracts into the particularity of herself, but finds the same problematic enacted at the level of her own individual body. If our skin is what "delineates us from other bodies," the other body is already installed at the exact moment and precise place at which I find myself; this other who is not me delineates my own boundary. The body belongs to the self to the extent that it "delineates us from other bodies," and thus the feminine finds her place as inescapably bordered by and bound to the place of the masculine, with the result that she cannot even extend into her own skin without feeling the press of the masculine on the other side of it.

But even though male and female are perfectly and inescapably joined, or perhaps *because* they are inescapably joined, Irigaray makes clear that we must not then understand them to be collapsible or substitutable. The shared border between male and female becomes the occasion of the shoring up of the boundary between them. And this boundary, this determinant of categorization, turns out to be bodily form, since "form and configuration also determine one's size and all that makes one body unsubstitutable by another." Irigaray, like Aristotle, reckons the body here as something more precise and distinct than merely the mass of matter of which it is comprised. Mapping my own body means feeling not only its weight, but its form and shape, and these latter are only perceptible as I feel the press of myself out toward the world where another body, another self, is located. We see again in Irigaray's text another surprising reversal: whereas what secures place in Aristotle is the substitutability of one kind of body for another, Irigaray points here toward the limits of that substitutability and suggests that the form and shape of the body secure for it an identity, though not a sameness, that allows and enables proximity. If one kind of thing is unsubstitutable for another, then two bodies might share the same space, inhabit the same place, with no fear of engulfing or annihilating each other. Though they are determined and constituted in relation to one another, their differences of form and configuration, their distinct morphologies secure and solidify their distinct identities. This last is crucial, for if one thing, in the act of replacing in space, takes over or overcomes another kind of thing, it is not only the thing that is vanquished, but place itself.

What does it mean to suggest that one body is unsubstitutable for another? And how can this help us make sense of sexual difference? I am most interested here in the ways that the singularity or unsubstitutability said to characterize bodies across sexual difference is secured by ascribing an interchangeability to bodies *within* sexual difference. The logic by which the male body is unsubstitutable for the female body is the same logic that would posit every male body as able to stand in for any other or viewing women, in some sense, as interchangeable parts of Woman. What is unsubstitutable about these bodies is not just any singular quality, not even the vicissitudes of size and shape, but their designation as "masculine" or "feminine." Irigaray writes: "For the masculine has to constitute itself as *a vessel* to receive and welcome. And the masculine's morphology, existence, and essence do not really fit it for such an architecture of place" (39). Understood in this way, it is not a difficulty of relation or a failure of imagination that makes the masculine unable to receive and welcome, it is rather the poor "fit" of the morphology of the masculine that Irigaray deems determinative. But what if we were to understand masculinity as something different from the male body, femininity as not reducible to the vessel of the womb? What if sexual difference were not parsed between the registers of morphology so neatly, so that masculinity might be less simply a matter of morphology but also a mode of relation?

Must sexual difference be legible at the surface of the body? And is sexual difference the same thing as "natural" sex? There are, of course, a number of ways to pose the question of sexual difference that would not reduce it to the category male or female, determined by bodily or genital morphology. One could, for example, formulate sexual difference in a way that would not require the identificatory possibilities it extended to relate mimetically to the dimorphic tendencies of genital morphology assumed to be the material markers of that difference. That is, if one thinks sexual difference in other than binary terms, the category can become unyoked from determinative bodily materiality in a way that makes it easier to resist the temptation to posit genital morphology as essentially determinative not only of sexual difference but also of the self. If sexual difference is categorically and functionally indistinguishable from *genital* difference, which is itself understood to manifest (as) a binary, than sexual difference is genital difference is genital dimorphism.

Like the goat-stag or the sphinx, Aristotle and Irigaray would seem to agree that the sexually undecidable does not exist and is located nowhere ("The non-existent is nowhere—where is the goat-stag or the sphinx?"). The goat-stag and the sphinx, who are themselves ambivalently located and fundamentally undecidable in terms of sexual difference, appear in the first sentence of book 4 in order to proclaim that they are located nowhere. Aristotle seems at first to be offering this monstrous couple to demonstrate that everything that exists must have its proper place. The passage as it stands, however, appears to be making this claim from the other direction: what secures the ontological primacy of place is precisely the fact that anything that is categorically undecidable cannot be located in any proper place. What renders a thing or being impossible is literally that it *has no place*. It is not quite that an understanding of place might be discerned by a thorough examination of existence, but rather that a proper orientation toward place can help us determine what things exist. We look around, in no place do we find a goat-stag or a sphinx, and this absence is evidence for our conclusion that such things do not exist.

We look around, we notice that the beings we encounter are male or female, and we make a swift and sure conclusion about the place of gender and of sexual difference. The feminine is the female is the one with a womb is woman, the masculine is male, and this of "morphology, existence, and essence." It remains to be determined, however, by what measure, what method of corporeal surveying the masculine or the feminine might be decided.

CORPOREAL SURVEILLANCE AND SEXUAL UNDECIDABILITY; OR, MINDING THE GAP

What if the bodies that we survey resist conforming to that most familiar of binaries, male and female? What if the objects of surveillance were transgendered bodies or other bodies that challenge the familiar divides by which we are accustomed to parsing sexual difference? Irigaray suggests that coexistence in place, the establishment of a place where masculine and feminine could reside together, is the ultimate goal of relation and can only be established once the distance between masculine and feminine is closed, "if the split between them (in the division of both work and nature) were bridged" (37), and she suggests a "corporeal surveying" as the method by which the establishment of this new place might become possible. The corporeal surveying Irigaray suggests would then close up the interval between the two bodies, span the gap between them, and allow masculine and feminine to coincide in sameness, in place.

And yet, even granting this interval exists (although Aristotle is quite deliberate in demonstrating that this interval is an illusion, a trick of form, in 211b, 1.15–20), it is unclear that the most productive response to this split, this gap, this embodied difference is to close it up. Indeed, we might think "corporeal surveying" as a method of apprehending not only the difference of the other, as Irigaray suggests, but also as a way of taking measure of the difference that inheres in my own flesh. Irigaray insists that we attend the difference that is always already installed at the level of not merely the blunt materiality of my body but also the labile boundary with the other that finally comprises my form. In this way, place becomes not the shared and self-identical space of sameness, but, more generatively and more radically, the place where I confront the otherness of the other without annihilating or canceling that difference or replicating the other in my own image.

What, then, are the effects of this corporeal surveying? It is attempted in order to close up the gap between the male and female, but I will suggest that this is only an incidental effect of the survey. Its aim is to find the outermost boundary of woman, which must be located and inhabited for woman to be able to establish place for herself. Locating this boundary is crucial for woman in particular because she is, for Irigaray, perpetually open, never closed off or sealed up. But the unbounded body can never be whole, whether that body is a mundane material object or the human form. Woman relies for her coherence on the boundary of difference that demarcates her singularity, the external edge of the masculine. What this corporeal surveying seems to show us is a condition of bodily being in which the masculine acts as place to house the feminine—an exact reversal of Irigaray's most familiar figuration of sexual difference—to define her borders and guarantee her existence. As place is coincident with the thing and boundaries are coincident with the bounded, so too is masculine necessarily always coincident with feminine, male always coincident with female. Whereas we are accustomed in Irigaray's work to understanding the feminine and the female as the condition of possibility for the masculine and the male, within this scene the masculine becomes the constitutive outside of the feminine, her condition of being.

Although Irigaray would seem to offer us the concept of the interval as a way of circumventing the logic of masculine form giving shape to the otherwise formless unboundedness of the feminine, we must stray far from the Aristotelian model to consider this possibility, as it requires an impossible extension between bodies. As these bodies are shown to be always in necessary continuity with another, we then have man and woman inescapably conjoined *as a direct result* of Irigaray's insistence that these bodies are male and female.

TO BE MORE THAN TWO

Thus is magically guaranteed an indissoluble nearness between two categories that are at first posited as entirely separate. The insistence on the radical boundedness of each kind of being across the divide of sexual difference secures for each not only a coherent and concrete identity but also an eternally proximate point of contact and place of meeting. This suggestion that the relation between members of different categories will be nearer and more vital than the relation between members of the same category is a particularly Aristotelian formulation, encapsulated in his observation that "bodies which are united do not affect each other, while those which are in contact interact on each other" (212b, 130). It is the same logic that underlies Irigaray's proclamation that "man and woman is a most mysterious and creative couple" (199).

Striking as the consequences of this position are for theorizing relations across sexual difference, they turn out to be still more stark when we consider relations among people who are nominally "of" the same sexual category. That is: relation within sexual difference turns out to be no relation at all. Woman's position relative to another woman can only be one of sexual indifference. There has been much contention on this point, and her work on ethical relations and sexual difference has been located at various points on the spectrum between heteronormative and homophobic. Irigaray has responded to charges of this kind by affirming the primacy of sexual difference, suggesting homosexuality is a question of sexual *choice* rather than sexual *difference* and that the problem of sexual difference is as primary for homosexuals as it is for heterosexuals. Their homosexuality, in Irigaray's eyes, is merely a flight from this problem, not a renegotiation of its terms.

This is absurd for a number of reasons: its insistence that sexual choice and sexual difference are strictly separate and separable realms, its figuration of "choice" as the proper rubric for understanding homosexuality, further emphasizing her view of both heterosexuality and proper gendering as compulsory. Perhaps most alarming is the assertion that homosexuality is a flight from difference, merely love of the same that has no relationship of difference at work within it. In order to achieve an ethical relationship, Irigaray has said that it is necessary for a couple *to be two*; as she understands things, this is not something that a gay or lesbian couple—or some other, queerer pairing—can ever quite manage.

And yet, even as she appears to be dismissing homosexuality as a flat and frictionless nonrelation, her own theory of relation offers the tools for describing its possibilities otherwise. What is presented as an insurmountable dilemma becomes immediately more potent and promising if we reconfigure the location of the sexuate border that Irigaray proposes, if we shift its *place*. For if we do not restrict our scope to the categories of male and female as they are most strictly conceived, and extend our consideration to the myriad ways in which gender is performed even within the category of, for example, femaleness, we can begin to discern differences, perhaps even difference itself. These are differences that are emphatically bodily, and undeniably material, even as they are also psychic, emotional, and relational differences.

What seems useful—crucial, even—within Irigaray's schema is its insistence on locating difference at the heart of relation, in insisting on the importance and generative power of the border between self and other. This boundary between male and female is characterized by Irigaray at times as a vaporous gulf, an immaterial divide or chasm that cannot be spanned, and at other times as a tactile boundary, as palpable and dense as flesh. But in insisting on the importance of the divide of sexual difference, what or who is served in drawing that divide only and always between male and female?

If we take the example of a butch/femme couple and note that they may exemplify different and contrasting modes of comportment, styles of embodiment, methods of bodily inhabitation, and affective tendencies, what investments demand the withholding of the term *sexual difference* as a descriptor of these oppositions? In a relationship between a transman and a straight woman, is it not clear that the difference between them is decidedly bodily and resolutely "sexuate"? Acknowledging the sexual difference between a couple consisting of a transman and a gay man in relation allows us to resist the easy collapse of all masculinities into one undifferentiated category of male, while, at the same time, recognizing that each member of this couple is indeed a man. These pairings can help us conceive of sexual difference without requiring that one sex be quarantined away from another. The trans body can also help us understand the traversal of sexual boundaries not as an unrepresentable breach but as a negotiation of difference. Recognizing that movement is possible across the borders of male and female means that the bodily envelope cannot only be understood as the symbolic marker of the absolute otherness of sexual difference. Indeed, transition itself can be understood as a means of "reclaiming the skin," the project that Irigaray enjoins women to undertake.

Irigaray's corporeal survey of sexual difference concerns itself with the primacy and place of difference and can show us that that even inhabiting one's own body necessitates an encounter with sexual difference. But it misunderstands the place of sexual difference, locating it always *over there*, in that other who is a perpetual mystery to me and never reachable or knowable. This impossibility of any true encounter with sexual difference, the assertion that it may be proximate to me but can never be known or understood, renders my sexual being closed and isolated away from difference, even as I endeavor to engage with it. When each sex is given its own proper domain, which the other can never traverse, the place of sexual difference is always beyond the scope of understanding, just out of grasp. The effect is finally an inoculation against sexual difference in the guise of an engagement with it.

It may in fact be true that there is a certain ineffable power, some enthralling and catalyzing force, in sexual difference. But it seems important to remember, as *Penelope Deutscher reminds us, that the concept of sexual difference—particularly as the ground for an ethics or politics—is always animated by the tension between its possibility and its impossibility.[7] It is imperative to consider the ways in which this difference does not reside only in the contrast between male and female, where these are both understood as immutable designations. If we are to give difference its due as a vital force, as Irigaray invites us to, we must also acknowledge that femininity is compossible with the category of male, that the masculinity expressed within some iterations of femaleness is as ontologically robust as any other kind of masculinity. To exclude these pairings from the realm of ethical, productive, generative relation is to understand both sex and difference in the most reductive and biologistic of terms. Genders that find no easy home within the binary system are still animated by difference. Sexual undecidability does not condemn the subject to placelessness, but rather locates difference at the heart of both subjectivity and relation.

*Deutscher: A Politics of Impossible Difference: The Later Work of Luce Irigaray Ithaca Cornell Univ. Press 2002

6

SEXUAL INDIFFERENCE AND THE PROBLEM OF THE LIMIT

THE PHANTOM TRANSSEXUAL

Elizabeth Grosz's "Experimental Desire: Rethinking Queer Subjectivity" opens with a quotation from Jasper Laybutt, a "'male lesbian,' female-to-male transsexual" who ruminates about the categorical significance and the ontology of queerness, issues that are the essay's central concern:

> To me, queer transcends any gender, any sexual persuasion and philosophy. Queerness is a state of being. It is also a lifestyle. It's something that's eternally the alternative. To both the gay and lesbian mainstream. What's queer now may not be queer in five years' time. If transgender queer was accepted by both communities, then there would be no queer. It's a reflection of the times you live in.[1]

Though the questions he poses animate Grosz's essay, Jasper Laybutt himself disappears after his epigraphical introduction.

And even as the category of "transgender queer" that Laybutt invokes frames Grosz's discussion about queerness, power, and corporeality, it, too, drops out of the conversation after the first page. Though perhaps unremarkable on its own, the epigraph at the beginning of "Experimental Desires" becomes more significant when read alongside the conclusion of Grosz's *Volatile Bodies*, in which transsexuality appears for the first time in the text in the final three pages. The MTF transsexual that Grosz invokes to conclude *Volatile Bodes* forms a parallel and a pair with the FTM who introduces "Experimental Desires," twin instances of phantom transsexuals who quite literally mark the limits of Grosz's "corporeal feminism."

This chapter will examine the deployment of transsexuality within feminist reimaginings of sexual difference and corporeal materiality, asking what corporeal and identificatory possibilities are produced by this structure and what possibilities are held at bay. The position of the transsexual at the physical boundaries of the text is symptomatic of the position of transsexuality in relation to much feminist theorizing about corporeality and sexual difference. The phantom transsexual is never properly inside Grosz's theory, yet is nevertheless a constant, if unspeakable, presence within her work, which questions traditional philosophical notions of the body's corporeal limits and attempts, with a good deal of success, to significantly expand the horizons of what "counts" as a body. I want to argue that this notion of the limit is not only challenged but also transferred, and the interrogation of the limits of bodily plasticity ends up reconfigured as a question about the limits of gender plasticity and the possibilities of gender plasticity are foreclosed in order to secure the body as a site that is, paradoxically enough, capable of almost limitless reconfiguration.

Volatile Bodies is a radical and important rethinking of corporeality. Like Paul Schilder, Didier Anzieu, and other theorists of bodily topography with whom she engages, Grosz argues that all of the subject's effects can be just as easily accounted for using the topography of the body, the corporeal surface, as a model rather than representing the psyche through metaphors of depth and interiority. Grosz also maintains that the body is central to questions of subjectivity rather than merely the inert raw material out of which social and cultural forces fashion a subject. Unlike Anzieu and Schilder, however, Grosz insists that sexual difference is not incidental to embodiment and subjectivity, but constitutive of both. Grosz's project is in several respects antimaterialist and crucially feminist, and what her analysis seems to offer is the possibility of a body that is pliable, labile, open to constantly shifting and shiftable identifications, transformations, and reworkings—a body that can exceed even the confines of its own skin. She is, at first, so cautious about pronouncements on the materiality of the body, and suspicious enough about deployment of the category of the biological, that she refuses to grant any ontological certainty to the category: "The biological body, if it exists at all, exists for the subject only through the mediation of an image or series of (social/cultural) images of the body."[2] The biological body, Grosz suggests, is either a social construct or is only rendered legible through the mediation of images, where those images represent both the individual body and social and cultural ideas of what a body means. Though these positions are not identical—one grants a "biological body" and one does not—they are functionally equivalent in that they place the body as always already suffused with culture and only available to the subject through the mediation of that culture.

"NONPHYSICALIST MATERIALISM" AND GENITAL DIMORPHISM

The relation between body and subject presented here is familiar enough territory, as we have seen in chapters 1, 2, and 3: I can only have access to my body through the mental image that I have of my body, an image that is extremely fluid and possesses only a tenuous cohesion to the biological body. This body image is not incidental to the lived body; it is the only means one has to experience that body. Grosz demonstrates, as she leads us through discussions of Head and Schilder's neurological works, that that body image gives us our bodies and our identities, rather than the other way around. It is, Grosz states "the precondition and raw material of a stable, that is, symbolic, identity" (44).

Grosz is arguing against theorizations that understand the body as the "raw material of subjectivity," a tendency she criticizes as it appears in the work of Foucault, de Certeau, and others (118, 155). The raw material of subjectivity is not the "stuff" of the material body, but rather the body image, which "is capable of accommodating and incorporating an extremely wide range of objects. Anything that comes into contact with the surface of the body and remains there long enough will be incorporated into the body image" (80). Grosz is not jettisoning materialism in her attempt to counter the "raw material" line of reasoning, but rather trying to reconfigure it. She proposes replacing biological materialism with what she calls "nonphysicalist materialism." The precise contours of "nonphysical materialism" remain unclear; Grosz is never explicit about how the physical and the material might be parsed so that the latter might be delivered free from the constraints of the former. But what Grosz seems to be arguing, along with Judith Butler, is that one can affirm the materiality of the body without recourse to a precultural or "natural" body. Grosz explicitly and repeatedly rejects the notion of a "natural" body, insisting that what is figured as the "organic" body is, in fact, an already cultured body "passing" as "natural."

Coincident with the assertion that the biological body cannot be affirmed without recourse to the cultural mediations that deliver it is the assertion that sexual difference, which is often located at this same level of the natural or biological, is similarly constructed and just as dependent on cultural mediation. "There is no natural body to return to, no pure sexual difference one could gain access to if only the distortions and deformations of patriarchy could be removed" (58). It is the myth of the biological body that gives rise to the myth of "pure sexual difference," and Grosz is suspicious of both. Her conclusions here derive support from her readings of neurobiological accounts of the body, but also from psychoanalysis, which

> makes clear . . . the body is in no sense naturally or innately psychical, sexual, or sexed. It is indeterminate and indeterminable outside its social constitution as a body of a particular type. This implies that the body which it presumes and helps to explain

is an open-ended, pliable set of significations, capable of being rewritten, reconstituted, in quite other terms than those which mark it, and consequently capable of reinscribing the forms of sexed identity and psychical subjectivity at work today.

(60–61)

Though bodies do possess a "weighty materiality" that is undeniable, Grosz stresses that "biology must be understood as psychologically pliable" (28).

But not *too* pliable, not *infinitely* pliable. *Volatile Bodies* theorizes a body that is unpredictable, unstable, excessive, a body whose "capacity for becoming cannot be known in advance, cannot be charted" (124). And yet, as the text proceeds, Grosz becomes increasingly hesitant about offering a body that is unconstrained by some sort of physical limit. "The body is constrained by its biological limits—limits, incidentally, whose framework or 'stretchability' we cannot yet know, we cannot presume, even if we must presume some *limits*" (187). She continues:

while there must be some kinds of biological limit or constraint, these constraints are perpetually capable of being superseded, overcome, through the human body's capacity to open itself up to prosthetic synthesis, to transform or rewrite its environment, to continually augment its powers and capacities through the incorporation into the body's own spaces and modalities of objects that, while external, are internalized, added to, supplementing and supplemented by the "organic body" (or what culturally passes for it), surpassing the body.

(187–188)

Grosz is simultaneously affirming the possibility of a body that transforms itself and its environment, a body that surpasses itself, a body that could become nearly anything, and expresses anxiety at the prospect of such a body. We must have limits, after all, else the materiality of the body be lost altogether. And the limit that no body can exceed, Grosz eventually concludes, is the limit of sexual difference.

Sexual difference is not just the condition of possibility for identity, where the subject is a precipitate or effect of the "pure difference" of genital morphology, it is the condition of both the ontology and epistemology of bodies: "This notion of sexual difference, a difference that is originary and constitutive, is not, strictly speaking, ontological; if anything it occupies a preontological—certainly a preepistemological—terrain insofar as it makes possible what things or entities, what beings, exist (the ontological question) and insofar as it must preexist and condition what we can know (the epistemological question)" (209). And Grosz eventually makes quite clear that sexual difference is a *material* difference. Even as Grosz sustains her argument against thinking bodies as the "raw material" of subjectivity, the stakes of the argument shift over the course of *Volatile Bodies*; whereas she begins by suggesting that understanding the body as the raw material of subjectivity neglects the psychic dimensions that are crucially formative of the body and the self, her argument concludes by charging that the raw material argument is inattentive to the importance of *the material body itself*. What begins as an argument cautioning against overinvesting the materiality of the body with the power to create subjectivity becomes, in a curious turn, a complaint about the ways in which it is credited with too little power. In the first instance, the body should not be thought as *raw material* because that rawness is fictive—the body is always already a product of culture. But, in the second instance, *raw* becomes an unsatisfactory adjective for the opposite reason, suggesting that materiality is unformed or unfinished, which denies the substantial effects that it produces without cultural mediation.

To this end, Grosz suggests that describing sexual difference as the effect of cultural inscription upon the material stuff of the body is insufficient because such an assumption "is to deny a materiality or a material specificity and determinateness to bodies. It is to deny the postulate of a pure, that is, material difference. It is to make them infinitely pliable, malleable" (190). Sexual difference is already there, before the operation of culture, in the "very real bodily differences" of the two sexes, a "pure difference" that is irrefutably material.

The extension of the body Grosz seemed to offer in the beginning of *Volatile Bodes* retracts as she rejects the notion of an infinitely pliable body as that which might threaten to escape or erase sexual difference. The body then becomes fixed and rigid concerning the question of sexual difference, in marked contrast to the flexibility that characterizes it in other registers and situations. My body schema might be so fluid as to include the feather in my hat or the stick I hold. Whatever apparatus I take up and use with or as my body *becomes* my body—but my body cannot "become" outside sexual difference. One can exceed, even shatter, the confines of the body, the boundary between the body and the world, but the sexually specific parts of the body, the "parts" it was born with, can never be transformed or superseded. The material stuff of the body might be "reworked," but no such transformation is possible in the realm of sexual difference, which cannot be reworked, only, it seems, reckoned with.

"WHETHER MALE OR FEMALE OR SOME OTHER TERM . . . "

Must sexual difference be legible at the surface of the body? And is sexual difference the same thing as "natural" sex? There are, as we saw in chapter 5, a number of ways to pose the question of sexual difference that would not reduce it to the category of either "pure" or "natural" materiality. One could, for example, conceive of sexual difference in a way such that it would not require felt sex to match up with perceived sex to match up with external gender to match up with internal gender and so on. That is, if one thinks sexual difference in other than binary terms, the category can become unyoked from "natural" materiality in a way that makes it easier to resist the temptation to posit genital morphology as essentially determinative of the self. But the formulation of sexual difference on which Grosz eventually settles is categorically and functionally indistinguishable from *genital* difference.

There are points at which Grosz seems to leave open the possibility that sexual difference might be considered in other than binary terms and thus be thought unyoked from the determinative force of genital dimorphism. She does suggests that "there are (at least) two kinds of body" (22), where the parenthetical qualification, though weak, does seem to afford some room for those bodies that are not normatively sexed. Yet these fleeting and empty placeholders, which seem to promise the possibility of alternatively sexed subject positions, or even an alternative domain of the sexual imaginary, must, in the end, remain empty. It is not that Grosz fails to consider the possibilities of sexual subject positions other than "man" or "woman": she explicitly states that any gradation in between male or female—what she terms the "Tiresian position"—cannot be theorized, because it is phenomenologically unlivable (191). And the evidence used to confirm this phenomenological unlivability is the experience of the transsexual.

The intersexual and the transsexual again function as phantoms in the text, both standing in for—and excluded from the text on the grounds of—the monstrous impossibility of any subject position in between or outside any "proper" sex, rendered unlivable by their lack of footing in the subject-producing matrix of sexual difference. But, if the impossibility of living as both or neither a male or a female (the "Tiresian position") renders the intersexed body merely unmentionable, the transsexual body is, for Grosz, something more pernicious. The category of woman is, in many ways, fairly fluid before Grosz's discussion of transsexuals: she is reluctant to offer a definition of female sexual specificity, pointing to—but refusing to elucidate—either the "very real differences" or the different "experiences" of the two sexes. This "alternative account" of sexual specificity would require "new forms of representational practice outside of the patriarchal frameworks" (188), and Grosz states that this is a project for the future.[3]

But, if it is still impossible to tell what a woman *is*, it is quite easy to determine what a woman *isn't*, as the following quotation makes clear:

> There will always remain a kind of outsideness or alienness of the experiences and lived reality of each sex for the other. Men, contrary to the fantasy of the transsexual, can never, even with surgical intervention, feel or experience what it is like to be, to

live, as women. At best the transsexual can live out his [*sic*] fantasy of femininity—a fantasy that in itself is usually disappointed with the rather crude transformations effected by surgical and chemical intervention. The transsexual may look like a woman but can never feel like or be a woman. The one sex, whether male or female or some other term, can only experience, live, according to (and hopefully in excess of) the cultural significations of the sexually specific body. The problematic of sexual difference entails a certain failure of knowledge to bridge the gap, the interval, between the sexes. There remains something . . . unpredictable, and uncontainable about the other sex for each sex.

(207–8)

We are returned to the language of gaps and intervals familiar from Irigaray's descriptions of relations across sexual difference, returned to the description of normative gender as a realm of catalyzing mystery. Perhaps more surprisingly familiar is the stereotypical figuration of the transsexual that emerges from this passage: the common characterization of the transsexual, always assumed to be a "biological" male, enmeshed in a hapless and hopeless fantasy about her own bodily materiality, a fantasy indicative of the transsexual's tenuous hold on the reality of the materiality of the body. Most odd is the dual use to which that stereotype is put. The transsexual becomes the constitutive outside that secures the legibility and coherence of the category of woman. The very fact that a transsexual never can get there is what creates and secures the location of "woman" for women. The phenomenon of transsexuality allows Grosz to point to the "mysterious remainder" that persists between the sexes, the interval between them that can never be bridged.

It is important to note that the theory of transsexuality presented here, and the implication it has for theorizing sexual difference, hinges on an internally derived *feeling* rather than externally observable morphology. A transsexual, Grosz argues, cannot be a woman because "he" can never feel like a woman. The move to make internal feeling the basis on which a sexual identity can be assumed (or, in this case, barred) is hard to reconcile with the rest of Grosz's account of embodiment. The internal feeling that Grosz describes is a sensation that seems, on the one hand, quite vague and unlocatable, and this by virtue of the fact that it is described in purely negative terms.

We are never told what it might mean to "feel like or be" a woman—is this a bodily feeling? a psychic one? is it constant or variable? is it conceptual? erotic? do all women "feel like" women? We are only assured that a transsexual can never get there. As we have seen in Chapter 4, this is exactly contrary to what most MTFs report: not only do MTFs "feel like women," but most assert that they have never felt like men. Whether they are MTFs or FTMs, whether they identify as men, as women, or as some other term, it is the persistence and strength of *feeling* that creates their sense of identity. Indeed, that persistent feeling of gendered identification is the cornerstone of the clinical definition of transsexuality. The confident assertion of the motivations, desires, and feelings of transsexuals is a remarkable way to end a text that takes such care not to represent the experiences of women in a totalizing way. On the other hand, this feeling, undefined as it might be, is characterized by a certainty so unshakable that it is capable of securing not only an individual identity but the very categories of "man" and "woman," from which the transsexual is now ejected. The sudden appearance of "feeling" in the text, and the primacy of place it is given in this passage, would seem to frustrate Grosz's attempt to ground sexual identity in morphology and materiality.

Perhaps, however, the move away from materiality is not as much of a departure as it seems. On the surface, Grosz's final emphasis on feeling seems to move sexual identity out of the register of bodily materiality and into the more elusive register of bodily feeling and, if we are to believe Grosz's report about the feelings of the hypothetical transsexuals to which she refers, ensures that the category of "woman" remains closed to them. If genital morphology were sufficient to determine sexual identity, as Grosz maintained, there would be no way to deny a postoperative transsexual's claim to "be" a woman, if she had the morphological appearance of a woman. Any transsexual who had undergone genital surgery would simply be passing from one sex to another. Grosz's response to this possibility seems twofold: to claim that transsexuals' post-transition bodies are marked by a crudeness that separates them from normatively gendered bodies and, more broadly, that it is feeling rather than genital configuration that confers sexual identity.

The charge that a neophallus or a neovagina is "crude" seems to be a judgment unrelated to the technology of the very complex processes of sex reassignment. Why are the transformations that a transsexual undergoes characterized as "crude," a judgment that is not leveled against any of the numerous other instances in the text of bodily modification, many of which are more technologically "crude" (tattooing, piercing, scarification, etc.) than sex reassignment surgeries? The asserted crudeness of a neophallus or neovagina has less to do with the technological or medical specificities of reconfiguring flesh and more to do with the specificity of the bodily region so configured. Grosz is generous in extending the possibilities of meaning making and self-transformation to bodily reconfigurations that intervene at the surface of the body, but attempts to transform or resignify the sexually specific regions of the body, rather than its surface, are judged as crude. Thus one might transform the surface of the body in order to live "according to (and hopefully in excess of) the cultural significations of the sexually specific body," but any attempt to transform the flesh of that body, rather than the cultural significations that inscribe it, is seen as a misguided project. Any hope that one might live "in excess of" the sexually specific body, as Grosz enjoins us to do, seems dim indeed, coming as it does on the heels of Grosz's indictment of the MTF transsexual for attempting to do just that.

What transsexuals teach us, Grosz maintains, is that there is an unbridgeable gap between the sexes, that there remains something "unpredictable, and uncontainable about the other sex for each sex." Since Grosz concludes *Volatile Bodies* with the assertion that each sex represents for the other an unknowable mystery, we would do well to return to feminist philosophy's most ardent proponent of mystery between the sexes, Luce Irigaray.

Grosz's theorization of bodily materiality and sexual difference owes a debt to Luce Irigaray in at least three respects, the most obvious of which is the postulation of an indigestible remainder between the sexes which renders each sex mysterious and unknowable to the other. Perhaps more subtle, but equally important, are the congruences between Grosz's and Irigaray's accounts of the relation between sexual difference and materiality. That relation hinges on invocations of the categories of naturalness and purity and the functional equation of bodily materiality with both. The importance of the conjoined categories of purity and nature for thinking sexual difference is emphasized when considering that one of Grosz's primary critiques of transsexuality is that it is a bodily *violation* and a hopeless attempt to alter or augment bodily materiality as it is *naturally* given.

In her early work *This Sex Which Is Not One*, Irigaray argues that the commodification of woman, and her place (or, properly speaking, *lack* of place) within the symbolic order instantiates a division that gives woman not one body, but two: "*A commodity, a woman, is divided into two irreconcilable bodies*: her 'natural' body and her socially valued, exchangeable body, which is a particularly mimetic expression of masculine values."[4]

The sex that is not one is characterized by a *body* that is not one, and Irigaray's presentation of this irreconcilable but inseparable pair of bodies is motivated by an impulse to challenge the symbolic through which woman, and the female body, is constituted, but within which she has no place. The female body becomes the site at which the tension between the social and "natural" material realms is made manifest. Irigaray describes a social realm that exists alongside, yet is "irreconcilable" with, the "natural" order that governs materiality. A woman is not a natural body saddled with an overlapping layer of social value: these realms are so distinct that they not only exclude one another, but each produces and constitutes a body. A woman's social "body" is seen as a reflection of "masculine values," but Irigaray is not constituting the natural as a privileged site; it has no more claim on the body than the social—perhaps even less, since the category of the natural is bracketed off in quotation marks, either offered only conditionally or pointed to as not fully realized or realizable, as a phantasm or fantasy of the social. Irigaray thus presents a radically *de*naturalized picture of woman as partially a social body and partially a natural body and would seem—in this text, at least—to be articulating a relation between woman and body that is far removed from essentialism.[5]

If the status of the natural as the grounds for embodiment is more complex than it might at first seem, the status of bodies within *This Sex Which Is Not One* is perhaps even less clear. A woman-as-commodity is *divided* into two bodies. There is no indication that woman is embodied before this division: it is the division itself that appears to constitute her, not even as a body, but as "bodies." It seems difficult to assert that these bodies are even corporeal at all, appearing as they do both simultaneously and after the appearance of the woman herself.

Do these bodies matter? Perhaps Irigaray has gestured toward an answer: "*Women-as-commodities are thus subject to a schism* that divides them into the categories of usefulness and exchange value; into matter-body and an envelope that is precious but impenetrable, ungraspable, and not susceptible to appropriation by women themselves; into private use and social use" (176).

So: one of these bodies is matter and one is not. There is a natural "matter-body" and a social "envelope-body" in which the matter is contained. This appears at first to frame the "woman question" within the traditional dichotomy of woman/body/nature in opposition and subordinate to what is masculine and social. However, the natural materiality of the female body is legible only to the extent that it retains its connection to the social body, its other half. Women-as-commodities "*are a mirror of value of and for man.* In order to serve as such, they give up their bodies to men as the supporting material of specularization, of speculation. They yield to him their natural and social value as a locus of imprints, marks, and mirage of his activity" (177). The commodity, the woman, cannot possess any sort of unmediated natural materiality at all. The natural is given over to the social and functions as a mirror of the man's value, a record of his activity. The woman-as-commodity, as mirror, loses herself in this mirroring function.

The materiality of the body, if it was ever there to begin with (and it is not clear that such a previously existing natural matter can easily be assumed as a predicate of this operation), evaporates through the process of commodification. "A super-natural, metaphysical origin is substituted for its material origin. Thus its body becomes a transparent body, *pure phenomenality of value*" (179). Nature's function as a concept becomes a purely anaclitic one: it serves as a prop upon which the mirror of the social can rest and assists the woman/commodity in her passage from the natural to the social, a passage that, Irigaray notes, "never takes place simply" (185).

The relation between the material and social aspects of the female can be seen in the figure of the virginal woman, who is a special kind of commodity. Instead of existing as a natural material body encased in a reflective social envelope, she is nothing *but* that mirroring envelope.

> *The virginal woman, on the other hand, is pure exchange value.* She is nothing but the possibility, the place, the sign of relations among men. In and of herself, she does not exist: she is a simple envelope veiling what is really at stake in social exchange. In this sense, her natural body disappears into its representative function. . . . Woman, for her part, as medium of exchange, is no longer anything but *semblance.* The ritualized passage from woman to mother is accomplished by the *violation of an envelope*: the hymen, which has taken on the value of *taboo*, the taboo of virginity. Once deflowered, woman is relegated to the status of use value, to her entrapment in private property; she is removed from exchange among men. . . . *Neither as mother nor as virgin nor as prostitute has woman any right to her own pleasure.*
>
> (186–87)

To be denoted as virgin is to be cordoned off into the realm of exchange value, which is always a reflection of masculine value. Her natural, material body "disappears into its representative function" that is, its function as a medium of exchange. The woman herself disappears along with her body. "She does not exist"; she is a reflective envelope that contains only emptiness. The virgin is a reserve for the accumulation of increased exchange value. In *Marine Lover* Irigaray describes virginity this way:

> This is the way with exchanges among man/men. Take possession, make use of, use up. With excess spoiling the object. The bonus that overturns value: virginity. Which—among man/men—is nothing more than the dissimulation of the product and its testing. Really taken away from nature is: the mother's daughter, and the nearness they shared. . . . He transforms the need or the desire for nearness into an exchange value-wrapping.[6]

Virginity, as it is presented in both these works, excludes the possibility of a woman's desire and even the possibility of the woman herself, locating her outside the exchange through which the body and self are delivered. The virginal is figured here as a void, a restrictive wrapping of masculine signification that is, at its core, empty.

In contrast, Irigaray's more recent *Je, Tu, Nous* presents quite a different picture; virginity not only possesses a material substance, is something other than empty circuitry and receptacle for value, but it is a positively valenced something that women, Irigaray suggests, ought to value. Virginity is refigured as that which enables woman to take possession of her own identity and her own body.

> Virginity and maternity involve spiritual dimensions that belong to me. These dimensions have been colonized by masculine culture: virginity has become the object of commerce between fathers (or brothers) and husbands, as well as a condition for the incarnation of the masculine divine. It has to be rethought as a woman's possession, a natural and spiritual possession to which she has a right and for which she holds responsibility. Virginity must be rediscovered by all women as their own bodily and spiritual possession, which can give them back an individual and collective identity status (and, among other things, a possible fidelity in their relationship with their mother, which would thereby escape the commerce between men). . . . Women must develop a double identity: virgins and mothers. At every stage of their lives.

Since virginity, no more than female identity, isn't simply given at birth. There's no doubt we are born virgins. But we also have to become virgins, to relieve our bodies and souls of cultural and familial fetters. For me, becoming virgin is synonymous with a woman's conquest of the spiritual.[7]

The most striking difference between discussions of the virginal in *This Sex Which Is Not One* and in *Je, Tu, Nous* is the language of property and ownership that is decried in the former and celebrated in the latter as the only means by which a woman can "have" the materiality of her own body. Virginity *belongs* to women, it is a *property* to which she has a *right*. Armed with these tools of maternity and virginity, woman can accomplish the "conquest of the spiritual." Though Irigaray never specifies exactly what is vanquished in this conquest, the battle must be fought so that women can free themselves of "cultural and familial fetters." Virginity here exists prior to masculine culture's efforts to control it. It is no longer a social construct, but a natural possession that does not come into being through the operations of the symbolic order but exists and belongs to the woman prior to its cultural colonization.

The notion of the virginal body as purely social, an empty envelope from which the natural and material is evacuated has transformed into a notion of virginity in which the natural, material body is foremost. In this scheme it is the social realm instead of the "natural body" that disappears. Occupying the place previously held by the social realm is the category of the spiritual, a dimension that belongs to woman, yet remains something she must conquer, even as it is possessed (though how one would possess or repossess a dimension is never made clear). There is no "culture" at work in this virginity; "culture" is simply the force that wrested possession of an already existent and natural virginity away from women and put it into use as a value-laden object to mediate exchange among men. Once virginity has been repossessed, it is used in the service of freeing women's bodies and souls from the fetters of culture.

Characterizing Irigaray as offering a virginity comprised wholly and only of body is perhaps somewhat unfair; she does loosen the concept a bit from its bodily moorings with her notion of "becoming virgin." Women are virgins at birth, this virginity is lost and must be rediscovered "at every stage" of life. This rediscovery is crucial because it not only allows women to develop a relation to the spiritual realm and to their mothers, but "can give them back an individual and collective identity status." So: this is an identity, singular and plural, that, like virginity, woman once possessed but was somehow wrested from her, presumably through masculine culture. The return of this lost identity to the woman cannot, it seems, take place without the rediscovery of virginity.

Even for a generous reading that assumes identity is here not *identical* to virginity—that is, the identity that is returned to her consists of something more than the virginity that delivers it—the rediscovery gives women back an identity constituted by and inextricable from that virginity. The celebratory tone with which Irigaray lauds this newfound identity's capacity to free woman from the fetters of culture would seem to be premature if this identity is, first and foremost, a *collective* identity for women, to whose disconcerting implications we will now turn.

THAT MYSTERIOUS REMAINDER

In "Commodities Among Themselves," Irigaray continues to explore the terrain of exchange mapped out in "Women on the Market" and asks the question "How can relationships among women be accounted for in this system of exchange?"[8] The answer, it seems, is that such relations are not possible within systems of exchange; moreover, the woman can have no relation *with herself* within this system, insofar as she exists within exchange "only as an occasion for mediation, transaction, transition, transference, between man and his fellow man, indeed between man and himself."[9] Woman exists as a circuit through which male homosocial bonds are established, bonds upon which the social order is predicated.

Relations between women are possible only outside this system of exchange, only when the "commodities" refuse to go to market. Irigaray suggests "'another' kind of commerce," one in which "use and exchange would be indistinguishable" (197).[10] In "When Our

Lips Speak Together," Irigaray performs this relation that "Commodities Among Themselves" gestures at, addressing a female other from "out of their [masculine] language" of commodification, exchange and sameness. Women have been absent from themselves "spoken machines, speaking machines. Enveloped in proper skins, but not our own."[11] The virginal woman is a creation of the masculine symbolic, a "closed, impenetrable" system that precludes the possibility of relation.

> Speak to me. You can't? You no longer want to? You want to hold back? Remain silent? White? Virginal? Keep the inside self to yourself? But it doesn't exist without the other. Don't tear yourself apart like that with choices imposed on you. *Between us*, there's no rupture between virginal and nonvirginal. No event that makes us women. ... Cut up, dispatched, finished: our pleasure is trapped in their system, where a virgin is one as yet unmarked by them, for them. One who is not yet made woman by and for them. Not yet imprinted with their sex, their language. Not yet penetrated, possessed by them. Remaining in that candor that waits for them, that is nothing without them, a void without them. A virgin is the future of their exchanges, transactions, transports. A kind of reserve for their explorations, consummations, exploitations. The advent of their desire, Not of ours.[12]

Virginity is a categorization that must be transcended or shrugged off in order to afford the possibility of communication, desire, and relation outside the masculine economy. Outside the system of exchange, between women, the category of the virgin dissolves.

If there is a certain recuperative possibility located in this "between" or "among" women, it is a possibility that requires the evacuation of difference, and this would seem to have dire implications. Irigaray seems at times to think women as either interchangeable pieces of "woman" or—if that states the case too strongly—at least self-identical to each other. Though Irigaray herself seems at times to revel in the possibility of a relation between women in which they are "neither one nor two" (see especially "When Our

Lips Speak Together" at the end of *This Sex*), the implication of such collapsibility is disturbing, situated as it is within a theory in which *difference* is of paramount importance. Relations between women are lacking this crucial element of difference, which is, for Irigaray, necessary in order to make relationships ethical or even interesting. This leads her to formulations such as "man and woman is a most mysterious and creative couple. This isn't to say that other couples may not have a lot in them, but that man and woman is the most mysterious and creative. . . . You can love the difference, but only if you're able to love those who are the same as yourself."[13] Same-sex relations thus function as a circuit through which the heterosexual bond is established, a curious reformulation of the notion of woman's function within heterosexuality as the mediating circuit for homosexual bonds that Irigaray proposes in "Commodities Among Themselves" and "Women on the Market."

Difference—that most crucial term within Irigaray's schema—is secured through sameness, through the insistence on a "collective identity" for women. Difference between men and women is possible only because of the evacuation of difference from within the category of woman, the effective collapse of the body itself.

RETHINKING THE LIMIT: DYSPHORIA AND DIFFERENCE

Irigaray's work and her theorization of the primacy of sexual difference has been crucial in shaping conversations about gender and sex within feminist theory. Her assertion that each sex represents a mystery for the other and that there is an unbridgeable divide between them has also been central to feminist theory even within theories that seek to explore the limits of the category of sex. Perhaps it is not a surprise that one of feminist and queer theory's most contentiously debated issues has been the question of transgender, since it suggests that the divide of sexual difference can indeed be bridged or, alternately, can be a limit to the very idea of sexual difference.

In "Of Catamites and Kings: Reflections on Butch, Gender, and Boundaries" Gayle Rubin recounts some of the struggles within the lesbian community to come to terms with female masculinity, particularly with those butches who decide to transition and become FTMs. Rubin aims to "discuss, clarify, and challenge some prevalent lesbian cultural assumptions about what is butch" (466) and, in her discussion of FTMs, attempts to complicate some of the more simplistic notions of sex and gender operative in the lesbian community. She critiques a categorical understanding of sex which figures it as a territory whose boundaries must be constantly policed, and offers instead a continuum model as a way to understand sexual difference that does not necessitate the exclusion of those at its margins. Rubin's fondness for the continuum (also apparent in the "continuum of deviance" she offers in her groundbreaking article "Thinking Sex") leads to the presentation of a continuum within a continuum as a means of explaining female masculinity and dysphoria. Butches, she suggests, are often dysphoric, and she explains that she uses *dysphoria* as "a purely descriptive term for persons who have gender feelings and identities that are at odds with their assigned gender status or their physical bodies. "Individuals who have very powerful gender dysphoria, particularly those with strong drives to alter their bodies to conform to their preferred gender identities, are called transsexuals" (467).

The continuum of female masculinity, which runs from soft butch to transsexual, is thus intertwined with a continuum of bodily dysphoria, which runs from mild discomfort to the transsexual's "strong drive" for bodily modification. The presentation of gender and dysphoria as parallel trajectories accomplishes two things: it unmoors identity from bodily morphology and it proposes a model in which a firm boundary between male and female is impossible to fix.

Rubin maintains that if butches and FTMs differ from each other this is a difference of degree or gradation rather than a difference of category. One's status as a transsexual in this account is less determined by where one finds oneself on the gender continuum than on one's relative position on the *dysphoria* continuum—not dependent on the configuration of the body, but rather one's feeling (of/about/in) his or her own body. Thus a butch and an FTM might *look* identical in terms of both presentation and morphology—and the difference between them would be a matter of identification. Rubin suggests that this difference is often quite subtle, noting that "some butches are psychologically indistinguishable from female-to-male transsexuals, except for the identities they choose and the extent to which they are willing or able to alter their bodies. . . . The boundaries between the categories of butch and transsexual are permeable" (473).

A "permeable boundary" between butch and FTM is precisely the possibility that worries some feminists grappling with the issue of transgender. In "Sexualities Without Genders and Other Queer Utopias," Biddy Martin offers a hope, and many worries, about the state of sexual difference within feminist theory. Her hope is to "multiply the permutations of gender with sexual aims, objects, and practices . . . so that identifications and desires that cross traditional boundaries do not efface the complexities of gender identities and expressions."[14] Her worries—about the category of "queer theory" and its tendency to valorize flux, about the figuration of gender as that which must be escaped, about the signifying capacities of the body—are worries about the limits of sexual difference and the ways that limit is challenged, or perhaps even eroded, by attempts to theorize butch and transgender. Martin writes in direct response to Rubin's "Of Catamites and Kings" and takes issue with the continuum model of understanding female masculinity:

> While the political purpose of such a continuum seems clear and compelling, namely, to challenge the stigma attached to transsexualism, and while it is true that butch lesbians have been associated historically with gender dysphoria or dysfunction, I would suggest that making gender dysphoria or gender dysfunction too central to butchness constructs butchness in negativity, curiously makes anatomy the ground of identity, and suggests that femmes, by contrast to butches, are at least implicitly gender conformist.[15]

Though she sympathizes with the political aims of the continuum model and is in agreement with Rubin about the need to "challenge the stigma attached to transsexualism," her primary objection is that the model puts butches too close to transsexuals within the continuum. The danger of this proximity, as Martin sees it, is that it infects the butch with a negativity, a dysphoria, that properly characterizes the transsexual but need not describe the butch.

The central question would seem to be: what is it that "crosses" if one allows for the possibility of movement between male and female as identificatory categories? If there is a "permeable boundary" between male and female, what is it, exactly, that permeates that boundary? The most obvious answer would seem to be that it is the transgressively gendered subject that permeates gender boundaries as sie travels between (and perhaps beyond) gendered boundaries. But Martin's objection to the continuum model seems to hinge on something more subtle than this. Within Martin's account, what permeates or passes from transsexual to butch is an infection of sorts, a dysphoria transmitted though proximity on an identificatory continuum.

Martin's anxiety is not focused on individuals who cross or pass, but rather centers on the dangers they pose to those who do not, those (such as femmes or nondysphoric butches) who remain within ostensibly more "traditional" gender configurations. Those dangers are, on the one hand, that transsexuals "efface the complexities of gender identities and expressions," through their very crossing, which renders those complexities less legible. On the other hand, transsexuals function as a contaminating force that infects and envelops butches in negativity. Thus transsexuality, as a category, usurps and renders invisible the category of butch both by its separateness (butch becomes invisible in the face of its dissimilarity from more "extreme" gender transgressions of the transsexual) and by its permeability (butch becomes invisible because of its dysphoric similarity to transsexuality).

To circumvent both these dangers, either the effacement of feminine specificity or the dysphoric collapse of butchness into transsexuality, Martin calls for a return to the body. Specifically, she asks us to attend to the *limits* of the body, the limits of what it cannot signify, and the limits of sexual difference it defines. Martin concludes her reading of Judith Butler's "The Lesbian Phallus and the Morphological Imaginary" by suggesting that "perhaps still more is required, namely, that the body constitute more of a drag on signification, *that we pay more respect to what's given, to limits*, even as we open the future to what is now unthinkable or delegitimated, that we do this in order to generate a notion of difference that is not fixed or stable in its distribution across bodies, but is also not dispensable."[16]

The call for an "open future" in which "what is now unthinkable or delegitimated" becomes possible is certainly a hopeful one, yet it is curious that this "open future" is secured only through a reliance on bodily limits, which then become reinscribed as gender limits. The role of the body here—as a drag on signification, as that which queer theory, with its valorization of flux, has disrespected—is to function as a stabilizing force, to return us to a relation between body and identity that, if not determinative of identity, is at least predictive of it.

What might it mean to "pay more respect" to the body as it is given, and to its limits? Martin answers by citing Joan Nestle, who "refuses to characterize butchness in terms of masculinity, insisting on butches as women in search of ways to honor their bodily sense of themselves" (91). In the case of butches, a return to the body is a return to the limit (or ruse?) of gender plasticity, a material reminder of her inescapable location on the "female" side of the binary of sexual difference. To honor her bodily sense of herself, Nestle thinks, and Martin seems to agree, a butch must eschew masculinity, which would be a disembodied flight from the body's own limits. What is asked of the butch here is for her to affirm her female body, which, though it might be represented or inhabited in a number of ways, constitutes an absolute limit at the level of identification. A butch might "play at" masculinity, the argument seems to be, but her body knows better. Indeed, it is hard to conceptualize the relationship presented here between butch and body as one capable of anticipating the embodied identifications that might be possible in the "open future"; the "drag" of the body would foreclose those possibilities, rather than making them possible. And, for a butch who does not want to reject masculinity, would this "respect" for the givenness of the female body feel more like glum resignation than a happy embodiment of the "complexities of gender identification"? One sees just how much easier it became to negotiate this terrain after Jack Halberstam offered the rubric of "female masculinity," thereby asserting the fundamental compossibility of the two categories.

Thus far I have presented a critique of several formulations of sexual difference that rely on notions of the limit to secure that difference, where the limit is sometimes understood as a bodily fact, sometimes a categorical impossibility. In either case, transsexuality becomes the constitutive outside of sexual difference. It is tempting to conclude that the various permutations of sexual difference that have emerged from feminist theory offer few tools for theorizing transgender, or even that the very concept of sexual difference is incompossible with transsexuality. But this would be too hasty; perhaps theories of sexual difference might be reworked to provide helpful ways of theorizing transsexuality and ensure that the categories through which we make sense of sex might themselves be capable of reflecting the lived experiences of the non-normatively gendered.

What if we took seriously Irigaray's insistence on the generative power of sexual difference as that which makes relationality possible, without positing an absolute identity within any sex as the ground for that difference? That is: what if we understood sexual difference without banishing difference itself from the categories of male or female? Is it possible to think sexual difference as something that need not be located at the level of sex at all? Might this position be akin to what Biddy Martin suggests in her description of "a notion of difference that is not fixed or stable in its distribution across bodies, but is also not dispensable"? And might this difference be employed as a means of establishing an ethical relation to the non-normatively gendered other, rather than as a means of keeping difference at a safe distance from normative gender categories? If it is true, as Judith Halberstam contends, that "transgender is the gender trouble that feminism has been talking about all along,"[17] then it would seem crucial for feminism to reconcile itself to modes of gender that are differently lived, to take that difference seriously, rather than relegating it to the realm of abjection and pathology.

4

BEYOND THE LAW

7

WITHHOLDING THE LETTER

Sex as State Property

A train arrives at a station. A little boy and a little girl, brother and sister, are seated in a compartment face to face next to the window through which the buildings along the station platform can be seen passing as the train pulls to a stop. "Look," says the brother, "we're at Ladies!"; "Idiot!" replies his sister, "Can't you see we're at Gentlemen." . . . For these children, Ladies and Gentlemen will be henceforth two countries towards which each of their souls will strive on divergent wings, and between which a truce will be the more impossible since they are actually the same country and neither can compromise on its own superiority without detracting from the glory of the other.

— JACQUES LACAN, "*THE AGENCY OF THE LETTER IN THE UNCONSCIOUS OR REASON SINCE FREUD*"

For there to be purloined letters, we wonder, to whom does a letter belong?

— JACQUES LACAN, "*SEMINAR ON 'THE PURLOINED LETTER'*"

LADIES AND GENTLEMEN . . .

It is a commonplace to speak of gender transition as a border crossing of sorts. The figuration of a transperson traversing a border in her passage from one gender to another is perhaps the most common trope used to describe transition in both literary and theoretical works, those written by transpeople and nontranspeople alike. In this final chapter I want to move beyond the observation that transpeople have been the figures of border crossing to claim that this figuration has implications that have not been much explored and I want to look at two of them. First, understanding transgender as a "border crossing" figures gender itself as a kind of bounded territory—gender not just as *a* property of bodies but as *property itself*—and I'd like to explore both the possibilities and the difficulties of this metonymic landscape. Second, I want to suggest that this figuration has had implications for the way that policy decisions about transpeople have been conceived and implemented. In the first half of the chapter, I look at a text that describes transpeople in just this way: *Conundrum* by Jan Morris, an autobiographical work that has come to function as the model for many of the trans autobiographies that have followed. In the second half, I look at a proposal by the New York City Board of Health offered in November of 2006 and withdrawn just a month later that would have allowed transpeople to amend the gender designated on their birth certificates without providing documentation of genital surgery. I want to claim that this New York City proposal and its defeat has more to say about what kind of a thing gender is than it does about what kind of subjects transpeople are and that transpeople are treated as a limit case for the understanding of what sex is and to whom it belongs.

"FOREIGN PARTS BEYOND THE LAW"

Conundrum, published in 1974, was not the first autobiography to tell the story of gender change through first-person narration, but it was the first to gain a relatively wide readership. The book's popularity, and Morris's subsequent brief notoriety as the world's most famous transperson, was certainly one of the reasons that *Conundrum* has become a foundational text in trans studies, another was Morris's skill as a writer. She had a successful career as a journalist and writer as James Morris before the publication of the autobiography and continued to write history and travel literature after her transition. *Conundrum* did much to establish the structural conventions of trans autobiography, the order and manner in which the journey from mistaken to true sex is related to the reader, and many trans autobiographies adhere to this same form: descriptions of the gender dilemmas of early childhood, an adolescent latency period, occasional escape from gender norms into some consuming pursuit or career, the decision to transition, and finally the sense of relief and peace gained from that transition. Accompanying the narrative throughout is a careful disarticulation of the question of sexual desire from the question of gender, a conceptual clarification that persists to this day in trans autobiography in an attempt to rectify the still common conflation of gender identity (am I male or female?) and sexual orientation (am I gay or straight?). The legacy of *Conundrum*, however, is not only a structural one; there are thematic and narrative elements of this text that persist in interesting and often unsuspected ways in cultural understandings of and responses to transgenderism. Foremost among these is the way that gender is analogized to a country, and membership in one or the other gender is an allegiance figured as a kind of nationalism.

It is easy to think of writing that proceeds in the other direction, by analogizing a country to gender. Literature in general and travel literature in particular abounds with descriptive examples that invest this or that city or forest or plain with a gendered character, claims that often map on imperialist or nationalist enterprises in rather blunt ways. Morris does indeed engage in this kind of gendering, and quite self-consciously so. For example, of Venice: "Like Oxford, Venice was always feminine to me, and I saw her perhaps as a kind of ossification of the female principle." As Morris continues the description, her prosopopoeia takes a reflexive turn: "—a stone equivalent, in her grace, serenity, and sparkle, of all that I would like to be." The city of Venice is personified as female and analogized to a human being to the extent that "she" has a gender, a femininity displayed with an ease the narrator envies. The narrator herself feels she cannot properly lay claim to any gender; the masculinity that her external appearance would seem to confirm is a source of chafing misery to her internal sense of femininity, and the femininity she feels constitutes her innermost self is not materially realizable. The exile from gender Morris experiences, and her anticipation of arriving at a proper gender, is described in these terms: "All I wanted was liberation, or reconciliation—to live as myself, to clothe myself in a more proper body, and achieve Identity at last. . . . It seemed only natural to me, and I embarked upon it only with a sense of thankfulness, like a lost traveler finding the right road at last."

That Morris describes this exile from gender in the language of land and property is not unusual—she is a travel writer, after all. It seems natural then that the language of land and travel lent itself to describing the more abstract conundrum of gender, but perhaps more surprising is that it is the conundrum of gender that occasions the travel to begin with. Morris opens the book by describing her childhood habit of wandering the Welsh border country alone, finding her internal sense of self externalized in the unmeeting sides of the land:

> If I looked to the east I could see the line of the Mendip Hills, in whose lee my mother's people, modest country squires, flourished in life and were brass-commemorated in death. If I looked to the west I could see the blue mass of the Welsh mountains, far more exciting to me, beneath whose flanks my father's people had always lived . . .
>
> Both prospects, I used to feel, were mine, and this double possession sometimes gave me a heady sense of universality, as though wherever I looked I could see some aspect of myself—an unhealthy delusion, I have since discovered, for it later made me feel that no country or city was worth visiting unless I either owned a house there or wrote a book about it. Like all Napoleonic fantasies, it was a lonely sensation too. If it all belonged to me, then I belonged to no particular part of it.
>
> (5)

This topographia of doubled vision and isolation, of standing on a no-man's-land or physical border from which she surveys the sweep of different landscapes, is recalled throughout the narrative, and even restaged several times in different places. We find it iterated most notably on Mount Everest, where in 1953 Morris accompanied Sir Edmund Hillary and Tenzing Norgay on the first climb ever to reach the top of the mountain. About the trip she says, "I think for sheer exuberance the best day of my life was my last on Everest."

Eventually, though, Morris comes down from Everest and decides that she needs to stop her travels, at least for a while. "I spent half my life traveling in foreign places" she writes, "and have only lately come to see that incessant wandering as an outer expression of my inner journey." Morris understands her life of travel to have been born of a kind of alienation from gender, and the need to stop is also figured as an expression of this inner journey; as she grows increasingly troubled by her conundrum, feeling exiled from sex and unable to express her gender, her travels prove increasingly unsatisfying. She decides to settle in England, with the thought that forgoing travel and becoming rooted in one familiar place will allow her to solve her conundrum, to undergo transition, and to emerge finally as Jan.

Morris hopes that fixity in physical place will allow her to move past what she terms "the frontier between the sexes" (116) in another turn of phrase that both metaphorizes and literalizes sex through landscape and nation. But Morris's hope that ending her geographical wanderings and taking up residence in just one place will also allow her to consolidate her gender cannot be realized because of the regulatory criteria determining who is be eligible for transition, the gatekeeping function of standards of care with which all transsexual people are painfully familiar. At the time, the surgeons in England who specialized in sex reassignment surgery (SRS) required the patient to meet several criteria: soundness of mind, fitness of body, a history of at least several years living in the new gender, and Morris satisfied all these. It was the final requirement of the surgeons at which Morris balked: they would not perform the surgery so long as Morris remained legally wed to "his" wife Elizabeth. The logic went something like this: before surgery Morris was understood to be a man, and surgeons would intervene to alleviate Morris's gender dysphoria through surgery only with the assurance that the surgery itself would not "create" a lesbian relationship from what had previously been a heterosexual marriage. That clear distinction between sex—I belong either to the male or female sex and am recognized as either a man or woman—and sexuality now begins to blur, a blurring that does not occur through the behavior or at the behest of the transperson herself but rather is enacted as a result of the homophobic logic governing the medical management of transsexuality.

The choices facing Morris were several: she could stay at home in England and remain married but forgo SRS, an option that seemed to secure an increasingly unhappy future. Or she could dissolve an admirable and happy marriage in order to secure a legally tenable sex. In the end, Morris refused both these choices. She repeatedly insisted that she was not and never had been either a lesbian *or* a homosexual, and she judged that in order to avoid *becoming* a lesbian she and Elizabeth "must be divorced in the end." But that end had not yet arrived, and Morris was disinclined to purchase her gender at the price of her marriage. She refused to divorce Elizabeth, thus rendering herself ineligible for SRS in England. She writes: "After a lifetime of fighting my own battles I did not feel in a mood to offer my destiny like a sacrifice upon the benches of Her Majesty's judges. . . . We would end our marriage in our own time, lovingly, and I would go for my surgery, as I had gone for so many consolations and distractions before, to foreign parts beyond the law."

Finding "foreign parts beyond the law" becomes Morris's destination and the object of her trip. Sex reassignment surgery will consist of constructing a new body for Morris comprised of "foreign parts," and as a result her body itself will become an object "beyond the law." Morris departs England for Morocco in July of 1972. Leaving England and decamping for Casablanca means swapping one letter for another: leaving national borders and becoming, again, itinerant, leaving the country so that she might change the sex yet keep the wife, leaving for "foreign parts beyond the law" in order to remain married in the eyes of the law. Thus she is able to change her sex only through giving up either sexual identity or national identity. Though her sojourn to Morocco is temporary and she will eventually return home, she will not return to England the same person who left it—James Morris's exile from England is final, even when Jan Morris returns home.

Once in Morocco, Morris sets off in search of Dr. B—, a well-known surgeon in Casablanca. The surgical interventions that she seeks require skill and expertise yet also exist outside the law; the clinics where she will find care are not regulated in the same manner as British clinics, and their very porousness is what secures their success. Indeed, Morris regards this lack of gatekeeping as a method of saving lives, as these clinics take in transpeople who, for various reasons, are denied care in their own countries. The story she tells of her fellow travelers who land in Casablanca posits a transsexual diaspora of sorts, "who over the years, had rescued hundreds, perhaps even thousands, of transsexuals from their wandering fate. Denied, all too often, surgery in their own countries, the more desperate sufferers roamed the world in search of salvation to Mexico, to Holland, to Japan" (135).

Morris offers fantastic, ornate descriptions of Casablanca in general and Dr. B—'s clinic in particular—she thinks of it as "some city of fable, of phoenix and fantasy, in which transubstantiations were regularly effected" (136). She continues:

> The clinic was not as I imagined it. I had rather hoped for something smoky in the bazaar, but it turned out to be in one of the grander modern parts of the city, one entrance off a wide boulevard, the other on a quiet residential back-street. Its more ordinary business was gynecology of one sort and another, and as I waited in the anteroom, reading *Elle* and *Paris-Match* with a less than absolute attention, I heard many natal sounds, from the muffled appeals of all-too-expectant mothers to the anxious pacings of paternity. Sometimes the place was plunged in utter silence, as Dr. B— weighed somebody's destiny in his room next door; sometimes it broke into a clamor of women's Arabic, screechy and distraught somewhere down the corridor. At last the receptionist called for me, and I was shown into the dark and book-lined presence of the Maestro . . .
>
> I was led among corridors and up staircases into the inner premises of the clinic. The atmosphere thickened as we proceeded. The rooms became more heavily curtained, more velvety, more voluptuous. Portrait busts appeared, I think, and there was

a hint of heavy perfume. Presently I saw, advancing upon me through the dim alcoves of this retreat, which distinctly suggested to me the allure of a harem, a figure no less recognizably odalisque. It was Madame B—. She was dressed in a long white robe, tasseled I think around the waist, which subtly managed to combine the luxuriance of a caftan with the hygiene of a nurse's uniform, and she was blonde herself, and carefully mysterious. . . . Powers beyond my control had brought me to Room 5 at the clinic in Casablanca, and I could not have run away then even if I had wanted to. . . . I went to say goodbye to myself in the mirror. We would never meet again, and I wanted to give that other self a long last look in the eye, and a wink for luck. As I did so a street vendor outside played a delicate arpeggio upon his flute, a very gentle merry sound which he repeated, over and over again, in sweet diminuendo down the street. Flights of angels, I said to myself and so staggered back to my bed, and to oblivion.

(136–140)

These few pages of the book, Morris's rather baroque observations of Casablanca, have traveled beyond the book itself. The scene of Morris's arrival at the clinic is retold, for example, at the beginning of Sandy Stone's groundbreaking essay "The *Empire* Strikes Back." Stone refers to the "'oriental,' almost religious narrative of transformation" Morris offers, and there is something about the confluence of sex and nation here, of the fantastic and the factual, of magic and science, of East and West, that continues to resonate even in contemporary trans writing. But as to the question of what drove Morris to the clinic in the first place—what led to her conclusion that her gender conundrum, prior to transition, was not only unsolvable but unlivable—the answer, again, lies in transit.

WITHHOLDING THE LETTER

The scene of Morris at the clinic figures transition as an almost magical event: she goes to sleep as James Morris and wakes as Jan. We can be sympathetic to the author's impulse to forge the narrative with a scene of gender transition that mimics the apparent ease, naturalness, and finality of sex as it is usually given at birth. But transition from one sex to another is not a singular event, as the rest of the text makes clear: it is rather a shorthand designation for a constellation of acts—some legal, some medical, some behavioral, some social—a long project whose successful "end result," though never truly finished, brings about the congruence of sex and gender in a way that is satisfying to the patient herself and recognizable to those around her. And each of these categories of sexed signification can be parsed into still more discrete units: "sex reassignment surgery," for example, is not a single surgical procedure but several, sometimes dozens, of surgeries on various parts of the body, no single one of which can be singled out as the cause of a legibly sexed body.

The phrase *sex change surgery* (or *the* surgery) is a misnomer, since genital surgery is less significant to most everyday social interactions than top surgery. This makes gender have in truth less to do with *sex*—understood to refer to the configuration of genitals—than it does with comportment, clothing, behavior, and social recognition. Culture often insists that sex equals genitals. But in the workings of culture, sex attribution has almost nothing to do with genital configuration. As Freud observed, the first determination we make about a person we pass on the street is an instantaneous *male or female?* and in nearly every case we make that determination with no information at all about genital configuration. Genital configuration as a determinant of either sex or gender happens exactly once—at birth—for normatively gendered people. But for transpeople it happens a second time as they try to conform their bureaucratic sex with their phenomenological sex. This illustrates that genital configuration as a means of determining sex is appealed to only when there is already some kind of gender trouble at issue, when an individual is already unreadable in some way. For instance, a male soldier returning from Iraq with a pelvic injury does not suddenly find his sex under dispute though his genitals may be reconfigured or gone altogether; no one questions his sex *because* no one questions his gender.

In Morris's case, she attempts to amend the sex designation on her official documents in 1971, a year before her surgery. Procuring new "official" documents of her identity proves surprisingly simple, much more simple, as we will see, than the process is today. The most difficult aspect of Morris's life up until that point had been negotiating public spaces when those documents insisted she was not the gender that she appeared to be. Indeed, Morris's decision to transition is finally motivated by a desire to have the official and bodily presentations of her gender coincide. Her liminal gender presents the most difficulty when she is also in a physically liminal space. Airports in particular cause much anxiety; Morris is at this moment preoperative, taking hormones, living as a woman full time and passing as a woman most, though not all, of the time. She relays the scene of anticipation and dread in the security line at the airport in the cheerful, matter-of-fact style that characterizes most of her recountings:

> I found the androgynous condition in some ways a nightmare, but in others an adventure. Imagine if you can the moment when, having passed through customs at Kennedy Airport, New York, I approach the security check. Dressed as I am in jeans and a sweater, I have no idea to which sex the policemen will suppose me to belong, and must prepare my responses for either decision. I feel their silent appraisal down the corridor as I approach them, and as they search my sling bag I listen hard for a "Sir" or a "Ma'am" to decide my course of conduct. Beyond the corridor, I know the line divides, men to the male frisker, women to the female, and so far I have no notion which to take. On either side a careful examination would reveal ambiguities of anatomy, and I would be plunged into all the ignominies of inquiry and examination, the embarrassments all round, the amusement or contempt, the gruff apologies and the snigger behind my back. But "Sir" or "Madam" comes there none, and through the curtain I diffidently go, to stand there at the bifurcation of the passengers undetermined. An awful moment passes. Everyone seems to be looking at me. Then: "Move along there lady, please, don't hold up the traffic"—and

instantly I join the female queue, am gently and (as it proves) not all that skillfully frisked by a girl who thanks me for my co-operation, and emerge from another small crisis pleased (for of course I have hoped for this conclusion all along) but shaken too. It is a precarious condition. One must live not for the day, but for the moment, swiftly adjusting to circumstance.

(109–110)

Morris describes here her "precarious condition," a precarity inhering in the fact that the work of gender in her case has become so legible and transparent, that her labor in the service of a gender norm, when made visible by a mundane procedure like an airport security line, cannot fade into her natural comportment. The gender liminality in which Morris is caught comes into clearer focus. For Morris's *own* sense of her gender is anything but liminal; her felt sense of self as a woman is persistent and certain. She pauses at the fork in the line not because she is uncertain which gender she is, but out of a recognition that the question of which line she belongs in is a matter of how she is read rather than how she feels. That is: at every moment she scans the faces, comportment, and behavior of everyone around her in an attempt to successfully read how successfully they are reading her. She is safe whether she passes successfully as a woman or is read as male, in either case. The peril comes if she is "read" as transsexual, as having no proper gender at all.

We can understand this moment of anxious hesitation before the gendered bifurcation of the airport security line as exemplifying the process of gender itself. That process is neither purely bodily nor purely volitional, but created—and enforced—through other peoples' expectations and interpretations of one's bodily appearance and behavior. Doesn't "the materiality of the body," as the phrase goes, enter into the configuration? Surely yes. However, the deployment of that phrase is often a coded way of pointing to the genitals and insisting that the "truth" of a body's gender must be located there. But a body's materiality, as the airport screening demonstrates, encompasses more than just its genitals; genitals are far less relevant to the determination of gender than other aspects of the body that are no less material by virtue of being more malleable. Hairstyle, way of walking, style of dress, pitch of voice, in addition to body shape and size, are crucial in determining gender in a way that genitals almost never are. It might be argued, and many have, that while gender is malleable in this way, sex cannot be. The claim that gender is a social role where sex is a bodily fact depends for its coherence on the characterization of sex as material and biological and gender as behavioral and cultural. But sex, too, has a cultural life, and the bureaucracy of sex as it is illuminated through the experiences of transpeople shows that, while it may be a bodily category, sex is always something else too.

The danger of being read as genderless, as an exile from gender, becomes compounded in this case because Morris is issued documents—*travel* documents, specifically—that withhold the status of sex altogether, offering only a stubborn blank where the *m* or *f* should be. Morris's experience highlights the fact that the matter of changing sex *is* largely a matter of paperwork, those bureaucratic machinations that are set in motion when she informs the state that she is now Jan Morris, rather than James. And though her transformation of sex as a matter of public record and paper documentation happens in a piecemeal way, she discovers that the passport is a special case:

> Now I told the state of my condition [preoperative, taking hormones, living full time as a woman]—the Department of Health and Social Security, the Passport Office. Unbending from the dour austerity of its addresses in Whitaker's Almanac, it responded with an unexpected flexibility. When the time came, the Establishment assured me, my new sexual role would be officially recognized. In the meantime, I might be issued with new documents to see me through the transitional phase. My bank, to whose manager I had long before confided my secret, laconically changed me from a Mr. to a Miss. The Oxford County Council gave me a new driving license. The Welfare Officer of the Passport Office sent me a passport *without any indication of sex at all*—compounding as it happened, during my last year of intersexual travel, the mystification of foreign officials.
>
> (121; EMPHASIS MINE)

What are we to make of that blank on the passport, its silence on the question of the sex of its bearer? What is withheld when the letter *m* or *f* is removed from the document? And from whom is it withheld? This heteroglossic collection of papers would seem to be offering a number of different, and even conflicting, reports about the sex of Jan Morris. In the case of the documents of identification, they are able to either confirm or betray gender, the possibility of betrayal attested to by the fact that the state is willing to seal those documents that confirmed James Morris as a man. But if the bank records have no difficulty in asserting that Jan Morris is a woman, if the driver's license reassigns her sex without complication, the same is not true of the passport. The passport demurs altogether on the question of sex, withholding the letter, its silence on the question of sex acts as though it were bearing the evidence of a gendered status that her body itself no longer bears. Note, too, that it is only by withholding the letter that the passport could signal its bearer as improperly gendered. At this point in her transition, she could ostensibly "pass" as James, however briefly, in order to, say, make it through the security line at the airport, but there is no way to embody the absence of gender that the passport accuses her of, no way to "pass" as genderless. Morris is condemned to dislocatedness at the level of sex by the same document that promises to locate her precisely at the level of the nation.

What kind of a thing is sex in this bureaucratic exchange? It is curiously at odds with gender in this case, for no performance of gender is convincing enough, no display of femininity sufficient, to stand in for the designation of "sex" that is determined and withheld by the document. Sex is something that the documents themselves enact, and sex becomes performative in the sense that the *m* or the *f* on the document does not merely report on the sex of its bearer but becomes the truth of and bestows the bearer's sex.

Whether it is the knowledge of sex or whether it is sex itself, the assigned letter on the document functions as a kind of property. In this instance, sex is not a kind of bodily property that suggests or confers ownership, as we saw in the last chapter, not a property belonging to the individual in question. Sex is not private property, but rather property *that belongs to the state itself.* Morris points to this dilemma in her description of being shown her federal record, dramatically sealed:

> There is, for example, the conflict of self-determination—the degree to which a human being is entitled to choose his own identity. I felt a slight chill when the man from the Ministry, delivering my new social security card, showed me my own dossier, taped and sealed with wax, ready to be delivered to the national register at Newcastle. "Nobody," he said, "will be allowed to look inside that file without special permission"— but I noticed that he did not invite *me* to see inside it either.
>
> (171)

THE AGENCY OF THE LETTER

Lacan's essay "The Agency of the Letter in the Unconscious or Reason Since Freud" is its own kind of border operation, its subject located halfway between reason and the unconscious, halfway between writing and speech.[1] There is much privileging of the spoken in his argument, and this is the essay wherein Lacan tells us that "what the psychoanalytic experience discovers in the unconscious is the whole structure of language."[2] How should we understand what the "letter" is, according to Lacan?

> Quite simply, literally [*a la lettre*]. By "letter" I designate that material support that concrete discourse borrows from language. This simple definition assumes that language is not to be confused with the various psychical and somatic functions that serve it in the speaking subject—primarily because language and its structure exist prior to the moment at which each subject at a certain point in his mental development makes his entry into it.
>
> (147)

We are warned not to confuse language "with the various psychical and somatic functions that serve it in the speaking subject," that is, cautioned against taking any particular instance of speech from any particular speaker and misattributing the power of the word to any single utterance. This is a tricky business, and the line we are asked to hold here is thin: surely we need to understand our deployments of language as purposeful, meaningful, and powerful. But Lacan is showing us that language prefigures us, exists even before we deploy it and therefore shapes the conditions of possibility for us to speak. This is why, within the psychoanalytic scene, the phrase *entry into language* is so common, and not simply as metaphor: we enter it in the sense that its rules are already fixed and its terms already set, though we carry our own little freedom into that scene. So to does language enter us, or the "signifier enter the signified," as we shall see.

As Lacan continues his description, the abstraction of the "letter" resolves into something more and more like that *m* and *f* on a birth certificate or a passport:

> Thus the subject, too, if he can appear to be the slave of language is all the more so of a discourse in the universal movement in which his place is already inscribed at birth, if only by virtue of his proper name. Reference to the experience of the community, or to the substance of this discourse, settles nothing. For this experience assumes its essential dimension in the tradition that this discourse itself establishes. This tradition, long before the drama of history is inscribed in it, lays down the elementary structures of culture. And these very structures reveal an ordering of possible exchanges which, even if unconscious, is inconceivable outside the permutations authorized by language.
>
> (148)

If "The Agency of the Letter in the Unconscious" is best known for the metaphorical pronouncement that the unconscious is structured like a language, the unconscious is not the only psychic structure that Lacan analogizes to language; he also explicates the letter through analogizing it to *gender*. What is true of language is also true of gender: it is given at birth, not just handed to us but inscribed into us, and inscribed through the legacy of a proper name.

In order to illustrate our misapprehension of the ways that language works, Lacan gives an illustration, famous from Saussure, of the word *tree* accompanied by the image of a tree. We are accustomed to thinking that signification works by pairing a signifier with a signified; the picture of the tree and the word *tree* are connected by unmediated equivalence. He counters this illustration with a second diagram of two doors, one with the word *LADIES* printed above it and one with the word *GENTLEMEN* printed above it. Lacan uses this "invented" example to show how the relation between the word and the thing is not simply indexical. *LADIES* does not refer indexically to the door below it, but rather complementarily to the word *GENTLEMEN* beside it. With this example, Lacan shows that the word does not positivistically encompass the thing, singularly and without rupture, but rather that the word exists in a chain of signification, relating to other words. In the case of the bathroom doors Lacan describes, the "urinary segregation" that they enact is not an effect of the particularity of those individual doors, but rather an effect of the already accepted practices and customs of gender recognition and refusal. As we have seen in earlier chapters, those two doors are not gender itself, yet they are enacting proper gendering through their specificity.

THE "FACTUAL RECORD": SEX CHANGE AND GENDER CERTIFICATION

If we return to Jan Morris's experiences with the letter and its agency, we might be tempted to view her case as a special one and understand the particularity of her passport and its blank where a designation of sex should be as evidence only of the anomaly of her situation. But the state's response to transgendered people in the United States, almost forty years later, is in many respects remarkably similar to what Jan Morris experienced. The sealing of records that Morris describes, for example, was the last step in the medical management of transsexuality according to the standard of care for intersexual and transsexual patients for many years. That sealing of a transperson's official records, undertaken by the state, was paralleled by the recommendation that the transperson destroy all her personal effects, letters, photographs, etc.—anything that would attest to the individual's "former life." Sandy Stone refers to this as the singular way that the transgendered subject is "programmed to disappear."[3]

In November 2006 the New York City Board of Health and Mental Hygiene considered a proposal aimed at amending its regulations concerning transgendered and transsexual people.[4] The proposal was supported by advocates for transpeople critical of the regulations in place. They argued that the current rules for the issuance of official documents to match the gender of transpeople were based on outdated standards and misinformation about transpeople in particular and sex in general. In fact, the present NYC proposal dates back to 1971, the same year that Jan Morris was wending her way through the tragicomedy of sex identity and state certification on the other side of the Atlantic.

The regulations that govern reissue of identity documents in New York vary according to which document is specified. The Social Security Administration requires proof of genital surgery to issue an amended license, for instance, while the Department of Motor Vehicles does not. They also vary according to jurisdiction: New York City and New York State both require evidence of genital surgery in order to correct a birth certificate, but they require *different* genital surgeries and demand different criteria for confirmation. In order to have a birth certificate updated, New York City requires medical evidence of a vaginoplasty (the creation of what is termed a "neovagina") for transwomen or a phalloplasty (creation of a "neophallus") for transmen. Like every state that allows for the emendation of a birth certificate, New York State requires proof of sex reassignment surgery in order to carry out that emendation.[5] But New York State uses different, less strict criteria than New York City, requiring MTFs to undergo only a penectomy (removal of the penis) and FTMs a hysterectomy and double mastectomy (removal of the uterus and breasts). New York State will issue a corrected birth certificate with the gender a transperson is living in only if that person can show proof that she has removed the genitals that, according to the state, properly "belong" to the other sex; without this procedure, the state issues a blank birth certificate.

A transwoman is thus required to fashion her own *body* as a blank in order to gain a document that is not itself a blank; the document will not speak her sex until her body fails to. Sex in this instance is a designation that belongs to the state, to be conferred on an individual only when she has, in the most literal sense, scraped her body clean of any evidence that she was once a member of the "other" sex. In these instances, the power to adjudicate the sex of the body in question is in the hands of the state. This power to adjudicate sex is no less authoritative when in the hands of the very surgeon responsible for crafting that body into a form recognizable by the state. In some cases *it is the surgery itself, rather than the body part in question*, that is the most salient factor to the granting of a document change, not the existence of the part resulting from that surgery. The matter of body parts and their veracity is a complicated one where SRS is concerned. A transwoman friend of mine experienced significant breast development after going on hormones, breasts that would have been perfectly passable had they been attached to a normatively gendered female. The surgeons responsible for her SRS rejected her passable breasts, insisting that they be removed and replaced with breast implants in the course of her treatment, on the grounds that what she had grown could not have been breasts. The reasoning behind this decision: sex reassignment surgery transforms a male into a female, therefore she was a man up until SRS, and men cannot grow breasts. According to the surgeons, what they could craft out of silicone were "real breasts," but the appendages that her own body grew, though they might have looked exactly like breasts, were merely gynecomastia, the abnormal development of the mammary tissue in a male. The breasts that her body grew were duly removed, and replaced by "real" surgically crafted breasts.

Some members of the panel of experts convened by the New York City Board of Health objected even to these standards for amending a birth certificate as too permissive, and suggested that a birth certificate should never be changed. Dr. Arthur Zitrin, a psychiatrist on the panel, suggested that there were no circumstances under which a birth certificate should be amended: "They should not change the sex at birth, which is a factual record. If they wanted to change the gender for all the compelling reasons that they've given, it should be done perhaps with an asterisk." I'd like to spend some time unpacking this statement, which demonstrates quite compactly the logic governing the bureaucratic management of transsexuality.

When Zitrin states, "They should not change the sex at birth," he means that transpeople and their advocates should not be allowed to intervene in or correct the documentation of the sex they were assigned at birth. Zitrin is offering this pronouncement in the rhetorical form of an ellipses, collapsing the distance between sex and recordkeeping in an attempt to suggest that the birth certificate functions as a safeguard for the bodily evidence, present at birth, of a person's sex. But his words are perhaps even more accurate taken literally; the commandment literally turns sex into a factual record, a matter of paperwork. Zitrin objects to the proposal as written because it is, in his estimation, tampering with the official history, the "factual record," of a person's sex. He proposes instead a newly designated sex, marked with complexity or compromise by an asterisk. He understands the *m* or *f* on the birth certificate to be the recording of a natural fact—a baby is born, its sex is either male or female—and this fact of *sex* does not change, no matter what the individual does with *gender*. The distinction Zitrin draws between sex and gender seems a crucial one: "gender," as he uses it, describes an attribute that might be changeable or vary over time or have some tenuous and not entirely clear relation to the morphology of the body and thus is positioned against the bodily "fact" of sex. The birth certificate itself functions as historic evidence of that unchanging fact, and Zitrin sees the state in the role of guardian; refusing to amend the birth certificate is done in the service of safeguarding the official record, protecting the unchanging truth of *sex* from the suspicious vagaries of *gender*. Indeed, if an individual has changed or wishes to change gender—and Zitrin says this might be done for "compelling reasons"—he suggests that "it should be done perhaps with an asterisk." In other words, *sex* should carry an asterisk to let us know that this sex is not quite legitimate, not in fact sex at all, but only *gender passing as sex*.

Though the factual record does indeed register births divided starkly into either male or female, we might pause to consider how that factual record comes to exist. Neonatal sex itself is not the unambiguous binary that Zitrin believes, as any pediatric urologist could testify. Consider, for example, the cases of infants born with ambiguous genitalia. They are assigned a sex, *m* or *f*, where that bureaucratic designation is not merely an immaterial marker of a material bodily fact, not an indexical label congruent with some nonlinguistic material thing, but a corrective to that bodily material, an imposition of meaning that those genitalia themselves do not manifest or realize without that linguistic supplement. Those infants often undergo so-called normalizing surgical procedures immediately after birth, cosmetic but medically unnecessary surgeries designed to bring the appearance of the genitals into congruence with that assigned sex. Intersex people and transpeople demonstrate that sex is assigned rather than discovered, interpreted even as it is documented, and thus offer a challenge to the notion that gender may travel, but sex is firm ground. To the extent that we conceptualize sex as a fixed binary, we do worse than misrecognize or misrepresent those sexes that manifest outside that binary. We cast them as nonexistent, as impossible as the goat-stag or the sphinx. The position that Zitrin authors imagines itself to be a kind of corrective to a too-liberal interpretation of gender that would let people amend it at will. I want to underscore what I think is the most surprising thing about this position: the fidelity to the "factual record" Zitrin champions requires a logically startling but necessary betrayal of materiality.

This is not the only legislation that seeks to align transpeople's sex with their paperwork, rather than aiming to have their paperwork reflect their sex. At the behest of the Department of Homeland Security, the Social Security Administration has for the past several years been sending out what are known as "no-match letters." A no-match letter is sent to an employer when the information that they submit to the SSA about an employee—name, gender, date of birth, social security number—does not match the information the

SSA has on file for that employee. Transpeople can be the recipients of no-match letters when the gender designation on their documents doesn't match the sex on their birth certificate. As we have seen, since different jurisdictions have different criteria for granting a change of sex designation, it might not be possible for a transperson to rectify the mismatch himself. But transpeople are ancillary, even accidental targets of the no-match letter, whose actual purpose is to force employers to find and fire illegal (that is, undocumented) workers by uncovering fraudulent Social Security Numbers. The no-match letter targets transgressions of citizenship, but unwittingly finds itself targeting transgressions of gender at the same time.

SEXUAL SYNECDOCHE IS A MISTAKE

The most significant aspect of the no-match letter lies in the identity of the discrepant objects. But what is the mismatch of which the letter accuses its addressee? What exactly is failing to match up? Even though the people flagged by no-match letters in these instances are transgendered, the mismatch is not between their physically apparent gender and their documented gender. Imagine that the driver's license, voter registration, and physical appearance of a muscular, bearded fellow who received a no-match letter might all say "male," but the "mismatch" comes about when the gender spoken by the preponderance of the documented and physical evidence fails to match the gender spoken by the birth certificate, which remains "female." Thus the mismatch may be between a gender, male, that is real, embodied, and apparent and a gender that has never described either the feeling or even the appearance of the person so described. The question then becomes: what does it mean to insist on the preservation of the gender of "factual record," *even when that gender has no phenomenological life at all?* In this case it redescribes the domain of gender, which is no longer the felt sense of the individual, nor the perceptions of the outside world, but rather the province of the factual record, a matter of documentation rather than bodily materiality or social perception. In the case of the birth certificate, sex is state property, and the *m* or *f* bestowed on the infant by the state acts like a sexual characteristic that trumps any other, an immutable designation that demands the body of the subject to conform to it, and not the other way around.

Though the withholding of the letter in each of these cases is similar to Jan Morris's descriptions of her experiences in her dealings with the state, the aims of the policing discourse on gender and its distribution seem to have changed, perhaps as a result of the ways in which cultural anxieties have also changed. Being "programmed to disappear," once the injunction for transpeople, now seems itself to be the threat. If what Morris experienced was a certain requirement to become invisible, what the New York City proposal and the Social Security no-match letters seem to be advocating is the opposite, by insisting that the waywardly gendered remain marked and thus identifiable as such. The primary anxiety today is not that transpeople will fail to pass, but that they will pass *too well*—that they will walk among us, but we will not be able to tell them apart *from* us, an anxiety that mirrors current apprehensions about nationality, border control, and the war on terror with uncanny precision. The fortification of national identity, like the fortification of gender identity, requires banishing uncertainty, and the tightening regulations concerning transpeople suggests again just how thin rhetorics of freedom can turn out to be.

When we inquire about the power of the letter in cases of gender and transition, it may seem at first as if we err when we speak of *the* letter in singular, so numerous and varied are its designations around the vast cultural apparatus that authorizes gender. Indeed, that apparatus is so extensive and intricate, so varied and pervasive, that it is in the end nothing different from culture itself. There is the letter as sign and the letter as dispatch. When transpeople speak of their "letters," they are often referring to the documents of certification issued them by psychiatrists declaring them competent to transition. These letters are required by the standards of care and put the issue of agency and the letter into some vexation: the letter in effect certifies that the individual named in them is a transsexual and should therefore be allowed to *become* a transsexual.

There is also the letter as it determines mode of address, the single letter of separation that determines the Mrs. or Miss or Ms.

or Mr. of gender as a salutary event. There is *m* or *f*, the letter that seems to confirm the truth of what is unremarkably visible and then marked and iterated, though not always faithfully duplicated, on birth certificate, social security card, school ID, driver's license, phone bill, insurance card, house deed, medical record, death certificate. Indeed, sometimes it is only the last that finally speaks a gendered truth to which the individual herself might attest, which is why Gwen Araujo's mother struggled after her daughter's death to have the state issue an official change of name and gender that was withheld in life. In this constellation of letters, each singular letter attests to its own gendered truth. Most remarkable about the fecundity of this proliferation is that the entire constellation of signs is animated in the service of resolution into one singular sign: the XX or XY of chromosomal sex, the titular sex endowed by a Mr. or Mrs. or Miss or Ms., and the *m* or *f* on each different document of gender must in the end resolve itself into one solitary letter. As a sign, that *m* or *f* may be referring to the gender identity of the individual concerned. It may also be pointing to something else, since sex can mean my felt sense of my gender, my gender as it was assigned at birth, my gender as it is currently perceived by other people, my genetic makeup (chromosomal sex), my secondary sex characteristics (phenotypic sex), my external morphological sex (genitals, visible), my internal morphological sex (testes and prostate if male, vagina, uterus, and ovaries if female), my hormonal sex . . . and so on.

What all these varied letters promise is nothing less than sexual synecdoche, the assurance that we ought to understand the letter, that part of sexual signification most imbedded within the logics and policies of state and local governance and furthest out of reach of the individual's control, as telling the truth entire of that person's sex. But when we take the letter designating sex to mean sex itself, we confer a recognition that is, inevitably, a misrecognition. Lacan would have us believe that we can do no better when questions of recognition are at stake, and he may be correct. And yet we must. When there is a cultural imperative to corral and bend all these resignations to the service of a singular designation, the depth of that misrecognition puts the stakes at nothing less than life itself.

NOTES

1. THE BODILY EGO AND THE CONTESTED DOMAIN OF THE MATERIAL

1. Catherine Millot's roundly condemnatory *Horsexe* is one example; more recently, see Chiland, *Transsexualism*.

2. Freud, *Three Essays*, p. 7.

3. See also Elizabeth Grosz and Gail Weiss.

4. Silverman, *The Threshold of the Visible World*, pp. 9–10.

5. Shepherdson, "The Role of Gender," p. 170.

6. In her discussion of the mirror stage, Judith Butler also notes the ways in which the figure of the body in bits and pieces prefigures or anticipates a whole and coherent body: "To have a sense of a piece or a part is to have in advance a sense for the whole to which they belong. Although 'The Mirror Stage' attempts to narrate how a body comes to have a sense of its own totality for the first time, the very description of a body before the mirror as being in parts or pieces takes as its own precondition an *already* established sense of a whole or integral morphology." Butler, *Bodies That Matter*, pp. 81–82.

7. Anzieu, *The Skin Ego,* pp. 9–10.

8. Freud, *The Ego and the Id,* p. 19.

9. See also Laplanche's description of the body as "a limit" and "a sack of skin" in *Life and Death in Psychoanalysis,* p. 81.

10. See Grosz's essay "Psychoanalysis and Psychical Topographies," in *Volatile Bodies,* especially p. 37, and also *Jacques Lacan.*

11. Nietzsche's philosophy, Irigaray's feminist theory, and the phenomenology of Merleau-Ponty have all characterized psyche and body as a relation between surfaces rather than a relation of contained to container.

12. See Anzieu, *The Skin Ego,* p. 21. See also Tiemsmerma's *Body Image and Body Schema.* This exhaustive survey of the historical development of body image and schema also credits Schilder with coining the term *body image,* but notes that the term *body schema* was used by Bonnier in 1893.

13. Later theorists have tried to rectify this confusing proliferation of terms. For example, in "Body Image and Body Schema," Gallagher distinguishes between body image and body schema by noting that the body image is something that is capable of becoming an object of consciousness, while the body schema is a nonvolitional structure primarily operational below the threshold of consciousness. Head's "postural model," then, would belong in the latter category in that it is an unconscious organization rather than an image or representation. Head and Rivers, *Studies in Neurology.*

14. Schilder, *The Image and Appearance,* p. 7.

15. Schilder's influence has indeed been considerable on phenomenological writing about the body. Merleau-Ponty's *Phenomenology of Perception,* in which he claims that subjectivity itself is only possible through the construction of a coherent body image takes its theorization of the body image (and, in some cases, specific examples of the lability of the body image) directly from Schilder's text.

16. Silverman, *The Threshold of the Visible World,* p. 13.

17. Ibid.

18. Ibid.

19. Freud, *On Narcissism,* p. 84, cited in Butler, *Bodies that Matter,* p. 59.

20. Anzieu, *The Skin Ego,* p. 4.

21. Prosser, *Second Skins,* p. 245*n*55.

22. Silverman, *The Threshold of the Visible World,* p. 12.

23. On the dissolution of bodily coherence that results from deperson-alization and the withdrawal of libido from the body, see Schilder's case study of Helen Hoffman, "A Case of Loss of Unity in the Body-Image," *The Image and Appearance of the Human Body*, p. 158.

2. THE SEXUAL SCHEMA

1. This fantasy of a magical fusion of sexes, and its production of a body cleaved exactly in half, might be understood as the dominant fan-tasy about non-normative sexes, inclusive of both hermaphroditism and transsexuality, since the dually sexed creatures of Ovid's *Metamorphosis*. For a history of gendered bodies beyond the binary in classical antiquity, see Brisson, *Sexual Ambivalence*. For a depiction of how such fantasies of bodily division, in which sex cleaves the body into two halves, per-sist in depictions of hermaphroditism, see Grosz,"Intolerable Ambiguity." Compare the critical account of transsexuality offered in the final pages of Grosz's *Volatile Bodies,* discussed in chapter 6, this volume.

2. Phenomenology has been utilized variously by authors doing trans work. See Rubin, "Phenomenology as Method in Trans Studies." His most recent book is a sociological account of transmen that uses Merleau-Pon-ty's *Phenomenology of Perception*; he reads phenomenology's insistence on the perspectival situatedness of subjects as shoring up and fortifying both the speaking "I" and the truth claims of that "I." See Rubin, *Self-Made Men.*

3. Irigaray's is perhaps Merleau-Ponty's most trenchant critic here. See "The Invisible of the Flesh," her engagement with Merleau-Ponty's *The Visible and the Invisible,* in *An Ethics of Sexual Difference.* For a reading of Irigaray's engagement with Merleau-Ponty, see Tina Chanter, "Wild Meaning," in *Ethics of Eros,* and Penelope Deutscher, "Sexed Discourse and the Language of the Philosophers," in *A Politics of Impossible Dif-ference.* Butler suggests that Irigaray's trope of two sets of lips speaking finds its inspiration in Merleau-Ponty's *deux lèvres* in "Merleau-Ponty and the Touch of Malebranche." Butler offers a different reading of the intersection of phenomenology and feminism in "Sexual Ideology and Phe-nomenological Description." See also Alcoff's essay "Merleau-Ponty and Feminist Theory on Experience." For a more optimistic feminist consider-ation of Merleau-Ponty's theorization of flesh, see Diprose's reading of the

relational nature of Merleau-Pontian embodiment as offering the promise of a transformed ethics in *Corporeal Generosity*.

4. Young's essay, "Throwing Like a Girl," her follow-up essay, "Throwing Like a Girl, Twenty Years Later," and her piece "Pregnant Embodiment" remain singular as examples of both critiques of the presumptively male body in Merleau-Ponty and positive phenomenologies of specifically female embodiment. There also appears to be a new interest in using phenomenology for queer theory; see Ahmed's *Queer Phenomenology*.

5. For an example of this kind of critique, see Grosz, *Volatile Bodies*.

6. See Raymond, *The Transsexual Empire*, which reads the motivation for MTF transition to be sexual gratification, and, in particular, the sadistic sexual gratification of "becoming" a woman, a sadistic gratification that is, Raymond suggests, akin to rape.

7. Bailey's *The Man Who Would Be Queen* is one example of this trend. In an inversion of Raymond's theory, he asserts that bodily transitions of "transmen" (by which he means MTF transwomen) is a result of their attraction not to the women that they want to become and thus supplant, but to themselves reimagined as women. The theory of *autogynophilia*—the term originates with Ray Blanchard—recasts the theory of a sexual attraction to oneself in a different scientific genre. This fetal androgen bath theory of transsexual development suggests that transpeople are "made" by exposure to the wrong kinds of hormones in utero and is regarded positively by some transpeople (such as Anne Lawrence), though rejected by most, in the same way that the "gay gene" or "gay brain" research is regarded positively by some homosexuals: a single, and resolutely biological, explanation of the "condition" means that its sufferer cannot be thought as morally culpable for her homosexuality or transsexuality, which is a biological, and thus ostensibly immutable, "fact." The recent discourse insisting on both the biological basis of trans and asserting that it is fundamentally a sexual obsession with oneself replicates with surprising faithfulness the concept of inversion understood as a form of sexual narcissism that once dominated discourses on homosexuality. Though the structural similarities of these two misreadings are noteworthy, I don't want to suggest that transgender has replaced homosexuality in this regard, which would risk obscuring the fact that the narcissistic interpretation of homosexuality is still dominant in some circles even today.

8. The acronym LGBT demonstrates this conflation in its inclusion of transgender (and sometimes intersexuality in the case of LGBTI) with the other categories that denote sexuality rather than gender. For more on the

sometimes uneasy relations in what Dean Spade has called the "LGB fake T" community, see Stryker, "Transgender Studies."

9. Sandy Stone expresses both sympathy for this disengagement and doubt at its efficacy in "The Empire Strikes Back." Meyerowitz's *How Sex Changed* also explores accounts of early trans autobiographies in which the subject of sexual desire is either politely avoided or entirely disavowed.

10. For an extended consideration of this concept in philosophy and its particular implications for women, see Weiss, *Body Images*.

11. See my "Is There a Phenomenological Unconscious? Time and Embodied Memory in Merleau-Ponty" (forthcoming).

12. Freud, *Three Essays on the Theory of Sexuality*.

13. Merleau-Ponty's commitment to ambiguity in his discussions of the body has frustrated even his least identitarian critics. This is, for instance, Derrida's chief quarrel with Merleau-Ponty as outlined in *On Touching*.

14. For a consideration of the eye, the look, and their structuration of perception as well as a challenge to Sartre's theorization of the gaze, see Merleau-Ponty, *The Primacy of Perception*.

15. For reflections on the iconic place of Brandon Teena within the trans movement, see Halberstam's *In a Queer Time and Place*. See also BRANDON (1998–1999), a multimedia collaborative project by Shu Lea Cheang, Jordy Jones, Susan Stryker, and Pat Cadigan commissioned by the Guggenheim Museum and accessible at http://brandon.guggenheim.org. For a particularly nuanced reading of "the traumatic event that goes by the proper name of Brandon Teena" (72), see the "Queer Spectrality" chapter in Carla Freccero, *Queer/Early/Modern*.

16. Laqueur describes the way in which "the flesh in its simplicity seemed always to shine through," even when approaching bodies as historically contingent constructions in *Making Sex* (14).

3. BOYS OF THE LEX

1. This is, of course, an easy generalization; for an account of queer community formation as it is emerging elsewhere and otherwise, see Halberstam, *In a Queer Time and Place*.

2. This can also be read as both a citation and an inversion of Herb Ritts's famous photograph of a very feminine Cindy Crawford shaving a besuited k.d. lang.

3. Feinberg, *Trans Liberation*, p. 114.

4. Ibid., 10.

5. Green, "The Art and Nature of Gender," p. 59.

6. Prosser, *Second Skins,* p. 7. See chapter 1 for an extended discussion of Prosser's important interventions in debates about social construction and transgenderism within a psychoanalytic context.

7. Cromwell, *Transmen and FTMs,* p. 25.

8. Ibid., 42. For a view of the phenomenological body as that which is singularly capable of resisting or defying both ideology and social construction, as well as a comparison between phenomenological and Foucauldian approaches to trans embodiment, see Rubin, *Self-Made Men.*

9. Green, "The Art and Nature of Gender," p. 62.

10. Cromwell, *Transmen and FTMs,* p. 43.

11. Kate Bornstein, talk presented at the University of California, Berkeley, April 27, 2000.

12. Green, "The Art and Nature of Gender," p. 60.

13. Namaste, *Invisible Lives,* p. 9.

14. Cromwell, *Transmen and FTMs,* p. 43.

15. Husserl, *The Crisis of European Science,* p. 160.

16. Foucault understands the body to be produced through several different modes of regulation and control. Punishment is one of these modes; sexuality is another. See Foucault, *Discipline and Punish*, p. 155, and *The Use of Pleasure.*

17. *Discipline and Punish*, p. 215.

18. For more on gender transgression and public restrooms, see Munt, "Orifices in Space"; and *Toilet Training: Law and Order in the Bathroom* (2003), a film by Tara Mateik and the Sylvia Rivera Law Project.

19. Cromwell, *Transmen and FTMs,* p. 42.

20. Butler, *Bodies That Matter,* p. x.

21. Green, "The Art and Nature of Gender," p. 60.

22. John Colapinto's presentation of the John/Joan case in *As Nature Made Him*, although not a critique of transsexuality per se, is a particularly conservative example of this trend. "Nature" made John a boy, and social constructionists tried to turn him into a girl; their failure, Colapinto contends, shows the indisputability of the nature of sexual difference.

23. Hausman, *Changing Sex,* pp. 26, 3.

24. Millot, *Horsexe,* p. 141.

25. For autobiographical accounts of these negotiations, see Devor, *FTM.*

26. Hausman, *Changing Sex*, p. xi.

27. Elliot and Roen, "Transgenderism and the Question of Embodiment."

28. Husserl, *The Idea of Phenomenology*, p. 5.

29. Husserl, *Ideas I*, p. 112.

30. Natanson, *Edmund Husserl*, p. 58.

31. Husserl, *Ideas I*, p. 17.

32. Ibid., p. 110.

33. Natanson, *Edmund Husserl*, p. 26.

34. Ibid., p. 71.

35. Merleau-Ponty, *Phenomenology of Perception*, p. 79.

36. Husserl, *Ideas I*, p. 150.

37. Butler, *Gender Trouble*, p. 123.

4. TRANSFEMINISM AND THE FUTURE OF GENDER

1. *The Transgender Studies Reader*, edited by Stryker and Whittle, is an important milestone in this regard.

2. Brown, "The Impossibility of Women's Studies," p. 21.

3. These models are not monolithic, and there are other ways to organize the study of women, a fact reflected in the recent prevalence of departments and programs calling themselves "Gender and Women's Studies" or even "Women, Gender, and Sexuality Studies."

4. Wilchins, *Read My Lips*, p. 25.

5. Stryker, "Transgender Studies."

6. See Prosser, *Second Skins*; see also Namaste, *Invisible Lives*.

7. Stone, "The Empire Strikes Back."

8. Riley, *Am I That Name?*

9. Spade, "Remarks at Transecting the Academy Conference."

10. Marech, "Nuances of Gay Identities"; and Hampton, "Transsexual Ousted from Shelter Shower."

11. Vitello, "The Trouble When Jane Becomes Jack."

12. On Camp Trans, the alternative annual gathering protesting the ban, see Tea, "Transmissions from Camp Trans."

13. See Valentine, "The Calculus of Pain," in which he asks how violence against transgender people might be discussed or represented without making the trans itself synonymous with violence and death.

14. Kate Bornstein, talk, University of California–Berkeley, April 27, 2000. See also Bornstein, "Her Son/Daughter."

15. For an alternate origin story for the trans community, see Susan Stryker's documentary film *Screaming Queens: The Riot at Compton's Cafeteria* (2005), dir. Victor Silverman and Susan Stryker, which recounts the little-known event that predated the Stonewall riots by three years.

16. For a discussion of the "border wars" both within and outside queer communities, particularly in the wake of Brandon Teena's death, see Halberstam and Hale, "Butch/FTM Border Wars."

17. Halberstam, "Female Masculinity."

18. Hausman, "Recent Transgender Theory," p. 476–77.

19. Dobkin, "The Emperor's New Gender."

20. Butler, *Undoing Gender,* p. 65.

21. For one example of this position and a deft explication of lesbian ambivalence about the desire for masculinity, see Findlay, "Losing Sue."

22. Hansbury, "The Middle Men."

23. Althusser, "Ideology and Ideological State Apparatuses."

24. Butler, *Gender Trouble*, p.22.

5. AN ETHICS OF TRANSSEXUAL DIFFERENCE

1. Irigaray, "Place, Interval."

2. Ibid., p. 35.

3. Chanter opens her book *Ethics of Eros* by reformulating this statement to point to feminist contestations of the concept of sexual difference: "One of the most powerful categories of analysis that has served the needs of feminism in recent years is that of gender" (1).

4. Aristotle, *Physics IV,* 208a, l.30.

5. Irigaray, "Place, Interval," pp. 36–37.

6. On bodily boundedness, unboundedness, and corporeal surveying in Irigaray, see Grosz, *Volatile Bodies.*

7. Deutscher, *A Politics of Impossible Difference.* This is particularly apparent in her emphasis on the uncertain temporality of sexual difference: "Sexual difference could only be that which is to come. Difference does not lie between two identities, the male and the female. That should not be sexual difference" (121).

1. Grosz, "Experimental Desire" (1).

2. Grosz, *Volatile Bodies*, p. 41.

3. Grosz does, in chapter 7 of *Volatile Bodies*, "Intensities and Flows," outline a "Deleuzian feminism" that, among other things, would pose a critique to binarism, countering its either/or framework with a "both/and" one. The "Sexed Bodies" chapter that follows, however, finds her commitment to sexual binaries not challenged, but strengthened. She gestures toward the both/and paradigm as a possible way of rethinking "the subject, the social order, even the natural world" (181), yet does not extend this possibility to thinking sexual difference itself.

4. Irigaray, "Women on the Market," in *This Sex Which Is Not One*, p. 180.

5. Irigaray does, however, leave herself vulnerable to the charge of essentialism in other texts. For a history of Irigaray's place in the essentialism debates, see Naomi Schor, "This Essentialism Which Is Not One: Coming to Grips with Irigaray."

6. Irigaray, *Marine Lover*, p. 113.

7. Irigaray, *Je, Tu, Nous*, p. 116-117.

8. Irigaray, "Commodities Among Themselves," in *This Sex Which Is Not One*, p. 194.

9. Ibid., p. 193.

10. Ibid., p. 196, 197.

11. Irigaray, "When Our Lips Speak Together," in *This Sex Which Is Not One*, p. 205.

12. Ibid., pp. 211–12.

13. Irigaray, "For Centuries We've Been Living in the Mother-Son Relation . . . ," quoted in Grosz, *Sexual Subversions*, p. 178.

14. Martin, *Femininity Played Straight*, p. 78.

15. Ibid., p. 90.

16. Ibid., p. 82 (emphasis mine).

17. Judith Halberstam, "Why We Need a Transfeminism" remarks at "Transfeminisms" conference, University of California at Santa Cruz, February 23, 2002.

1. I should emphasize that, in turning to Lacan, I don't want to cede explanatory or interpretive control to psychoanalysis, nor do I think Lacan gives us any kind of code or key that helps explain transgender, but I do so rather with the hope that the experiences of transpeople might make Lacan's text perhaps more explicable and that his text in turn might help us reckon what the letter is in these instances and from whence its power emerges.

2. Lacan, "The Agency of the Letter in the Unconscious," in *Ecrits,* p. 147.

3. Stone, "The Empire Strikes Back" (295). There are reasons to be cautious in drawing too exact parallels between the ways that the British system manages a change of sex and the ways the American system does. For a description of the current state of trans law in the UK, see Stephen Whittle, a legal scholar who has written extensively about the UK gender recognition act and the legal status of transpeople in England.

4. For a comprehensive and insightful look at the legal reasoning behind sex certification for transpeople as well as the negotiations involved during the committee meetings in which the proposal was considered, see Currah and Moore, "'We Won't Know Who You Are.'"

5. See Spade, "Compliance Is Gendered."

BIBLIOGRAPHY

Ahmed, Sara. "Orientations: Toward a Queer Phenomenology." *GLQ: A Journal of Lesbian and Gay Studies* 12, no. 4 (2006): 543–574.

—— *Queer Phenomenology: Orientations, Objects, Others.* Durham: Duke University Press, 2006.

Alcoff, Linda Martin. "Merleau-Ponty and Feminist Theory on Experience." In Fred Evans and Leonard Lawlor, eds., *Chiasms: Merleau-Ponty's Notion of "Flesh,"* pp. 251–72. Albany: State University of New York Press, 2000.

Allen, Jeffner, and Iris Marion Young. *The Thinking Muse: Feminism and Modern French Philosophy.* Bloomington: Indiana University Press, 1989.

Althusser, Louis. *Lenin and Philosophy and Other Essays.* Trans. Ben Brewster. "Ideology and Ideological State Apparatuses," pp. 127–136. New York: Monthly Review Press, 1972.

Anderson, Benedict R. *Imagined Communities: Reflections on the Origin and Spread of Nationalism.* Rev. ed. New York: Verso, 1991.

Anzieu, Didier. *The Skin Ego.* Trans. Chris Turner. New Haven: Yale University Press, 1989.

Aristotle. *Physics*. Trans. R. P. Hardie and R. K. Gaye. Books 1–4. Oxford: Oxford University Press, 1930.

Bailey, J. Michael. *The Man Who Would Be Queen: The Science of Gender-Bending and Transsexualism*. Washington, DC: Joseph Henry Press, 2003.

Bender, Lauretta, Keiser, Sylvan and Schilder, Paul. *Studies in Aggressiveness, from Bellevue Hospital, Psychiatric Division, and the Medical College of New York University, Department of Psychiatry*. Genetic Psychology Monographs 5.18, nos. 5–6. Worcester, MA: Clark University, 1936.

Bergson, Henri. *Matter and Memory*. New York: Zone, 1991.

Bermúdez, José Luis, A. J. Marcel, and Naomi Eilan. *The Body and the Self*. Cambridge: MIT Press, 1995.

Bernstein, Fred. "On Campus, Rethinking Biology 101." *New York Times*, March 7, 2004.

Bindel, Julie. "Gender Benders, Beware." *Guardian Review*, January 31, 2004.

Bornstein, Kate. *Gender Outlaw: On Men, Women, and the Rest of Us*. New York: Routledge, 1994.

—— "Her Son/Daughter," *New York Times Magazine*, January 19, 1998, p. 70.

Braidotti, Rosi. *Nomadic Subjects: Embodiment and Sexual Difference in Contemporary Feminist Theory*. New York: Columbia University Press, 1994.

Brisson, Luc. *Sexual Ambivalence: Androgyny and Hermaphroditism in Graeco-Roman Antiquity*. Berkeley: University of California Press, 2002.

Brown, Patricia Leigh. "A Quest for a Restroom That's Neither Men's Room Nor Women's Room." *New York Times*, March 4, 2005.

Brown, Wendy. "The Impossibility of Women's Studies." In *Edgework: Critical Essays on Knowledge and Politics*, pp. 116–135. Princeton: Princeton University Press, 2005.

Butler, Judith. *Bodies That Matter: On the Discursive Limits of "Sex."* New York: Routledge, 1993.

—— *Excitable Speech: A Politics of the Performative*. New York: Routledge, 1997.

—— *Gender Trouble: Feminism and the Subversion of Identity, Thinking Gender*. New York: Routledge, 1990.

—— "How Can I Deny That These Hands and This Body Are Mine?" *Qui Parle* 11, no. 1 (1997): 1–20.

—— "Merleau-Ponty and the Touch of Malebranche." In Taylor Carman and Mark B. N. Hansen, eds., *The Cambridge Companion to Merleau-Ponty*, pp. 181–205. Cambridge: Cambridge University Press, 2005.

—— "Sexual Ideology and Phenomenological Description: A Feminist Critique of Merleau-Ponty's *Phenomenology of Perception*." In Jeffner Allen and Iris Marion Young, eds., *The Thinking Muse: Feminism and Modern French Philosophy*, pp. 85–100. Bloomington: Indiana University Press, 1989.

—— *The Psychic Life of Power: Theories in Subjection*. Stanford: Stanford University Press, 1997.

—— *Undoing Gender*. New York: Routledge, 2004.

Califia, Pat. *Sex Changes: The Politics of Transgenderism*. San Francisco: Cleis, 1997.

Cameron, Loren. *Body Alchemy: Transsexual Portraits*. San Francisco: Cleis, 1996.

Chanter, Tina. *Ethics of Eros: Irigaray's Rewriting of the Philosophers*. New York: Routledge, 1995.

Chiland, Colette. *Transsexualism: Illusion and Reality*. Middletown, CT: Wesleyan University Press, 2003.

Colapinto, John. *As Nature Made Him: The Boy Who Was Raised as a Girl*. New York: HarperCollins, 2000.

Cromwell, Jason. *Transmen and FTMs: Identities, Bodies, Genders, and Sexualities*. Champaign: University of Illinois Press, 1999.

Currah, Paisley, and Lisa Jean Moore. "'We Won't Know Who You Are': Contesting Sex Designations in New York City Birth Certificates." *Hypatia: A Journal of Feminist Philosophy* 24, no. 3 (2009): 113–35.

Damasio, Antonio R. *Descartes' Error: Emotion, Reason, and the Human Brain*. New York: Avon, 1995.

—— *The Feeling of What Happens: Body and Emotion in the Making of Consciousness*. New York: Harcourt Brace, 1999.

Davis, Lennard J. "Gaining a Daughter: A Father's Transgendered Tale." *Chronicle of Higher Education*, March 24, 2000.

Denny, Dallas, ed. *Current Concepts in Transgender Identity*. New York: Garland, 1998.

Derrida, Jacques. *On Touching—Jean-Luc Nancy*. Trans. Christine Irazarry. Palo Alto: Stanford University Press, 2005.

Deutscher, Penelope. *A Politics of Impossible Difference: The Later Work of Luce Irigaray*. Ithaca: Cornell University Press, 2002.

—— *Yielding Gender: Feminism, Deconstruction and the History of Philosophy.* New York: Routledge, 1997.

Devor, Holly. *FTM: Female-to-Male Transsexuals in Society.* Bloomington: Indiana University Press, 1997.

Diprose, Rosalyn. *Corporeal Generosity: On Giving with Nietzsche, Merleau-Ponty, and Levinas.* Albany: State University of New York Press, 2002.

Dobkin, Alix. "The Emperor's New Gender." *off our backs* 30, no. 4 (2000): 14.

Dreger, Alice Domurat. *Hermaphrodites and the Medical Invention of Sex.* Cambridge: Harvard University Press, 1998.

Elliot, Patricia, and Katrina Roen, "Transgenderism and the Question of Embodiment: Promising Queer Politics?" *GLQ: A Journal of Lesbian and Gay Studies* 4, no. 2 (1998): 231–261.

Epstein, Julia, and Kristina Straub. *Body Guards: The Cultural Politics of Gender Ambiguity.* New York: Routledge, 1991.

Evans, Fred, and Lawlor, Leonard, eds. *Chiasms: Merleau-Ponty's Notion of Flesh.* Albany: State University of New York Press, 2000.

Fanon, Franz. *Black Skin, White Masks.* New York: Grove, 1967.

Fausto-Sterling, Anne. *Myths of Gender: Biological Theories About Women and Men.* New York: Basic Books, 1985.

—— *Sexing the Body: Gender Politics and the Construction of Sexuality.* New York: Basic Books, 2000.

Feinberg, Leslie. *Stone Butch Blues.* Ithaca: Firebrand, 1993.

—— *Transgender Warriors: Making History from Joan of Arc to Dennis Rodman.* Boston: Beacon, 1996.

—— *Trans Liberation: Beyond Pink or Blue.* Boston: Beacon, 1998.

Findlay, Heather. "Losing Sue." In Sally Munt, ed., *Butch/Femme: Inside Lesbian Gender*, pp. 133–145. London: Cassell, 1998.

Foucault, Michel. *Discipline and Punish: The Birth of the Prison.* Trans. Alan Sheridan. 2d ed. New York: Vintage, 1995.

—— *Madness and Civilization: A History of Insanity in the Age of Reason.* New York: Vintage, 1988.

—— *The History of Sexuality*, vol. 1: *An Introduction.* Trans. Robert Hurley. New York: Vintage, 1980.

—— *The History of Sexuality*, vol. 2: *The Use of Pleasure.* Trans. Robert Hurley. New York: Vintage, 1990.

Freud, Sigmund. "Some Psychical Consequences of the Anatomical Distinction Between the Sexes." In *The Standard Edition of the Complete Psychological Works*, 19:248–258. London: Hogarth, 1953.

—— *The Ego and the Id*. Trans. James Strachey. In *The Standard Edition of the Complete Psychological Works*, 19:1–66. London: Hogarth, 1961.

Freud, Sigmund. *Three Essays on the Theory of Sexuality*. Trans. James Strachey. New York: Basic Books, 1963.

Freytag, Fredericka. *The Body Image in Gender Orientation Disturbances*. New York: Vantage, 1977.

Gallagher, Catherine, and Thomas Walter Laqueur. *The Making of the Modern Body: Sexuality and Society in the Nineteenth Century*. Berkeley: University of California Press, 1987.

Gallagher, Shaun. "Body Image and Body Schema: A Conceptual Clarification." In Donn Welton, ed., *Body and Flesh: A Philosophical Reader*. Malden, MA: Blackwell, 1998.

Gatens, Moira. *Imaginary Bodies: Ethics, Power and Corporeality*. New York: Routledge, 1996.

Green, Jamison. "The Art and Nature of Gender." In Felicity Haynes and Tarquam McKenna, eds., *Unseen Genders: Beyond the Binaries*, pp. 59–70. New York: Peter Lang, 2001.

Grosz, Elizabeth. "Experimental Desire: Rethinking Queer Subjectivity." In Joan Copjec, ed., *Supposing the Subject*, pp. 133-157. London: Verso, 1994.

—— "Freaks." *Social Semiotics*, 1, no. 2 (1991): 22–38.

—— "Intolerable Ambiguity: Freaks as/at the Limit." In Rosemarie Garland Thompson, ed., *Freakery: Cultural Spectacles of the Extraordinary Body*, pp. 55–68. New York: New York University Press, 1996.

—— *Jacques Lacan: A Feminist Introduction*. New York: Routledge, 1990.

—— *Sexual Subversions: Three French Feminists*. Sydney: Allen and Unwin, 1989.

—— *Space, Time, and Perversion : Essays on the Politics of Bodies*. New York: Routledge, 1995.

—— *Volatile Bodies: Toward a Corporeal Feminism, Theories of Representation and Difference*. Bloomington: Indiana University Press, 1994.

Halberstam, Judith. *Female Masculinity*. Durham: Duke University Press, 1998.

—— *In a Queer Time and Place*. New York: New York University Press, 2005.

—— "Transgender Butch: Butch/FTM Border Wars and the Masculine Continuum." *GLQ: A Journal of Lesbian and Gay Studies* 4, no. 2 (1998).

Halberstam, Judith, and C. Jacob Hale. "Butch/FTM Border Wars: A Note on Collaboration." *GLQ: A Journal of Lesbian and Gay Studies* 4, no. 2. (1998): 283–285.

Hampton, Adriel. "Transsexual Ousted from Shelter Shower for Sexual Orientation." *San Francisco Independent*, February 10, 2004.

Hansbury, Griffin. "The Middle Men: An Introduction to the Transmasculine Identities." *Studies in Gender and Sexuality* 6, no. 3 (2005): 241–264.

Haskell, Molly. "Midnight in the Garden of Male and Female: Edward Ball untangles a Charleston Mystery: who, and what, was the Southern belle Dawn Langley Hall?" *New York Times Book Review*, April 4, 2004, p. 10.

Hausman, Bernice Louise. *Changing Sex: Transsexualism, Technology, and the Idea of Gender*. Durham: Duke University Press, 1995.

—— "Recent Transgender Theory." *Feminist Studies* 27, no. 2 (2001): 465–490.

Head, Henry. *Aphasia and Kindred Disorders of Speech*. New York: Hafner, 1963.

Head, Henry, and W. H. R. Rivers. *Studies in Neurology*. London: Frowde Hodder and Stoughton, 1920.

Husserl, Edmund. *Ideas 1*. The Hague: Nijhoff, 1964.

—— *The Crisis of European Science and Transcendental Phenomenology: An Introduction to Phenomenological Philosophy*. Trans. David Carr. Evanston, IL: Northwestern University Press, 1970.

—— *The Idea of Phenomenology*. Dordrecht: Kluwer Academic, 1964.

Irigaray, Luce. *An Ethics of Sexual Difference*. Trans. Carolyn Burke and Gillian C. Gill. Ithaca: Cornell University Press, 1984.

—— "For Centuries We've Been Living in the Mother-Son Relation . . . " *Hecate* 9, nos. 1-2 (1983).

—— *Je, Tu, Nous: Toward a Culture of Difference*. Trans. Alison Martin. New York: Routledge, 1993.

—— "Place, Interval: A Reading of Aristotle, *Physics* IV." In *An Ethics of Sexual Difference*, pp. 34–55. Trans. Carolyn Burke and Gillian C. Gill. Ithaca: Cornell University Press, 1984.

—— *Sexes and Genealogies*. Trans. Gillian C. Gill. New York: Columbia University Press, 1993.

—— *Speculum of the Other Woman.* Trans. Gillian C. Gill. Ithaca: Cornell University Press, 1985.

—— *This Sex Which Is Not One.* Trans. Catherine Porter. Ithaca: Cornell University Press, 1985.

Kessler, Suzanne J. *Lessons from the Intersexed.* New Brunswick, NJ: Rutgers University Press, 1998.

Kirby, Vicki. *Telling Flesh: The Substance of the Corporeal.* New York: Routledge, 1997.

Lacan, Jacques. *Ecrits.* New York: Norton, 1981.

—— *Four Fundamental Concepts of Psychoanalysis.* New York: Norton, 1977.

Laplanche, Jean. *Life and Death in Psychoanalysis.* Trans. Jeffrey Mehlman. Baltimore: Johns Hopkins University Press, 1976.

Laqueur, Thomas Walter. *Making Sex: Body and Gender from the Greeks to Freud.* Cambridge: Harvard University Press, 1990.

Leder, Drew. *The Absent Body.* Chicago: University of Chicago Press, 1990.

Levy, Ariel. "Where the Bois Are." *New York Magazine,* January 5, 2004.

Lindemann, Gesa. "The Body of Gender Difference." *European Journal of Womens Studies* 3, no. 4 (1996): 341–361.

McCloskey, Deirdre N. *Crossing: A Memoir.* Chicago: University of Chicago Press, 1999.

MacKenzie, Gordene Olga. *Transgender Nation.* Bowling Green: Bowling Green State University Popular Press, 1994.

McLean, Sandra. "It's a Boi Thing." *Courier-Mail.* June 7, 2003.

Mantilla, Karla. "Men in Ewes' Clothing: The Stealth Politics of the Transgender Movement." *off our backs* 30, no. 4 (April 2000): 5.

Marech, Rona. "Nuances of Gay Identities Reflected in New Language: 'Homosexual' Is Passé in a 'Boi's' Life." *San Francisco Chronicle,* February 8, 2004.

—— "Throw Out Your Pronouns—'He' and 'She' Are Meaningless Terms in the Bay Area's Flourishing Transgender Performance Scene." *San Francisco Chronicle,* December 29, 2003, D1.

Martin, Biddy. *Femininity Played Straight: The Significance of Being Lesbian.* New York: Routledge, 1996.

Merleau-Ponty, Maurice. *In Praise of Philosophy.* Trans. John Wild and James M. Edie. Evanston, IL: Northwestern University Press, 1963.

—— *Phenomenology of Perception.* Trans. Colin Smith. London: Routledge, 1962.

—— *Signs*. Evanston, IL: Northwestern University Press, 1964.

—— *The Primacy of Perception: And Other Essays on Phenomenological Psychology, the Philosophy of Art, History and Politics*. Trans. Arleen B. Dahery et al. Evanston, IL: Northwestern University Press, 1964.

—— *The World of Perception*. Trans. Oliver Davis. New York: Routledge, 2004.

Merleau-Ponty, Maurice, and Claude Lefort. *The Visible and the Invisible: Followed by Working Notes*. Trans. Alphonso Lingis. Evanston: Northwestern University Press, 1968.

Meyerowitz, Joanne. *How Sex Changed: A History of Transsexuality in the United States*. Cambridge: Harvard University Press, 2002.

Millot, Catherine. *Horsexe: Essay on Transsexuality*. Brooklyn, NY: Autonomedia, 1990.

Mitchell, Juliet. *Psychoanalysis and Feminism*. New York: Vintage, 1974.

Mitchell, S. Weir. *Injuries of Nerves and Their Consequences*. Philadelphia: Lippincott, 1872.

More, K., and S. Whittle. *Reclaiming Genders: Transsexual Grammars at the Fin De Siecle*. Washington, DC: Cassell, 1999.

Morris, Jan. *Conundrum*. New York: Harcourt Brace Jovanovich, 1974.

Munt, Sally. "Orifices in Space." In Sally Munt and Cherry Smith, eds., *Butch/Femme: Inside Lesbian Gender*, pp. 200–209. Washington, DC: Cassell, 1998.

Munt, Sally, and Cherry Smyth. *Butch/Femme: Inside Lesbian Gender*. London: Cassell, 1998.

Namaste, Viviane K. *Invisible Lives: The Erasure of Transsexual and Transgendered People*. Chicago: University of Chicago Press, 2000.

Nataf, Zachary I. *Lesbians Talk Transgender*. London: Scarlet, 1996.

Natanson, Maurice. *Edmund Husserl: Philosopher of Infinite Tasks*. Evanston, IL: Northwestern University Press, 1973.

Nestle, Joan, ed. *The Persistent Desire: A Femme-Butch Reader*. Boston: Alyson, 1992.

Nestle, Joan, Clare Howell, and Riki Wilchins, eds. *Genderqueer: Voices from Beyond the Sexual Binary*. Los Angeles: Alyson, 2002.

Ovid and A. D. Melville. *Metamorphoses*. Trans A. D. Melville. New York: Oxford University Press, 1998.

Price, Douglas B., and Neil J. Twombly, eds. *The Phantom Limb Phenomenon: A Medical, Folkloric, and Historical Study: Texts and Translations of Tenth- to Twentieth-Century Miracle Accounts of the Miracu-*

lous *Restoration of Lost Body Parts*. Washington, DC: Georgetown University Press, 1978.

Prosser, Jay. *Second Skins: The Body Narratives of Transsexuality*. New York: Columbia University Press, 1998.

Rayfield, Tom. *Dear Sir or Madam*. London: JWT Direct, 1994.

Raymond, Janice G. *The Transsexual Empire: The Making of the She-Male*. New York: Teachers College Press, 1994.

Riley, Denise. *Am I That Name? Feminism and the Category of "Women" in History*. Minneapolis: University of Minnesota Press, 1988.

Rubin, Gayle. "Of Catamites and Kings: Reflections on Butch, Gender, and Boundaries." In Joan Nestle, ed., *The Persistent Desire: A Femme-Butch Reader*, pp. 468–482. Boston: Alyson, 1992.

Rubin, Henry. "Phenomenology as Method in Trans Studies." *GLQ: A Journal of Lesbian and Gay Studies* 4, no. 2 (1998): 263–281.

—— *Self-Made Men: Identity and Embodiment Among Transsexual Men*. Nashville: Vanderbilt University Press, 2003.

Schilder, Paul. *Introduction to a Psychoanalytic Psychiatry*. Trans. Bernard Glueck. New York: International Universities Press, 1951.

—— *On Psychoses*. New York: International Universities Press, 1976.

—— *The Image and Appearance of the Human Body: Studies in the Constructive Energies of the Psyche*. New York: International Universities Press, 1950.

Schor, Naomi, and Elizabeth Weed. *The Essential Difference*. Bloomington: Indiana University Press, 1994.

Shepherdson, Charles. "The *Role* of Gender and the *Imperative* of Sex." In Joan Copjec, ed., *Supposing the Subject*, pp. 158–182. London: Verso, 1994.

—— *Vital Signs: Nature, Culture, Psychoanalysis*. New York: Routledge, 2000.

Sherrington, Charles Scott. *The Integrative Action of the Nervous System*. Cambridge: Cambridge University Press, 1947.

Siegfried, J., M. Zimmermann, and René Baumgartner. *Phantom and Stump Pain*. New York: Springer, 1981.

Silverman, Kaja. *Male Subjectivity at the Margins*. New York: Routledge, 1992.

—— *The Threshold of the Visible World*. New York: Routledge, 1996.

—— *World Spectators*. Stanford: Stanford University Press, 2000.

Spade, Dean. "Compliance Is Gendered: Transgender Survival and Social Welfare." In Paisley Currah, Richard Juang, Shannon Minter, eds.,

Transgender Rights, pp. 212–241. Minneapolis: University of Minnesota Press, 2006.

—— "Mutilating Gender." In Susan Stryker and Stephen Whittle, eds., *The Transgender Studies Reader*, pp. 315–332. New York: Routledge, 2006.

—— "Remarks at Transecting the Academy Conference." http://www.makezine.org/transecting.html.

—— "Resisting Medicine/Remodeling Gender." *Berkeley Women's Law Journal* 18 (2003), pp. 15–37.

Stone, Sandy. "The *Empire* Strikes Back: A Posttranssexual Manifesto." In Julia Epstein and Kristina Straub, eds., *Body Guards: The Cultural Politics of Gender Ambiguity*, pp. 280–304. New York: Routledge, 1991.

Stryker, Susan. *Transgender History.* Berkeley: Seal, 2008.

—— "Transgender Studies: Queer Theory's Evil Twin." *GLQ: A Journal of Lesbian and Gay Studies* 10, no. 2 (2004): 212–215.

—— "The Transgender Issue: An Introduction." *GLQ: A Journal of Lesbian and Gay Studies* 4, no. 2 (1998): 145–158.

Stryker, Susan, and Stephen Whittle. *The Transgender Studies Reader.* New York: Routledge, 2006.

Sullivan, Nikki. *A Critical Introduction to Queer Theory.* New York: New York University Press, 2003.

Tea, Michelle. "Transmissions from Camp Trans." *Believer,* November 2003, pp. 61–81.

Thomson, Rosemarie Garland. *Freakery: Cultural Spectacles of the Extraordinary Body.* New York: New York University Press, 1996.

Tiemersma, Douwe. *Body Schema and Body Image: An Interdisciplinary and Philosophical Study.* Amsterdam: Swets and Zeitlinger, 1989.

Todes, Samuel. *Body and World.* Cambridge: MIT Press, 2001.

Valentine, David. *Imagining Transgender.* Durham: Duke, 2007.

—— "'The Calculus of Pain': Violence, Anthropological Ethics, and the Category Transgender." *Ethnos: Journal of Anthopology* 68, no. 1 (2009): 27–48.

Vitello, Paul. "The Trouble When Jane Becomes Jack." *New York Times,* August 20, 2006, p. 9.1.

Volcano, Del LaGrace, and Judith Halberstam. *The Drag King Book.* London: Serpent's Tail, 1999.

Wallon, Henri. *Les Origines du caractère chez l'enfant: Les préludes du sentiment de personnalité.* 2d ed. Paris: PUF, 1949.

Wallon, Henri, and Gilbert Voyat. *The World of Henri Wallon.* New York: Aronson, 1984.

Weiss, Gail. *Body Images: Embodiment as Intercorporeality.* New York: Routledge, 1999.

Weiss, Gail, and Dorothea Olkowski, eds. *Feminist Interpretations of Maurice Merleau-Ponty.* University Park: Penn State University Press, 2006.

Weiss, Gail, and Honi Fern Haber. *Perspectives on Embodiment: The Intersections of Nature and Culture.* New York: Routledge, 1999.

Welton, Donn. *Body and Flesh: A Philosophical Reader.* Malden, MA: Blackwell, 1998.

Whittle, Stephen. "Where Did We Go Wrong? Feminism and Trans Theory—Two Teams on the Same Side?" In Susan Stryker and Stephen Whittle, eds., *The Transgender Studies Reader*, pp. 194–202. New York: Routledge, 2006.

Wilchins, Riki Anne. *Read My Lips: Sexual Subversion and the End of Gender.* Ithaca: Firebrand, 1997.

Wills, David. *Prosthesis.* Stanford: Stanford University Press, 1995.

Young, Iris Marion. "Pregnant Embodiment: Subjectivity and Alienation." In *Throwing Like a Girl and Other Essays in Feminist Philosophy and Social Theory.* Bloomington: Indiana University Press, 1990.

—— "Throwing Like a Girl." In Jeffner Allen and Iris Marion Young, eds., *The Thinking Muse.* Bloomington: Indiana University Press, 1989.

—— "Throwing Like a Girl, Twenty Years Later." In Donn Welton, ed., *Body and Flesh: A Philosophical Reader.* Malden, MA: Blackwell, 1998.

Zaner, Richard M. *The Problem of Embodiment: Some Contributions to a Phenomenology of the Body.* The Hague: Nijhoff, 1964.

INDEX

Freud, Sigmund: 1, 2, 179; Didier Anzieu on, 25–31; and bodily ego, 3, 22, 41; Judith Butler on, 34; and castration anxiety, 112; Elizabeth Grosz on, 28; and spectacular identification, 128; on intersexuality (Freudian bisexuality), 14–22; Maurice Merleau-Ponty on, 47; Jay Prosser on, 38–39; Paul Schilder on, 29–31; and sex, 14–22; and sexuality, 57; Kaja Silverman on, 22

FTM (female-to-male): banned from Michigan Women's Music Festival, 106; in Jason Cromwell, 74; in Alix Dobkin, 110; FTM experience, 9, 154; in Elizabeth Grosz, 145–46; in Bernice Hausman, 110; and law, 187; in *New York Times*, 105–7; relation to butch, 164–65; relation to lesbians, 105–7; in Gayle Rubin, 164–65; in Henry Rubin, 119; and surgery, 112, 113, 187; and transition, 110, 112; and violence, 79, 110; *see also* men; transmen

Gallagher, Shaun, 196n14
gay: gay bars/clubs, 69–70; gay gene, 198n7; and gender identity, 173; in Elizabeth Grosz, 145; in Luce Irigaray, 142–43; and marriage, 103; and normativity, 106, 145; relation to queer, 101–2, 145; relation to trans, 106; and sexual difference, 142–43; as sexual identity, 49, 104, 173; in Susan Stryker, 106; and violence, 105, 127; in Riki Wilchins, 127; *see also* lesbian and gay studies
gender, 4, 19, 21–22, 35; 48, 70, 98, 114; and body, 2, 5, 14, 37, 38, 71, 74–77, 79, 118, 155, 181, 197n1; and fantasy, 125; and felt sense, 121, 124, 164; gender ambiguity, 15, 43, 117,

180; gender crossing, 5, 166, 171, 172; gender freedom, 104; gender identity, 49, 58, 83, 87, 102, 105, 120, 125, 127–28, 154, 165–66, 168, 173, 192, 193; gender ideologies, 75, 84, 85, 88; gender norms, 5, 105, 173, 181; gender plasticity, 7, 146, 167; gender presentation, 45, 72, 104, 108, 127, 175, 180, 183; gendered pronouns, 9; gender regulation, 8; gender studies, 82, 96, 97; gender trouble, 101, 105, 168, 179; gender variance, 3, 62; as historical category, 96; and language, 82, 171, 185, 186; and law, 172–73, 187, 191, 193, 203n3; and marriage, 104, 176; and nation, 173; non-normative gender, 1, 6, 8, 43, 44, 72, 75, 95, 104, 105, 109, 118, 166, 168, 183, 191, 200n18; normative gender, 2, 3, 8, 14, 16, 38, 41, 75, 76, 81, 103, 104, 109, 117, 124, 125, 133, 142, 153, 155, 168, 179, 188; and performativity, 28, 81, 85, 142, 183; and phenomenology, 191; post-gendered subject, 96; as property, 172; psychoanalytic accounts of, 13; and race, 100; and realness, 38, 71, 72, 85, 92, 114, 183, 193; and representation, 92; and restrooms, 79, 200n18; and sex, 163, 179, 189, 190; and sexuality, 100, 103, 104, 105, 113, 127, 198n8; and social construction, 73–75; and space, 79, 106; and theory, 71–74, 80, 88; and transition, 109, 115, 171–72, 179, 183, 189, 192; and travel, 174–75, 190
gender dysphoria, 3, 83, 164, 165, 175
genderqueer, 4, 79, 80, 120–22, 126, 165
Green, James, 74–76, 80–83, 88, 114